JO-KANG'ATO

A MODEL FOR CHRISTIAN UNITY IN THE ECCLESIAL LIFE OF THE CHURCH IN AFRICA

Hezron Otieno Adingo

authorHOUSE

AuthorHouse™
1663 Liberty Drive
Bloomington, IN 47403
www.authorhouse.com
Phone: 833-262-8899

© 2024 Hezron Otieno Adingo. All rights reserved.

No part of this book may be reproduced, stored in a retrieval system, or transmitted by any means without the written permission of the author.

Published by AuthorHouse 03/25/2024

ISBN: 979-8-8230-2423-5 (sc)
ISBN: 979-8-8230-2422-8 (hc)
ISBN: 979-8-8230-2421-1 (e)

Library of Congress Control Number: 2024906360

Print information available on the last page.

Any people depicted in stock imagery provided by Getty Images are models, and such images are being used for illustrative purposes only.
Certain stock imagery © Getty Images.

All scriptures were taken from the New Revised Standard Version of the Bible.

This book is printed on acid-free paper.

Because of the dynamic nature of the Internet, any web addresses or links contained in this book may have changed since publication and may no longer be valid. The views expressed in this work are solely those of the author and do not necessarily reflect the views of the publisher, and the publisher hereby disclaims any responsibility for them.

CONTENTS

Foreword ix
Preface xi
Acronyms xv
Introduction xvii

Chapter 1 The History of the Church: Ecclesial Unity and
    Disunity 1
  1.1 The Commencement of the Church 1
  1.2 The Church through the Ages 4
    1.2.1 The Church during the Patriarchal Period 4
    1.2.2 The Church during the Mosaic Period 6
    1.2.3 The Church in the New Testament Period 7
    1.2.4 The Church during the Patristic Times 9
    1.2.5 The Rise of the Papacy 14
    1.2.6 The Emergence of Denominationalism 15
  Conclusion 23

Chapter 2 Christian Unity as Understood in Various
    Ecclesial Traditions 25
  2.1 The Roman Catholic Church Tradition 27
  2.2 The Greek Orthodox Tradition 34
  2.3 The Evangelical Protestant Tradition 38
  Conclusion 49

Chapter 3 The Notion of Kinship in the African Church............ 51
   3.1 Previous Scholarship.. 51
      3.1.1 John Mary Waliggo 51
      3.1.2 Agbonkhianmeghe Orobator 54
      3.1.3 Charles Nyamiti, Bénézet Bujo, and Diane Stinton 56
   3.2 Kinship as an Aspect of the African Family..................... 59
   3.3 The Extended Family System among the Luo 62
   3.4 The Luos' Perspective of Community 65
   Conclusion... 67

Chapter 4 The Concept of Jo-kang'ato among the Luo of Kenya 68
   4.1 The Origin of the Concept of Jo-kang'ato 70
   4.2 The Impact of the Colonial and Western
      Missionaries' Activities on the Luo Unity 71
   4.3 The Ideals Embedded in the Concept of Jo-kang'ato 72
      4.3.1 Solidarity and Support for One Another 73
      4.3.2 A Sense of Belonging 79
      4.3.3 Meaningful Incorporation 82
      4.3.4 Teamwork 83
      4.3.5 Cooperation 84
      4.3.6 Selflessness 85
      4.3.7 Sound Leadership 86
      4.3.8 Intergenerational Connection 87
      4.3.9 Dispute Resolution Mechanisms 89
   4.4 The Relationship between the Concept of Jo-
      kang'ato and Ubuntu 91
   4.5 Using the Concept of Jo-kang'ato to Solve the
      Problem of Disunity in the Church 96
      4.5.1 The Effects of Christians' Engagement and
         Treatment of One Another as Jo-kang'ato 97
      4.5.2 The Relationship among Christian
         Denominations Arising from the Treatment of
         One Another as Jo-kang'ato 97

4.5.3 Ways through Which the Concept of Jo-kang'ato Could Address the Generational Gap within the Church 100
4.6 The Weaknesses and Strengths of Jo-kang'ato 102
4.7 Behavioral Symbols Affecting Christian Unity 111
Conclusion.. 117

Chapter 5 The Familial and Communal Ecclesial Models in Light of Selected Passages of the Scripture 119
5.1 An Overview of Ecclesial Models................................... 119
5.2 The Familial Model of the Church 121
5.3 The Communal Model of the Church 128
5.4 The Ecclesial Relationship Presented in the Selected Passages of the Scripture 131
   5.4.1 John 17:20–23 132
   5.4.2 1 Corinthians 12:12–27 145
   5.4.2.6 Care for the Weaker and Vulnerable Members (vv. 23–24)... 157
   5.4.3 Ephesians 2:12–22... 162
5.5 A Comparative Analysis of the Concept of Jo-kang'ato and the Scripture 179
Conclusion.. 186

Chapter 6 The Implications of the Concept of Jo-kang'ato for Christian Unity in the Ecclesial Life of the Church 188
Conclusion.. 193

Conclusions 195
Bibliography 209

FOREWORD

It is now widely accepted that one's reading of the scripture is shaped by theological and ideological presuppositions. Furthermore, each scholar or interpreter of the Bible has been formed within a certain cultural milieu. Our deep-rooted assumptions about "the way things really are" have been bred into us by our culture of origin. All Christians mix their culture with their faith and its practices. We can no longer cling to the idea that Christianity's core is cultureless. Thus, when I read in the scripture about our being adopted into God's family, my cultural assumptions shape my sense of the meaning of this metaphor. I know what a "family" looks like. But what if?

Biblical revelation does not provide us with clearly articulated, logical "doctrines." Instead, we find stories, metaphors, symbols, images, sermons, songs, letters, and poems. Part of the beauty and richness of the Christian movement is that whenever the Christian teaching is received and assimilated in new cultural situations, new insights and nuances are added. The Spirit sometimes shows us something about Jesus that we haven't seen before. We discover more about God and his ways when we hear his "mighty acts" articulated through the cultural "lenses" of yet another tongue, tribe, and nation. This is very good.

For this reason, I am thrilled to see this doctoral research carried out by Hezron Otieno Adingo being made available to the global theological fraternity. The global church is fortunate to have available the research carried out by a scholar who was socialized in the Luo community of western Kenya. When Dr. Adingo examines the scriptures regarding the unity of the church of God, he interprets the text through the eyes of a Luo. He sees and understands theological ideas based on the "lifeworld" of the African environment, which nurtured him.

Specifically, he explains to the rest of us an ancient Luo social construct, *jo-kang'ato*. To people shaped by the community on the shores of Lake Victoria in western Kenya, jo-kang'ato names dynamics that obviously fit the way things really are. I need this understanding.

Dr. Adingo's work will benefit the entire church. His research combines exegesis of the scripture and historical (Western) theology. It integrates social anthropology and empirical research among the Luo community. Dr. Adingo demonstrates competence in handling the accepted methodologies of theological research but adds a new model to enlighten us as we seek to grasp the rich cluster of metaphors and stories through which the Bible reveals God's will for the "church."

I am happy to commend the book to all who long to see Jesus's passion for the oneness of the church more fully manifest "on earth as it is in heaven." Perhaps the Spirit will allow us to grasp more of God's vision for "the bride of Christ" when we look through the eyes of this African brother.

Is Hezron O. Adingo's proposal that we envision a Christian community through the lens of jo-kang'ato correct? Wrong question. Ultimately, as Jesus tells us, it is "by their fruit" that the authenticity of a theological model should be assessed.

George Renner, PhD

PREFACE

Disunity remains the dilemma that the church in Africa continues to face. The parsimonious relationship among Christians is a reality at the interdenominational, denominational, and local church levels. The mission of the church in Africa is affected as a result. The anticlimax of the results expected upon the assumption of ecclesial leadership and control by the indigenous people following the departure of Western missionaries testifies to this fact.

Ecclesiologists have proposed a couple of models to address the problem, the prominent ones being the familial model, which has its basis in the scripture and advocates for the mutual relationship found at home as a pattern for ecclesial life, and the communitarian model. The two, however, do not provide a proper understanding of Christian unity in the ecclesial life of the church in Africa because the relationship prescribed by them is not intimate or broad enough in scope to meet the expectations of African Christians.

The misunderstanding arising from the failure of these ecclesial models in their current form contributes to the persistence and escalation of disunity. The lack of proper clarification also culminates in remote relationships among believers and even the disowning of one another. The model of the family itself is laden with Western cultural overtones, which reek of individualism whose characteristics are isolation, prejudice, and exclusion. These are catalysts of conflict among parishioners. The model of the community too distorts the meaning of unity and inculcates a strange kind of engagement that is neither scriptural nor African. It has an assumption as its basis as it leads people to hope that tranquility and meaningful coexistence will be realized even without input to solve outstanding issues. Both models manifest exclusivism, which provides fodder for domination manifested in elitism, clericalism, superiority complexes, mechanical relationships, and alienation among Christians. The limitations presented in the models render a book of this kind necessary.

An attempt has been made in this book to establish the connection between the Luos' concept of jo-kang'ato (kinship) and Christian unity by pointing out the bearing that the former has upon the latter. An implication for Christian unity by enrichment of understanding would be the outcome. This task involved determining the correlation between jo-kang'ato and the kind of relationship prescribed in the scripture for Christians within the ecclesial life of the church.

The exegeses of particular passages of the scripture and the culture of the Luo people through the interview data collected during my doctoral research from the village elders and church members across several denominations in Migori County, Homa Bay County, Siaya County, and Kisumu County, all found in the Republic of Kenya, facilitated the process. The study also relied on the Luos' anthropological works. A comparison was drawn, which affirmed the validity of jo-kang'ato in theological reflection. The approach helped enhance the understanding of unity among Christians in the ecclesial life of the church in Africa.

The motivation for writing this book was derived from the impact that African Christian theology continues to make among African believers as the enrichment of various Christian teachings takes place. I add my voice to those of other scholars who have provided an African touch in their theological reflections. The concept under investigation is based on African kinship, which is the fabric of African society. As an insider, I was inspired by the kind of unity that the concept of jo-kang'ato fosters among the Luo, the consequences of which are manifested in the various aspects of life: social, economic, religious, and political.

Jo-kang'ato holds the various social units among the Luo in the form of households, families, lineages, clans, and the entire tribe, and beyond together. The support system prescribed by the concept is also remarkable. The kind of unity it fosters could be a pattern for Christian relationships in the ecclesial life of the church. The concept of jo-kang'ato, therefore, instills a new sense into the understanding of Christian unity. Its themes could be replicated in the ecclesial life of the church to inform and improve the relationship among Christians, leading to unity among them at all ecclesial levels.

Hezron Otieno Adingo
London, March 2024

ACRONYMS

AICs	African Independent Churches
AIDS	Acquired Immune Deficiency Syndrome
COVID–19	Coronavirus Disease 2019
EP	Evangelical Protestants
FGM	Female Genital Mutilation
FORD KENYA	Forum for the Restoration of Democracy in Kenya
GO	Greek Orthodox
GOC	Greek Orthodox Church
HIV	Human Immunodeficiency Virus
KANU	Kenya African National Union
KPU	Kenya People's Union
LGBT	LGBTQ+ Lesbian, Gay, Bisexual, Transgender, Queer
LDP	Liberal Development Party
NDP	National Development Party
NT	New Testament
ODM	Orange Democratic Movement
OT	Old Testament
PT	Protestant Tradition
RC	Roman Catholic(ism)
RCC	Roman Catholic Church
SDA	Seventh-Day Adventist Church

INTRODUCTION

The ecclesial models of family and community enjoy prominence in the discussion of Christian unity as a pattern to relationships among believers in the various levels of the church. However, these models suffer from Western individualism, which limits their scope to the extent that they fail to make sense to African believers whose understanding stretches the same to encapsulate all the relatives, clan and village members, the whole tribe, and even those who are incorporated into their societies. Msafiri—a priest in the Roman Catholic Church (RCC) in Tanzania, for instance—points out the weakness of the familial model as follows: "When understood or interpreted from an exclusivistic Catholic oriented or Euro-American understanding, the family model can have very negative ecumenical consequences."[1] Tien, on his part, says that the familial model is supposed to demonstrate "the universality of the Church because it includes all peoples. Therefore, the new family of Christians should overcome the negative aspects of the human family."[2] The dominating attitude stemming from the familial model often results in the autonomy of the clergy manifesting in disregard for

---

[1] Aidan Msafiri, "The Church as a Family Model: Its Strengths and Weaknesses," Accessed August 24, 2020, https://pdfs.semanticscholar.org/6b59/813e7f8f77 89c4fb39a3a2e5cec6a427486a.pdf? ga=2.119494602.2116468974.1598167077-1515817833.1598167077.

[2] Ngo Tien, "The Church as Family of God: Its Development and Implications for the Church in Vietnam," (PhD thesis, Australian Catholic University, 2006), 25.

the priesthood of all believers and the treatment of parishioners in a condescending or patronizing manner.³ Furthermore, certain denominations have used this model to advance an argument that they are more family than the rest. The communitarian model, on the other hand, tends to promote contentment with division rather than promote an intimate relationship among Christians.⁴ According to Schmitt (cited by Radner), they do so with the consciousness of their misgivings outstanding, but somehow regulated, and as a "community of enemies," or people "who cannot reach agreement on important matters."⁵

Failure to inject this ecclesial model with a new sense could promote deprivation of a sense of belonging since it takes after the typical community where certain members continue to be regarded as aliens even when they have been around for a significant number of years.

The blurring of understanding of Christian unity in the ecclesial life of the church is because in their conventional form, the two models do not take into consideration the Weltanschauung of the African people, which is collectivist. Consequently, disunity manifested in various forms abounds in the church at different levels.

Unless an extension, modification, and even correction of the age-long understanding of these models takes place, the misunderstanding will continue, the consequence of which is the perpetuation of disunity, as the reference of family and community is claimed exclusively by denominations and Christians who then view one another as strangers. However, viewed from the perspective of the African person, they could enhance unity among Christians and save the church from disunity, which presently manifests in tribalism, nepotism, racism, classicism, regionalism, nationalism, clericalism, etc. It also renders needless the desire for a denominational merger as

---

³ Elochukwu Uzukwu, *A Listening Church: Autonomy and Communion in African Churches* (Eugene, OR: Wipf and Stock, 2006), 121–122.
⁴ Ephraim Radner, *A Brutal Unity: The Spiritual Politics of the Christian Church* (Waco, Texas: Baylor University Press, 2012), 455.
⁵ Ibid., 454.

a show of unity as it roots for a mutual relationship amid distinctions. In the process, the need for a mechanism that binds Christians in a way that they would regard one another in sibling terms becomes indispensable. That would involve listening to one another and benefiting from their engagements in a symbiotic manner. At the local church level, interacting that way enables openness, sincerity, and amicable ways of handling differences whenever they arise.

Disunity among Christians manifests in protracted disputes and prolonged bitterness and rivalry among believers, which often turns into breakups and the formation of offshoot groups headed by disenchanted leaders as the brethren feel uncomfortable remaining in the company of one another. Leadership wrangles are usually among the forms of disunity. Some of the major factors attributed to disunity among parishioners in Africa include the misappropriation of church funds, tribalism, and nepotism.

At the onset, certain behaviors are manifested, which include refusing to take part in the ordinances of the church and its other important functions, for instance, the Lord's Supper; storming out of meetings and holding similar events differently to counteract what the rival party is doing; and withholding tithes and offerings. The acceleration of disputes to higher proportions is usually a result of the failure to act upon them promptly and the refusal to listen to one another or dialogue to find solutions to contentious issues. The more the opportunity to talk to one another is ignored, the deeper the animosity penetrates. The most unfavorable outcomes could include, among other things, lawsuits and physical fights. Tension gets out of hand in most cases and the intervention of government agencies is sought. In many cases, sects and denominations are born out of the situation. All these contribute to the loss of vitality as the consequence of deflected attention from spreading the Gospel to litigations.

At the interdenominational level, the problem of disunity is so critical that hopes of churches ever agreeing again continue to dwindle with time. This state has arisen partly from the Christians' perception of "the Christian message."⁶ However, Christians can still talk to one another and work together toward the realization of what Lonergan refers to as "the redemptive and constructive roles of the Christian church in human society."⁷ The main concern, however, is that despite the glaring nature of the phenomenon of ecclesial disunity, a lack of significant scholarly interest in it continues. This is appalling since, from the inception of the Christian church, the problem of division has been receiving attention at different times. Such interests came to the fore in, among other ways, the establishment of heresiology, a theological discipline that looks into the teachings or beliefs of a given body of people who are thought to be propagating unorthodoxy.⁸ According to heresiologists, "to believe wrongly is to divide, and to divide is to attack the true faith."⁹ The current dilemma of disinterest and indifference is spelled out by Radner:

> The divided Church—to give her a single persona—forgets her division … the forgotten division—which multiplies into manifold divisions—is not for the sake of healing but for the sake of *ongoing* conflict, for the sake of remaining separate and allowing such separation to be unquestioned, to stand for the whole. Forgetting in the Church is a form of conflict, then, not reordering.¹⁰

Despite the tendency to underestimate ecclesial division, it is a challenge that needs to be addressed. Leithart points out that "the Church is divided into various camps defined by their differences from others. To suggest otherwise is a form of ecclesial idealism

---

⁶ Bernard Lonergan, *Method in Theology* (Toronto: University of Toronto Press, 1971), 367, 368.
⁷ Ibid.
⁸ Radner, *A Brutal Unity: The Spiritual Politics of the Christian Church*, 3-4.
⁹ Ibid., 4; Titus 3:10.
¹⁰ Radner, *A Brutal Unity: The Spiritual Politics of the Christian Church*, 6.

that easily becomes a form of ecclesial bullying."¹¹ For example, among Protestant denominations who claim to share many things in common—for instance, creed and doctrines—division continues to characterize the way allegiance or subscription to the various tenets is expressed.¹² Disunity also manifests in, among other ways, the "predatory relationship," which would sooner or later render churches that cannot cope with the stiff competition for members dysfunctional and inexistent.¹³ In the past, though, the scramble for members, as currently witnessed, was unheard of since believers understood themselves as one body that cannot hunt for itself and as parts of the same body that cannot compete with one another for membership.¹⁴

Parsimonious relationship among Christians in Africa is fueled by an arrogant attitude in the form of a superiority complex over other denominations, for instance, the mentality of being more biblically based in teachings than the rest of Christians.¹⁵ In Waruta's words, this is tantamount to "narrow-mindedness, parochialism and Biblicalism."¹⁶ The other factor is what Cleveland refers to as the "right Christian, wrong Christian" attitude, the consequence of which is the drawing of a wedge between believers and disapproval of each other.¹⁷ The tendency among Christians is that those belonging to their denominational persuasions are to be dealt with better than

---

¹¹ Peter Leithart, *The End of Protestantism: Pursuing unity in a Fragmented Church* (Grand Rapids, MI: Brazos Press, 2016), 38.
¹² Ibid., 2.
¹³ Bruce Marshall, "Who Really Cares About Christian Unity?" Accessed October 9, 2017, https://www.firstthings.com/.../who-really-cares-about-christian-unity.
¹⁴ Ibid.
¹⁵ Leithart, *The End of Protestantism: Pursuing Unity in a Fragmented Church*, 73, 74.
¹⁶ David Waruta, "Towards an African Church: A Critical Assessment of Alternative Forms and Structures," in *The Church in African Christianity: Innovative Essays* (Nairobi: Initiatives Publ., 1990), 36.
¹⁷ Christena Cleveland, *Disunity in Christ: Uncovering the Hidden Forces That Keep Us Apart* (Downers Grove, IL: InterVarsity Press, 2013), 12, 15.

the rest who are categorized as outsiders.[18] Viewing other Christian groups as our adversaries, though, results in unkindness toward them.[19] Since some Christians believe that their position is the best and the monopoly of truth abides with them, they seek ways of silencing those with different views. They label them as "heretics" and "black sheep" who ought to be dealt with as such rather than as "brothers" and "sisters" who need to be loved.[20] The labeling of other children of God thus results in a misrepresentation of Him rather than serving Christ's interests, bearing in mind that He reaches and accommodates all.[21]

Prompted by the misunderstanding of Christian unity in the ecclesial life of the church, which the familial and communitarian models have been unable to address, and the acceleration of disunity resulting from such failure, this piece of work becomes inevitable. The failure of the familial and communitarian models is due to their infestation with Western individualistic elements. The approach to Christian unity taken in this book is different because it utilizes an African concept to shed light on the two models, make them relevant, and use them to create a more biblical understanding of Christian unity. I have attempted to address this problem in a more meaningful manner using the concept of jo-kang'ato among the Luo of Kenya. While jo-kang'ato is familial and communitarian, it presents a terminus a quo from the conventional view of these social units. The concept brings to the fore the African people's broadened view of family and community, and in the process, the meaning of unity is deepened. With improved understanding, appropriate conduct ensues, and optimum conditions for the thriving of unity are created among Christians.

One of the intentions for producing this work was to identify the implications of the Luos' concept of jo-kang'ato and show how its adoption could help the church in Africa to achieve unity. There

---

[18] Ibid., 34, 35.
[19] Ibid., 118.
[20] Ibid., 118, 126, 131.
[21] Ibid., 15, 16.

are not many ecclesiological works, especially among the evangelical circles, done with the help of thought-forms of African nature.²² This is among the areas where much work is needed.²³ This work is a contribution toward that effort. This concept continues to bind people together, just like it did in the past. It is posited here that the kind of unity fostered by the concept of jo-kang'ato could be a pattern to Christian relationships in the ecclesial life of the church. The study established the following:

1. There is a positive and significant relationship between the concept of jo-kang'ato among the Luo of Kenya and the kind of relationship prescribed for Christians in the scripture, hence its potential to address disunity within the ecclesial life of the church in Africa.
2. There is a significant relationship between the extended family system (kinship) among the Luo of Kenya and the kind of relationship offered for Christians by the familial model of the church in relation to unity within the ecclesial life of the church.
3. There is a significant relationship between the community as understood and practiced among the Luo and the communal relationship that is expected of ecclesial life as a panacea to disunity within the church in Africa.

---

²² James Nkansah-Obrempong, *Visual Theology: Some Akan Cultural Symbols, Metaphors, Proverbs, Myths, and Symbols and Their Implications for Doing Christian Theology* (Saarbrucken: VDM Verlag Dr Muller, 2010), 65.
²³ Ibid.

CHAPTER 1
The History of the Church: Ecclesial Unity and Disunity

This chapter traces Christian unity in the ecclesial life of the church back to history with specific interest in the church's commencement and performance over the ages, beginning from the patriarchal period and into the Mosaic period, the New Testament (NT) period, the patristic times, the rise of the papacy, and the emergence of denominationalism.

1.1 The Commencement of the Church

The NT and Old Testament (OT) do not present divergent notions about the intrinsic nature of the church. In both dispensations, the church has existed as the faithful people of God.[24] In its visible form as an institution, both the upright and the wicked exist in it simultaneously.[25] However, Ryrie contends against the notion of the church's existence before the Day of Pentecost, which is a NT

---

[24] Louis Berkhof, *Systematic Theology* (Grand Rapids, MI: Wm. B. Eerdmans Publishing Co. 1938), 571–572.
[25] Ibid.

development.²⁶ Pope buttresses this position with an argument that Jesus taught about His church and established it in advance during His ministry in the world, but it did not come into place until after He had departed.²⁷ Pope says further, "He left a large body of instruction concerning it which waited only for the Day of Pentecost to disclose its fullness of meaning."²⁸ Berkhof contends that the basis of this premillenarian view is the failure to consider the definitions of the church in its entirety as presented in the scripture.²⁹ He observes that the proponents of this view are somehow lopsided as they understand the church as Christ's "body" but fail to grasp the fact that it is as well God's "temple" and "Jerusalem," which are OT terms despite their usage in the NT (1 Corinthians 3:16, 17; 2 Corinthians 6:16; Ephesians 2:21; Galatians 4:26; Hebrews 12:22).³⁰ Again, it is from the Hebrew word *qāhāl*, rendered as *ekklēsia* in the Septuagint and frequently appears in the OT, where the word *church* comes (Joshua 8:35; Ezra 2:65; Joel 2:16).³¹ In both testaments, the word for *church* refers to the "congregation" or "assembly" of those who believe in God.³² Moreover, while the Lord Jesus Christ promised that He would build His Church in the times to come (Matthew 16:18), He also spoke of it as an entity that was already in place (Matthew 18:17).³³ Berkhof asserts that there was a church in the OT that is related to the one in the NT, and in both cases, God's true people constituted it.³⁴

The understanding of the link between the church and the OT

---

[26] Charles Ryrie, *Basic Theology: A Popular Systematic Guide to Understanding Biblical Truth* (Chicago, IL: Moody Press, 1999), 462.
[27] William Pope, *A Compendium of Christian Theology: Being Analytical Outlines of a Course of Theological Study, Biblical, Dogmatic, Historical*, vol. 3 (London: Beveridge and Co, 1879), 262.
[28] Ibid.
[29] Berkhof, *Systematic Theology*, 571.
[30] Ibid.
[31] Ibid.
[32] Ibid.
[33] Ibid., 572.
[34] Ibid., 571.

also instills a sense of the kingship of Christ. The church is the domain of Christ, whose "subjects" are the believers.[35] The Belgic Confession affirms, "This Church has been from the beginning of the world, and will be to the end thereof; which is evident from the fact that Christ is an eternal King, which without subjects He cannot be."[36] This position is upheld in *The Heidelberg Catechism* thus: "That the Son of God, out of the whole human race, from the beginning to the end of the world, gathers, defends, and preserves for Himself, by His Spirit and Word, in the unity of the true faith, a Church chosen to everlasting life."[37]

The church's existence in both dispensations is also brought to the fore when understood as a "community of believers." The church is "a community" or group of people who cultivate faith in God down through the ages, right from the onset of the OT era to the present and future, when the history of the world will come to a climax.[38] Calvin's description is enlightening.

> Then, indeed, the Church includes not only the saints presently living on earth, but all the elect from the beginning of the world. Often, however, the name "church" designates the whole multitude of men spread over the earth who profess to worship one God and Christ. By baptism we are initiated into faith in him; by partaking in the Lord's Supper [sic] we attest our unity in true doctrine and love; in the Word of the Lord [sic] we have agreement, and for the preaching of the word the ministry instituted by Christ is preserved. In this Church are mingled many hypocrites who have nothing of Christ but the name and outward appearance. There are very many ambitious, greedy, envious persons, evil speakers, and

---

[35] Ibid.
[36] The Belgic Confession in Art. XXVII (ibid., 571–572).
[37] *The Heidelberg Catechism* in "Lord's Day XXI" (ibid., 571–572).
[38] Ibid.

some of quite unclean life. Such are tolerated for a time either because they cannot be convicted by a competent tribunal or because a vigorous discipline does not always flourish as it ought.[39]

It is worth noting, however, that the relationship referred to here is of a spiritual rather than physical nature.[40]

1.2 The Church through the Ages

1.2.1 The Church during the Patriarchal Period

During the time of the patriarchs, the "families" of those who believed in God formed the "religious" entities. The church was in the form of devout "households," and the male parents presided over worship as "priests."[41] The performance of religious rites and customs was not frequent even though there was an indication of the habitual declaration of God's name (Genesis 4:26).[42] God's "children" were differentiated from "the children of men," but with time, the latter became dominant.[43] When the deluge came upon the earth, God kept His Church, which was at the time Noah's family, safe from destruction.[44] The church remained in existence through Shem's descendants.[45] Later, as "true religion" was almost becoming extinct, God and Abraham had a "covenant," which required the latter's offspring to be circumcised and be distinct from the rest of the

---

[39] John Calvin, *Institutes of the Christian Religion*, vol. 1, ed. J. T. McNeill, trans. F. L. Battles (Louisville, KY: Westminster John Knox Press, 2011), 1021–1022.
[40] Act 7:38; Rom 11:17–21; Eph 2:11–16.
[41] Hans Küng, *The Church*, trans. Ray and Rosaleen (Ockenden, New York: Sheed & Ward, 1967), 137; Berkhof, *Systematic Theology*, 570.
[42] Berkhof, *Systematic Theology*, 570.
[43] Ibid.
[44] Ibid.
[45] Ibid.

people.⁴⁶ Abraham and his lineage were set apart as people who were special to God.⁴⁷ Berkhof states, "Up to the time of Moses the families of the patriarchs were the real repositories of the true faith, in which the fear of Jehovah and the service of the Lord was kept alive."⁴⁸

The patriarchal era was postlapsarian and therefore a difficult time as people were living with the consequences of disobedience. From the onset, however, God's portion for humanity had been unity and peaceful coexistence. Sin set the pace for disunity. One of the first demonstrations of the division was the strained relationship between Adam and Eve manifested in the former's response to God when asked to account for his actions. He blamed Eve for the blunder.⁴⁹ The developments marked the beginning of a long struggle with division and its dreadful consequences among humanity, which would spread through the ages as human history would be tainted by it.

The next episode was the crime committed against Abel by his brother Cain as a result of jealousy, envy, and selfishness of the latter.⁵⁰ Cain killed Abel as a way of venting his anger and disapproval of God's decision to accept the latter's offerings and abhor his own. Later, when asked by God to account for his deeds, he demonstrated an uncaring and irresponsible attitude. "I do not know; am I my brother's keeper?" was his response.⁵¹ Cain's behavior demonstrates the fact that a poor relationship with God results in a sour relationship with others. The refusal to be one another's keeper has been among the catalysts of disunity through the ages among Christians. Even after the worldwide deluge in the days of Noah, humanity continued to live in disobedience, culminating in the construction of the Tower of Babel and subsequent confusion of language and scattering.

---

⁴⁶ Ibid.
⁴⁷ Ibid.
⁴⁸ Ibid.
⁴⁹ Gen 3:11–13.
⁵⁰ Gen 4:1–10.
⁵¹ Gen 4:9.

1.2.2 The Church during the Mosaic Period

Following the Exodus event, the Israelites became not only "a nation" but also a church belonging to God.[52] Berkhof states, "They were enriched with institutions in which not only family devotion or tribal faith, but the religion of the nation could find expression."[53] During that time, the church was not an entity standing on its own but an entire nation under a human king.[54] Notwithstanding their expression within the national life, the church and the state did not fuse into a single entity as there were duties cut out for those serving within each entity; there was a distinction between "civil and religious" functions[55] Concomitantly, the Israelite nation formed membership of the church, and people drawn from Gentile nations were admitted by way of integration into Israel.[56] While describing the developments during the Mosaic period, Berkhof says, "In this period there was a marked development of doctrine, an increase in the quantity of the religious truth known, and greater clearness in the apprehension of the truth. The worship of God was regulated down to the minutest details, was largely ritual and ceremonial, and was centred in one central sanctuary."[57]

Obedience was a crucial matter for the OT church, for we see prophets on many occasions appealing to the Israelites to be obedient to the Lord's commands, as the absence of obedience would not only be a recipe for apostasy but would also cause them to lose unity. Adhering to God's instructions, on the other hand, would generate a peaceful coexistence among them as well as bolster their determination to resist the encroachment of paganism into their community. To neglect obedience in favor of their ways and

---

[52] Küng, *The Church*, 116; Berkhof, *Systematic Theology*, 570; Ex 19:3–6; Lev 26:12; Deu 7:6.
[53] Berkhof, *Systematic Theology*, 570.
[54] Küng, *The Church*, 137.
[55] Berkhof, *Systematic Theology*, 570.
[56] Ibid.
[57] Ibid.

devices would incur catastrophic effects. The division of their nation sometimes later attested to this fact.[58] Rehoboam succumbed to peer pressure and refused to listen to the voice of reason. His injudicious decision to lead by subjugation and intimidation caused him to lose the loyalty and allegiance of his subjects. It also led to secession and false worship among the people of God. This incident also demonstrates the contribution of poor leadership to ecclesial disunity. The refusal of the clergy to listen to the laity and poor decisions made by ecclesiastical leaders are among the significant causes of ecclesial disunity.

1.2.3 The Church in the New Testament Period

During the NT era, the church's scope widened beyond Palestine. This significant adjustment was a result of what Jesus had done and has produced a church that is no longer nationalistic but an entity that stands on its own.[59] The borderlines that limited it to the nation of Israel were removed, and it became a church for all people and nations.[60] To live up to the new principle and achieve its international scope, though, focus on its mission was inevitable as it would see the dissemination of the good news of Jesus's saving act around the globe to all.[61] Besides, the system of rites in worship also gave way to "spiritual worship."[62]

The church of the NT during its beginning in AD first century was united. Before the Pentecost, for instance, when the disciples waited for the Spirit to descend, they came together to pray, forgetting their differences.[63] Their unity also manifested in the

---

[58] 1 Kgs 12:1-16.
[59] Berkhof, *Systematic Theology*, 571.
[60] Kevin Giles, *What on Earth is the Church? A Biblical and Theological Inquiry* (London: SPCK, 1995), 11; Peter Osuchukwu, *The Spirit of Umunna and the Development of Small Christian Communities in Igboland* (Frankfurt: Peter Lang, 1995), 98.
[61] Berkhof, *Systematic Theology*, 571-572.
[62] Ibid.
[63] Act 1:12-14.

care for one another, kindness, and acts of charity.[64] It was not long, though, before differences emerged in that Christian community in the form of disenchantment arising from the distribution of food to the widows. Those of a Hellenistic background claimed that their colleagues of Hebrew heritage were receiving special favors.[65] The issue was resolved through the appointment of deacons to serve various social needs.[66] The quarrel between Paul and Barnabas over John Mark is also a display of disunity, though providential.[67] The sociological aspects of disunity among Christians during AD first century also manifested in personality cults, litigations against one another in the courts of law, unloving relations, etc.[68]

Theologically induced controversies too set upon the Christian church right from its early stages. The events culminating in the Council of Jerusalem, for instance, were due to theological differences in the church of God in Antioch. Unlike Paul and other apostles who taught unconditional reception of Gentiles into the fellowship of God's children, some troublemakers from Jerusalem insisted that converts from other nations must be circumcised in addition to being baptized ahead of their acceptance into God's family. Stott articulates the circumstances thus,

> So far it had been assumed that they would be absorbed into Israel by circumcision, and that by observing the law they would be acknowledged as *bonafide* members of the covenant people of God. Something quite different was now happening, however, something which disturbed and even alarmed many. Gentile converts were being welcomed into fellowship by baptism without circumcision. They were becoming Christians without also becoming Jews. They were

---

[64] Act 2:44; 4:32-37.
[65] Acts 6:2.
[66] Acts 6:2-6.
[67] Acts 15:36-41.
[68] 1 Cor 1:10-17; 3; 13.

retaining their own identity and integrity as members of other nations.[69]

Despite the fierce contestation that characterized the deliberations in Jerusalem, members agreed, and exclusion was discouraged.[70] The Pauline corpus is also awash with incidences of parsimonious relationships between Christian believers arising from divergent theological positions. For instance, there were glaring rivalries and disagreements over food and holy days, charismatic expressions, among other theological issues.[71]

1.2.4 The Church during the Patristic Times

It was during the ante-Nicene and patristic periods that the stage was set for "the doctrine of absolute uniformity," otherwise referred to as "mechanical unity."[72] This development was a result of heretical teachings and divisions, which sprang forth.[73] History shows that in the infant stages of the church, converts came from an array of settings, resulting in the interpretation of the scripture in ways that jeopardized its "integrity" through "syncretism."[74] In AD second century, for instance, the Gnostics came up with a theology that presented a severe danger to the church in its emphasis on "secret knowledge."[75] The other danger came from the Marcionites' church,

---

[69] John Stott, *The Message of Acts*, The Bible Speaks Today (Nottingham, England: Inter-Varsity Press, 1991), 240–241.
[70] Acts 15:1-30.
[71] Rom 14; 1 Cor 8; Rom 12:3-8; 1 Cor 12-14.
[72] Pope, *A Compendium of Christian Theology: Being Analytical Outlines of a Course of Theological Study, Biblical, Dogmatic, Historical*, 3:272.
[73] Pope has defined heresy as "the self-willed choice of some particular error and consequent departure from the Christian Confession."(Ibid.).
[74] Justo Gonzalez, *The Story of Christianity: The Early Church to the Dawn of the Reformation*, vol. 1 (Massachusetts: Prince Press, 1984), 58.
[75] Hans Jonas, *The Gnostic Religion*. (Boston: Beacon Press, 1958), 3-238; Norman Geisler, *Baker Encyclopedia of Christian Apologetics* (Grand Rapids, MI: Baker Books, 1999), 274.

which divorced Jehovah from the God of Christians.⁷⁶ The dilemma of heresy led the church to dig deeper into the Word of God and the formulation of a canon, creed, and apostolic succession.⁷⁷ The word Catholic was also coined to distinguish the legitimate or orthodox church from heretical groups.⁷⁸

During the imperial age, the church in North Africa was divided over the "lapsed." These, unlike the faithful few, would not lose their lives in the bloody persecutions meted out against Christians by Decius, so they gave in to paganism.⁷⁹ Among them were some bishops who handed over the Holy Scripture to the powers that be to be burned; they came to be known as *traditores*. When the surviving ones wanted to return to communion at the end of persecution during Constantine's reign, a section of the church (confessors) proposed a favorable reception for them (repentance as a prerequisite), while others insisted on a more rigid treatment.⁸⁰ Consequently, there was a split and the emergence of various camps led by Caecilian (mild) and Majorinus (rigorist), each of whom was regarded by their parties as a legitimate bishop of Carthage.⁸¹ Following Majorinus's death, Donatus of Casae Nigrae succeeded him and led the group for about fifty years.⁸² Constantine was in favor of Caecilian's camp, to which

---

[76] Sebastian Moll, *The Arch-Heretic: Marcion* (Tubingen: Mohr Siebeck, 2010), 47–70.

[77] Gonzalez, *The Story of Christianity: The Early Church to the Dawn of the Reformation*, 1:62–66.

[78] Avery Dulles, *The Catholicity of the Church* (Oxford: Clarendon, 1985), 3, 15-16; John Meyendorff, *Catholicity and the Church* (Crestwood, New York: St. Vladimir's Seminary Press, 1983), 7–8.

[79] Robert Workman, *Persecution in the Early Church* (London: Epworth Press, 1960).

[80] Gonzalez, *The Story of Christianity: The Early Church to the Dawn of the Reformation*, 1:152, 89, 151.

[81] James Sabine, *A Concise History of the Christian Church: From the Birth of the Saviour to the Commencement of the Nineteenth Century*, 3rd ed. (London: Burton and Briggs; Law and Whittaker, 1816), 125.

[82] William Frend, *The Donatist Church: A Movement of Protest in Roman North Africa*. (Oxford: Clarendon, 1952), 48-338.

he bestowed favors.[83] Later, the Donatists left the church following Constantine's conversion, claiming that the church had become an "ally of the Empire."[84]

In the West, the conflict over the lapsed pitted Novatian and Cornelius, the bishop of Rome, while Bishop Cyprian's decision to go into hiding during the persecution from where he sent letters to the flock in Carthage came into question.[85] Consequently, mixed perceptions arose concerning "the nature of the church and the validity of the sacraments."[86] There had also been conflicts in Rome regarding the treatment of perpetrators of fornication, pitting Hippolytus and Calixtus, the bishop, earlier on. Whereas the former opposed the acceptance of those involved, the latter favored forgiveness upon repentance.[87]

The arbitration of civil authorities on ecclesiastical matters began during Emperor Constantine's reign. Constantine regularly intervened to make sure that the church remained intact for the sake of the empire's unity.[88] One party would win the emperor's favor and have their way as the other got punished.[89] Such was the case during the "Arian controversy," which pitted a priest by the name of Arius and the Bishop Alexander of Alexandria; it later extended to calling for Constantine's action.[90] Arius saw a distinction between the Son and the Father contrary to Alexander's view of one substance,

---

[83] Sabine, *A Concise History of the Christian Church: From the Birth of the Saviour to the Commencement of the Nineteenth Century*, 125.

[84] Gonzalez, *The Story of Christianity: The Early Church to the Dawn of the Reformation*, 1:156–157.

[85] Frederic Farrar, Lives *of the Fathers: Sketches of Church History in Biography*, vol. 1 (Edinburgh: Adam and Charles Black, 1889), 274-311.

[86] Gonzalez, *The Story of Christianity: The Early Church to the Dawn of the Reformation*, 1:157.

[87] Ibid., 1:90.

[88] Hermann Doerries, *Constantine the Great* (New York: Harper & Row, 1972).

[89] Ibid.

[90] Elesha Coffman, and Patrick Rardon, "Saints and Heretics," *Christian History Magazine*, 2004.

which the Son had with the Father.[91] Arius was removed from the priesthood, but he mobilized sympathizers who protested against the bishop's decision.[92] The other bishops also sympathized with Arius, claiming that he was right and Alexander was wrong. Since this dispute could not be sorted out and peace secured between the two, Constantine convened the Council of Nicea in AD 325 composed of bishops drawn from the entire empire.[93] Subsequently, Arius was deposed and sent into exile with his sympathizers, including Eusebius of Nicomedia.[94] Soon, this became the fate of Athanasius and other bishops supporting the Nicene position.[95] Julian ("the Apostate") took advantage of the wrangling among Christians and introduced paganism.[96] In addition to the Council of Nicea, there was the Council of Constantinople held in AD 381, which dealt with disputes relating to Christ and the Holy Spirit's divinity.[97]

In medieval times, Eastern Christianity experienced a dispute centered on the issue of Jesus's embodiment of two natures that are linked: God and man. The arguments revolved around the convergence of two natures in Him and how this was to be comprehended. Whereas the Alexandrine group maintained that Jesus's divine nature has to be emphasized above His humanity even if the latter gets into jeopardy, the Antiochenes argued that Jesus would not be the Savior to save to the utmost if He were not 100 percent human as well, and that divinity should not overshadow

---

[91] Michael Barnes, "Timeline," *Christian History Magazine*, 2004.
[92] Gonzalez, *The Story of Christianity: The Early Church to the Dawn of the Reformation*, 1:161-162.
[93] Coffman, and Rardon, "Saints and Heretics"; Sabine, *A Concise History of the Christian Church: From the Birth of the Saviour to the Commencement of the Nineteenth Century*, 127-129.
[94] Barnes, "Timeline."
[95] Lewis Ayres, "The Final Act," *Christian History Magazine*, 2004; Coffman, and Rardon, "Saints and Heretics."
[96] Gonzalez, *The Story of Christianity: The Early Church to the Dawn of the Reformation*, 1:167.
[97] Ayres, "The Final Act"; Barnes, "Timeline."

humanity.[98] Other battles—for instance, over the patriarchy of Constantinople (mostly dominated by the Antiochenes)—came out of the two traditions.[99] Patriarchs were rewarding their friends to take on the Bishopric of Constantinople.[100] The solution was found in the Council of Chalcedon (also known as the Fourth Ecumenical Council) convened in AD 451.[101] Before, there had been the Council of Ephesus in AD 431.[102] Other councils were convened in the East to address endless doctrinal disputes. The Council of Constantinople held in AD 553 (also known as the Fifth Ecumenical Council) was one of such.[103] There was also a quarrel over the celibacy of the clergy pitting the West and the East, among other issues that have kept ecclesial unity far from realization.[104]

Despite the schisms that were going on during the patristic times, what stands out is that no reason was good enough to warrant estrangement from the church, not even internal conflicts and severance from it through willful action or as a result of expulsion.[105] During that era, Ignatius, "an Apostolic Father of the first century," set the rule which stated that "one episcopate was the only bond of union: meaning, however, only that in every church, the chief minister was the guarantee of order against schism and of sound doctrine as against heresy."[106] Irenaeus followed in the second century with a rule placing "One Church as the congregation of all churches under this episcopal government, the only organ of the Holy Ghost: where we have a singular combination of visible and invisible

---

[98] Gonzalez, *The Story of Christianity: The Early Church to the Dawn of the Reformation*, 1:252–253.
[99] Ibid., 1:254.
[100] Ibid.
[101] Barnes, "Timeline."
[102] Gonzalez, *The Story of Christianity: The Early Church to the Dawn of the Reformation*, 1:256.
[103] Ibid., 1:258.
[104] Ibid., 1:265.
[105] Pope, *A Compendium of Christian Theology: Being Analytical Outlines of a Course of Theological Study, Biblical, Dogmatic, Historical*, 3:272.
[106] Ibid.

unity."¹⁰⁷ In the third century (250), Cyprian, in his *De Unitate*, was particular enough to direct attention to Rome "as the centre of unity."¹⁰⁸ However, Cyprian renounced the dominion of Rome to make decisions and judgments on all matters, as was the case.¹⁰⁹

1.2.5 The Rise of the Papacy

The rise of the papacy was a gradual rather than an abrupt occurrence in history. With time, the bishop of Roman bishops began to have and exercise power over the church in its entirety, playing on a large scale the role resembling that of bishops to their respective churches.¹¹⁰ The "ecclesiastical" was adjusted to correspond to the political arrangement as it stipulated that "the Cæsar of a temporal universal empire must have for his counterpart the spiritual Cæsar, or the Vicar of Christ as the centre of unity and final appeal."¹¹¹ This move offended the Eastern churches, who protested it.¹¹² They also raised dislike for the incorporation of the *filioque* into the Nicene Creed and questioned the power or right to do so.¹¹³ Pope describes the developments:

> The breach between Eastern and Western Christendom has never been healed: it remains as a standing protest against the erroneous doctrine of unity. While Rome denounces the Protestant communities as out of the pale of the one body of Christ, the Orthodox Greek Church denounces Rome as the first of all Protestant dissenters, heretics, and sehismatics [*sic*].¹¹⁴

---

[107] Ibid., 3:272–273.
[108] Ibid., 3:273.
[109] Ibid.
[110] Ibid.
[111] Ibid.
[112] Ibid
[113] Ibid.
[114] Ibid.

The Protestant Reformation in the West on its side completely renounced the idea of "an external unity," advanced by both the Roman Catholic and Orthodox Churches.[115]

Following developments after the Reformation, it has become clear that the realization of ecclesial unity within the "visible church" is neither viable nor achievable unless it happens in the aspects of adherence to foundational teachings of Christianity, "worship, and discipline."[116] Consequently, Christianity in both the West and the East has lost hope of the possibility of coming back together as a single entity, for each side would only welcome such kind of arrangement if their conditions are followed.[117]

1.2.6 The Emergence of Denominationalism

Denominationalism and schism are intertwined; hence, it is impossible to discuss either of them exclusively. The former stems from the latter, which is the product of a breached external manifestation of oneness.[118] Pictet points out that schism is either "universal" or "particular."[119] In its former aspect, schism manifests through a rejection of universal "truths" that are fundamental to the Christian faith and are acknowledged by every believer, and the latter in a rejection of certain "truths" that are good yet not central.[120] According to Pictet, "all separation is not schism, although all schism is separation; but all unlawful separation is schism."[121] Many schisms have occurred as a consequence of heretical teachings.[122] At times,

---

[115] Ibid.
[116] Ibid.
[117] Ibid.
[118] Bénédict Pictet defines schism as "the breaking of those bonds which constitute the unity of the church" [Bénédict Pictet, *Christian Theology*. Translated by F. Reyroux (Philadelphia: Presbyterian Board of Publication), 367)].
[119] Pictet, *Christian Theology*, 367.
[120] Ibid.
[121] Ibid.
[122] Pope, *A Compendium of Christian Theology: Being Analytical Outlines of a Course of Theological Study, Biblical, Dogmatic, Historical*, 3:274–275.

though, schism becomes necessary and could be Spirit-led.[123] Pope articulates that point:

> Ecclesiastical schism may be taken up by Divine wisdom into the development of the kingdom of Christ: having been in fact not schism in the sight of God, or soon losing the taint. Apparent schism may be the only cure of heresy. Many minor heresies may co-exist with holding the Head. But where, on the one hand, there is such infidel subtraction from the faith, or, on the other, such superstitious addition to it, as neutralise the fundamentals, separation may be inevitable and lawful … Schism may be the sin of the community left as well as of the community leaving. But all this rises to the higher principle that the Holy Spirit is the Giver of life corporate as well as individual … As to heresy or self-willed and needless schism it is still one of the works of the flesh: (Galatians 5:19) condemned of itself.[124]

One of the two misconceptions about Christian unity is an overestimation of its significance to the point of perceiving it as "uniformity." The Spirit of God also uses "sects and divisions" to accomplish what Christ wants.[125] For instance, the advancement of good news and positive results gained in the missionary fields near and far has been a result of the toil of "Christian societies" working apart from one another.[126] The other positive aspect of denominationalism, which we cannot ignore, is that it gives no space for the society to be "monopolistic"—to dominate and control people's lives as it upholds "religion-cultural pluralism [sic]," which is known

---

[123] Ibid.
[124] Ibid.
[125] Ibid., 3:275.
[126] Ibid.

for its acceptance of one another and freedom of conscience.[127] It is by divine permission that diversities exist even denominationally, and in a way, such separation between Christians into denominations was a blessing in disguise. Leithart contends that "it [denominationalism] is in some mysterious way the creation of God ... It is God's good gift, and we should show proper gratitude ... Division is inevitable and not altogether a bad thing."[128] For Duffield and Van Cleave, "denominations may have been God's way of preserving revival and missionary fervor."[129] However, even with this understanding, the underestimation of Christian unity remains a mistake. Duffield and Van Cleave cautions as follows:

> The members of denominational churches, however, must keep in mind that the Church which is the Body of Christ is composed of all true believers, and that true believers must be united in Spirit to carry forward the Gospel of Christ in the world, for all will be caught up together at the Coming of the Lord. That local churches [sic] should band together for fellowship and missions is certainly a Bible truth. (2 Corinthians 8:1–19, 23, 24; Titus 1:5)[130]

Since the days of Cyprian, discourses about denominationalism have been dominated by propositions for organizational unity. While introducing the idea, Cyprian said that the ecclesial unity would come as a result of intimate unity with "the bishop of Rome."[131] The

---

[127] Leithart, *The End of Protestantism: Pursuing Unity in a Fragmented Church*, 57–59, 65, 66, 62, 63.
[128] Ibid., 6, 55, 62.
[129] Guy Duffield, and Nathaniel Van Cleave, *Foundations of Pentecostal Theology* (Los Angeles, CA: L.I.F.E. Bible College, 1983), 423.

[130] Ibid.
[131] Berkhof, *Systematic Theology*, 502; Reinder Bruinsma, *The Body of Christ: A Biblical Understanding of the Church* (Hagerstown, MD: Review and Herald Publishing Association, 2009), 62.

position has only made the animosity between denominations worse rather than helping to mend fences, as it provides an occasion for the RCs and Protestants to point fingers at each other during discussions on ecclesial disunity. For instance, Steve Bruce (cited by Radner) claims that division was premeditated by the Protestants, whose phrase "priesthood of all believers" demonstrates intentionality.[132] However, the need for separation between Roman Catholics and Protestants was necessitated and induced by severe circumstances, including the incorporation of pagan traditions into the once-pure church and bloody persecutions meted out against those loyal to the scripture by the papal system. Far from being a development driven by selfishness, as has been purported, the fragmentation was a by-product of an attempt to stick to God's will and stay away from error and adulteration of the Gospel.[133] The refusal of the church to listen and consider the concerns of the Protestants and to embrace reform made disunity more inevitable.[134] This trend continues to be among the factors that inform the springing forth of splinters. Denominations often arise because of the inappropriate response to "revival" by those wielding ecclesiastical power, as well as the felt need among the agents of revival to safeguard the purity of Christian teachings and spirituality.[135]

However, the inappropriate relationship is not just between the RCs and Protestants; the relationship among churches affiliated with the latter is not great either. Sometime after the exodus from the RCC, the architects of the Reformation could not stick together because of the divergence in theological positions. Martin Luther, John Calvin, Ulrich Zwingli, the Anabaptists, and Baptists took separate ways. In later times, "nontraditional forms of the church" (also known as free churches) have sprung forth in the south and the

---

[132] Radner, *A Brutal Unity: The Spiritual Politics of the Christian Church*, 3.
[133] Marshall, "Who Really Cares About Christian Unity?"; Duffield and Van Cleave, *Foundations of Pentecostal Theology*, 423.
[134] Duffield and Van Cleave, *Foundations of Pentecostal Theology*, 423; Marshall, "Who Really Cares About Christian Unity?"
[135] Duffield and Van Cleave, *Foundations of Pentecostal Theology*, 423.

West as a result of the failure of mainline ecclesiologies to appeal to members who subscribe to them.[136] Despite the dismissal of these "new" ("younger") churches by "older" churches as mere splinters, they have shown their influence and asserted themselves.[137] All these put the goal of the Reformation at bay—the protest continues.[138] There is no indication of an ecclesial unity happening in this age. Leithart articulates the situation even better,

> Some Christians will claim that reunion will occur when all the schismatics come back home to the mothership. Everyone should become Orthodox, or Roman Catholic, or Anglican, or Lutheran. I do not believe that this is a viable option, either practically or theologically … What is needed is not a return to one or the other existing churches but faith to walk in a way of being Church that does not yet exist. We must walk by faith to be what we will be. What is needed is a death to our present divisions so that we may rise reconciled.[139]

In Africa, denominationalism is a piece of baggage that was bequeathed by Western missionaries to Christians. At first, Western missionaries, on arrival on the African continent, showed unity among themselves despite their divergent nationalistic backgrounds and denominational affiliations.[140] However, when their efforts began to bear fruits among the locals and their leaders in terms of conversions, rivalry and conflict set in among missionary societies.[141]

---

[136] Veli-Matti Karkkainen, *An Introduction to Ecclesiology: Ecumenical, Historical & Global Perspectives* (Downers Grove, Illinois: InterVarsity Press, 2002), 39–78.
[137] Ibid., 59–60.
[138] Leithart, *The End of Protestantism: Pursuing Unity in a Fragmented Church*, 49, 48, 41.
[139] Ibid., 25, 26.
[140] Waruta, "Towards an African Church: A Critical Assessment of Alternative Forms and Structures," 33.
[141] Ibid.

The dissemination of the Gospel became a means of enlarging the scope of their respective Christendoms by way of triumphing, conquering, subjugating, and assimilating.[142] African Christians emulated and carried this trend forward when they took over the task of promulgating the Gospel, leading to unfriendliness and undesirable treatment of one another.[143] While describing the developments of that time, Waruta says that "the era of denominationalism and religious competitiveness dawned in Africa."[144] Since then, disunity remains the greatest dilemma that the church in Africa continues to face. In the face of indifference in the academy regarding this phenomenon, it threatens the very existence and mission of the church. Waruta describes the situation further as follows, "The dynamism anticipated in the Church at independence in the early 1960s has given way to denominational isolationism and more statism at the expense of dynamic spirituality and ecumenism."[145] Rather than working as different members of the Lord's body, Christians have allowed the range of different things that distinguish them to tear them apart and jeopardize the course of the church.[146]

Since an amalgamation of denominations is untenable and unnecessary in this age, the church's only option is to fit itself in a continuum whereby Christians of different denominational persuasions agree to coexist without animosity, acrimony, tension, superiority complex often characterized by the "I am more biblical than thou" mentality, and the undue quest for internally homogenous churches.[147] Bruinsma describes the unity expected of the Church in the following terms:

---

[142] Ibid., 40.
[143] Ibid., 33.
[144] Ibid.
[145] Ibid., 40.
[146] Cleveland, *Disunity in Christ: Uncovering the Hidden Forces That Keep Us Apart*, 20, 25.
[147] Bruinsma, *The Body of Christ: A Biblical Understanding of the Church*, 62; Sidney Mead, "Denominationalism: The Shape of Protestantism in America," in *Denominationalism* (Eugene, OR: Wipf and Stock, 2010), 75–76; Leithart, *The End of Protestantism: Pursuing Unity in a Fragmented Church*, 73–74.

> It is a "tie that binds," but not in ecclesiastical handcuffs. This unity is not primarily theological agreement (even though this is an important goal). It is far more than a spirit of camaraderie—it is a spiritual communion that is rooted in divine gift love: agape ... Yet let us, in pointing to the spiritual nature of this unity, not forget that it has also very concrete this-worldly ramifications.[148]

It is possible to be mutual and in fellowship while maintaining the quality of distinctive teachings and uniqueness.[149] To achieve this kind of harmony, Green and DeJonge propose a reckoning of various existing ecclesial units as smaller and "visible" entities that are part of a larger and "invisible" body called the church.[150] The unity of this kind hinges on several factors that bring or tie Christians to one another. Since the church is both "external" and "internal," these factors are also of either type. In Pictet's description, some of the ties are "essential" and some "accidental."[151] The "internal" ties consist of "the unity of the Spirit" (Ephesians 4:3; 1 Corinthians 12:13).[152] Pictet maintains that "the Spirit is the soul of the church; by this unity of the Spirit two or more societies, which are animated by this same Spirit, constitute one body, though they may be unknown to

---

[148] Bruinsma, *The Body of Christ: A Biblical Understanding of the Church*, 63.

[149] Paul Murray, *Receptive Ecumenism and the Call to Catholic Learning: Exploring a Way For Contemporary Ecumenism* (Oxford: Oxford University Press, 2010); Leithart, *The End of Protestantism: Pursuing Unity in a Fragmented Church*, 167, 168; James Quinn, "Pluralism and the Unity of the Church," n.d, www.theway.org.uk/Back/15Quinn.pdf 276; Augustin Bishwende, *Eglise - Famille de Dieu Dans La Mondialisation: Theologie D'une Nouvelle Voie Africaine D'evangelisation*. (Paris: L'Harmattan, 2006), 307–311, 317–326.

[150] Clifford Green and Michael DeJonge, eds., *The Bonhoeffer Reader* (Minneapolis, MN: Fortress Press, 2013), 571.

[151] Pictet, *Christian Theology*, 366–367.

[152] Ibid.

each other; thus we ourselves form one body with other churches in distant parts of the world."[153]

There is also "the unity of faith" (Ephesians 4:5), which implies shared teachings about "salvation," as spelled out in the Word of God and accepted "by faith."[154] The distortion of biblical teachings and the misuse of ordinances have no place in it and are tantamount to a "universal schism."[155] Pictet refers to the other as "the unity of charity or love," which facilitates unity among all believers who are in unity with Christ.[156] This unity sets in through love—one cannot be in unity with Christ and fail to be in unity with others in love.[157] There is also "the unity of hope" (Ephesians 4:4)—that is, of the substance of hope, what believers will receive in paradise—"we are all called" for this (Ephesians 4:5).[158]

"Outward" ties, which are also essential, consist of "the unity of sacraments"—for instance, "baptism" (Ephesians 4:5)—and "the unity of ministry."[159] "Accidental bonds" could include concurrence in every teaching, similar rules, polity, or "discipline."[160]

Whenever disputes related to teachings arise, discussions should take place to find a solution.[161] Conversations leading to "understanding" among those involved ought to take place to reduce the rift where possible and lead to unity in principle aspects.[162] At the same time, freedom to exercise judgment on nonfundamental

---

[153] Ibid.
[154] Ibid.
[155] "Universal schism" is a rejection of truths that are common and enjoy universal acceptance among believers, and core to Christianity. (Louis, Berkhof, *Systematic Theology*, 573; Pictet, *Christian Theology*, 367).
[156] Pictet, *Christian Theology*, 366–367.
[157] Colossians 3:14.
[158] Pictet, *Christian Theology*, 366–367.
[159] Ibid.
[160] Ibid., 367.
[161] Donald Bloesch, *The Church: Sacraments, Worship, Ministry, Mission* (Downers Grove, IL: InterVarsity Press, 2002), 300.
[162] Ibid.

issues should be allowed, and love should be shown all the way.[163] Separation should be a final resort when all available avenues of resolving disagreements have been employed to no avail.[164] It is a step that is taken with reluctance.

Conclusion

Ecclesial disunity is not unique only to the present time. Church history is littered with instances of disunity among Christians throughout the ages. The church, at various times right from its commencement, dealt with this problem in ways that African Christians could emulate in the present. In both the OT and NT dispensations, the church exhibited very strong familial and communitarian features in its life right from the patriarchal to the Mosaic through to the apostolic and patristic periods. These features enhanced intimate connections among Christians that the relationships arising from the two models presently are short of as the Western mindset informs them. Whenever the familial and communitarian aspects of the church were taken away, disunity and problems set in, as demonstrated in Adam and Eve's case; in the relationship between Cain and Abel; in the secession of Israel from Judah; in quarrels among believers during the apostolic times; in tussles over doctrinal issues and leadership wrangles during the patristic era; and the schism in the Catholic Church, which caused the departure of Protestants from it. The severance of the Eastern Orthodox Church from the RCC is also among those moments. The current situation in ecclesial life is a product and the aftermath of historical developments. However, the developments also present familial aspects of the relationship among the people of God. The component of jo-kang'ato was there during the patriarchal period when families comprised the church and handed faith down to

---

[163] Ibid.
[164] Augustus Strong, *Systematic Theology* (Philadelphia: American Baptist Publication Society, 1907), 903.

the next generations. In the Mosaic period, Israel demonstrated jo-kang'ato as a theocratic society and a national church. At the beginning of the NT church in AD first century too, Christians engaged one another as members of one community where spiritual and material resources were shared. In most cases, the disputes that arose were viewed as sibling rivalry, and solutions were worked out. For instance, in the misunderstanding between the Hebrew and Hellenistic women, the apostles formulated the process of resolution, while at the council in Jerusalem, the elders—that is, senior leaders of the church—heard and determined the theological case presented by delegates from each side of the spectrum. The concept of jo-kang'ato also came into play in the broadened scope of the church during the apostolic era when extension and inclusivity happened. However, the component of jo-kang'ato was marred during the patristic times by the Arian controversy and subsequent theological conflicts. The situation was aggravated by the rise of the papacy and subsequent denominationalism.

CHAPTER 2

Christian Unity as Understood in Various Ecclesial Traditions

Unity has been defined by Wehmeier as "the state of being in agreement [sic] and working together; the state of being joined together to form one unity."[165] The definition has been extended by Thomas Aquinas to include the absence of "separation."[166] As used in this work, unity does not refer to a conglomeration or confederacy of people who act in the same way into a single social unit with centralized ecclesiastical leadership. If you go by history, especially developments during the Middle Ages when Constantine and rulers after him reigned, the benefits of constructing an outfit of that nature are dismal in comparison to the demerits.[167] An ideal Christian unity lets people and churches keep their unique God-given features, thus making them lively rather than uninteresting.[168] The "spiritual" or "inward" aspects are stressed rather than the "external" aspects. At

---

[165] Sally Wehmeier, ed., *Oxford Advanced Learner's Dictionary* (New York: Oxford University Press, 2005), 1614.
[166] Thomas Aquinas, *Summa Theologica*, trans. Fathers of the English Dominican Province (London: Burns Oates & Washbourne, n.d.).
[167] James Boice, *Foundations of the Christian Faith: A Comprehensive & Readable Theology* (Downers Grove, IL: InterVarsity Press, 1986), 583; Berkhof, *Systematic Theology*, 573.
[168] Berkhof, *Systematic Theology*, 571, 572.

the local church level, that unity allows the parishioners to participate fully in the ecclesial life of the church as opposed to reserving the right to do so to an individual or a group of clergies.

Unity is among the marks of the church that set forth its true nature or character.[169] For Küng, these marks are the "dimensions" of the church since they speak of what the real church looks like.[170] If we go by this description, it could be said that when the church is united, it simply manifests its intrinsic characteristics. There exists only one church—one set by Christ and enabled to be effective and noticeable through the showers of God's Spirit.[171] However, as with other marks of the church, Christian unity is related to love. A unity that is devoid of love begets "tyranny," which is a characteristic of the hierarchical churches and takes the form of callousness and autocracy.[172] As Boice puts it, the consequence of love for other Christian believers is unity in that "by love we discern that we are bound together in that bundle of life which God himself has created within the Christian community."[173] Bloesch emphasizes this point further:

> Christians are commanded to love each other despite differences of race, gender, privilege, and social, political and economic background (John 13:34–35; Galatians 3:28–29), and to be of one mind wherever possible (John 17:20–21; Philippians 2:2; Romans 14:1–15:13). We know that divisions among Christians hinder our witness in the world, and we desire greater mutual understanding and truth-speaking in love.[174]

---

[169] Pictet, *Christian Theology*, 366.
[170] Küng, *The Church*, 269.
[171] Bloesch, *The Church: Sacraments, Worship, Ministry, Mission*, 100.
[172] Boice, *Foundations of the Christian Faith: A Comprehensive & Readable Theology*, 585.
[173] Ibid.
[174] Bloesch, *The Church: Sacraments, Worship, Ministry, Mission*, 300.

Harmony is lacking among theologians presently on how the marks are to be understood.¹⁷⁵ The subject of ecclesial unity is especially an area where such divergence of thought continues to manifest.

The contentious issue among scholars with respect to Christian unity is whether it is supposed to be understood institutionally or it is an "invisible fellowship of the saints on earth and in heaven."¹⁷⁶ The divergence of views is often informed by the ecclesial traditions the scholars subscribe to. In Volf's words, though, "the differentiation of various Christian traditions is not simply to be lamented as a scandal, but rather welcomed as a sign of the vitality of the Christian faith within multicultural, rapidly changing societies demanding diversification and flexibility."¹⁷⁷ Generally, Christian unity is a dominant discussion to date among theological scholars and in the ecclesial life of the church as a whole.¹⁷⁸

2.1 The Roman Catholic Church Tradition

As far as the church fathers were concerned, the Catholic Church comprises every true section of Christ's church that is bonded to one another externally and visibly under a body of bishops as the unifying factor.¹⁷⁹ With time, this understanding of the church in terms of an exterior entity gained momentum and support. This development was accompanied by the laying of more stress on the hierarchy within it, which realized its highest achievement as a dispensation with the arrival of the papacy.¹⁸⁰ As Jay puts it, the church turned into a "highly structured organisation centred on the

---

¹⁷⁵ Ibid., 39.
¹⁷⁶ Ibid.
¹⁷⁷ Miroslav Volf, *After Our Likeness: The Church as the Image of the Trinity*, Sacra Doctrina (Grand Rapids, Michigan; Cambridge: William B. Eerdmans Publishing Company, 1998), 21.
¹⁷⁸ Bloesch, *The Church: Sacraments, Worship, Ministry, Mission*, 41.
¹⁷⁹ Berkhof, *Systematic Theology*, 562.
¹⁸⁰ Ibid.

papacy, for which increasingly the claims of primacy and supremacy were made."[181] Cyprian himself said that ecclesial unity would be achieved as a result of intimate unity with "the bishop of Rome."[182] In line with this perspective, the church is not a church unless it is a "hierarchically organised ecclesia," and unity occurs around the clergy.[183] This view is based on the Vatican I's (1869–1870) position of the church as a group of people who are not on the same level.[184] This thought is captured so well in the definition of the Church within the Roman Catholic (RC) circles: "The congregation of all the Faithful, who, being baptised, profess the same faith, partake of the same sacraments, and are governed by their lawful pastors, under one visible head on earth."[185] This worldview comes out even clearer in Berkhof's enlightening explanation of the RCC hierarchy, whereby he says that Roman Catholicism differentiates *ecclesia docens*—"the Church consisting of those who rule, teach, and edify"—and the *ecclesia audiens*, "the Church which is taught, governed, and receives the sacraments."[186]

As per this view, what makes up the church is the ecclesia docens rather than the ecclesia audiens. Berkhof explains further that the reason behind it is that the ecclesia docens "shares directly in the glorious attributes of the Church" while the ecclesia audiens "is adorned with them only indirectly."[187] The prominence of the clergy in that hierarchy is so great that they are referred to as the soul of the church.[188] Devine's definition of the soul of the church brings this to the fore in that he views it as "the society of those who are called to

---

[181] Eric Jay, *The Church: Its Changing Image Through the Twenty Century*, vol. 1 (Atlanta: John Knox Press, 1980), 97.
[182] Berkhof, *Systematic Theology*, 502.
[183] Ibid., 572.
[184] Avery Dulles, *Models of the Church* (New York: Doubleday, 1974), 31.
[185] Berkhof, *Systematic Theology*, 562.
[186] Ibid., 362.
[187] Ibid., 562.
[188] Ibid.

faith in Christ, and who are united to Christ by supernatural gifts and graces."[189] Berkhof elaborates the situation even further:

> Its real center is not found in the believers, but in the hierarchy with its concentric circles. There is first of all the broad circle of the lower clergy, the priests and other inferior functionaries; then the smaller circle of the bishops; next the still narrower one of the archbishops; and, finally, the most restricted circle of the cardinals;—the entire pyramid being capped by the Pope, the visible head of the whole organisation, who has absolute control of all those that are under him. Thus the Roman Catholic Church presents to the eye a very imposing structure.[190]

The position of the RCC is connected to the emphasis on the visible dimension of the church over the invisible. While the RCC theology does not refute the church's "invisible" dimension, prominence is given to its visible state to the extent of almost eclipsing the former.[191] The RCC tradition favors the application of the reference "church" on a "visible" fellowship of Christians.[192] Its theology maintains that "there is no salvation beyond the pale of the one visible institution."[193] As Moehler puts it, "the Catholics teach: the visible Church is first,— then comes the invisible: the former gives birth to the latter."[194] In

---

[189] Arthur Devine, *The Creed Explained, Or, An Exposition of Catholic Doctrine* (Hardpress Publishing, 2012), 259.
[190] Berkhof, *Systematic Theology*, 572.
[191] Pope, *A Compendium of Christian Theology: Being Analytical Outlines of a Course of Theological Study, Biblical, Dogmatic, Historical*, 3:281; Berkhof, *Systematic Theology*, 563, 562.
[192] Berkhof, *Systematic Theology*, 562.
[193] Pope, *A Compendium of Christian Theology: Being Analytical Outlines of a Course of Theological Study, Biblical, Dogmatic, Historical*, 3:231.
[194] Johann Moehler, *Symbolism: or Exposition of Doctrinal Differences Between Catholics and Protestants, as Evidenced by their Symbolic Writings*, 2nd ed, vol. 2 (London, 1847), 108.

other words, the *mater fidelium* ("mother of believers") status precedes *communio fidelium* ("community of believers").[195] Moehler agrees, though, that in a way, the "internal church" comes first before "the exterior one," and people are members of the former before they could be members of the latter.[196] That position is captured in the statement "one Ruler of the church invisible, Christ; and one Ruler of the visible, the successor of St. Peter."[197]

Presently, in the RC theological circles, the "marks of the church" are being reconsidered with the resolutions of the Vatican Council II coming into play.[198] The interrogation of the conventional premise of unity, which is taking place already, is part of these developments. This is almost displacing the view that has enjoyed prominence over the years, whereby the action of becoming RCC members is seen as the avenue for achieving unity.[199] It has dawned on scholars of late that authentic unity has to do with the "conversion" of each church to Christ and the good news about Him.[200] In line with the current trend, Dulles, in particular, contends that the kind of ecclesial unity to be expected ought not to be understood in the "external" sense demonstrated institutionally and visibly but in the sense of "the interior unity of mutual charity leading to a communion of friends."[201]

Christian unity, as understood in Roman Catholicism, is also informed by the perception of Catholicism. Karl Barth made a pronouncement about Catholicity that the Christian church is "catholic, or it is not the Church."[202] In most cases, RCC scholars have understood the unity of the church and continue to do so in light

---

[195] Berkhof, Systematic Theology, 563.
[196] Moehler, Symbolism: or Exposition of Doctrinal Differences Between Catholics and Protestants, as Evidenced by their Symbolic Writings, 109.
[197] Pope, *A Compendium of Christian Theology: Being Analytical Outlines of a Course of Theological Study, Biblical, Dogmatic, Historical*, 3:281.
[198] Bloesch, *The Church: Sacraments, Worship, Ministry, Mission*, 40.
[199] Ibid., 41.
[200] Ibid.
[201] Dulles, *Models of the Church*, 122.
[202] Karl Barth, *Church Dogmatics*, Vol. IV/1 (Edinburgh: Clark, 1956), 702.

of Catholicity. By the word Catholic, the universality of the church is meant.[203] However, this term has been employed in the history of the church in varying ways. From the earliest time, the scripture envisaged a time when religious entities from every nation (yet not dependent on their national elements) would come together.[204] Local churches are parts of that Catholic fellowship (Revelation 1:4).[205] However, in the middle of the second century, when the word Catholic came into use, connotations that are not alluded to by the scripture were incorporated into it.[206] It was employed in differentiating the sole, "universal," and true believers from the disjointed elements, subscribing to heresies and adherents of schismatic groups that have fallen out with Catholicism.[207]

While the term Catholicity is not meant to be employed by Christians exclusively to refer to a given entity, the RCC has taken ownership of it, for they claim that they are "the one and only church, outside of which there is no salvation."[208] However, whereas the church is universal, it is regional and specific too.[209] Pope is articulate as he relays that fact,

> The Church is also Local or Particular: it exists in independent and even isolated forms, whether as it respects individual, or connexional, or national bodies; and it may, holding the catholic verities, maintain in its Confession truths that are not catholic, and adopt un-catholic usages, without impairing its catholicity. For the one Church of Christ is at once adapted for every variety of mankind and influenced in its turn

---

[203] Pope, *A Compendium of Christian Theology: Being Analytical Outlines of a Course of Theological Study, Biblical, Dogmatic, Historical*, 3:282.
[204] Ibid., 3:283.
[205] Ibid.
[206] Ibid.
[207] Ibid; Volf, *After Our Likeness: The Church as the Image of the Trinity*, 265.
[208] Pope, *A Compendium of Christian Theology: Being Analytical Outlines of a Course of Theological Study, Biblical, Dogmatic, Historical*, 3:283–284.
[209] Ibid.

by every variety of human life. It is not more certainly Universal than it is Particular.[210]

Furthermore, while Catholicity is about the church's "universality and inclusivity," it also speaks of the unbroken link with past ecclesial "traditions."[211]

Catholicity has gained a new shape and meaning in present times in the RC theology. The departure from the exclusive and discriminative understanding has been the consequence of the works of recent theologians. Küng presents this new perspective in his argument when he says that "the catholicity of the Church ... consists in a notion of entirety, based on identity and resulting in universality. According to this view, unity and catholicity go together; if the Church is one, it must be universal, if it is universal [sic] it must be one. Unity and catholicity are two interwoven dimensions of one and the same Church."[212] He contends further that it is incumbent upon both the "mother church" and "daughter churches" to regain the Catholicity of the church.[213] He advances his argument:

> The so-called "Catholic Church" will never achieve the necessary unity or catholicity of the Church without sorting out its relationship to the Churches which directly or indirectly have sprung from her, and on her side making peace with them. All the movements towards reform and renewal within the Church, which we must all welcome, will remain incomplete if the connections ... with the other Churches are ignored. If on the other hand these connections are examined sympathetically and taken

---

[210] Ibid.
[211] Bloesch, *The Church: Sacraments, Worship, Ministry, Mission*, 101–102.
[212] Küng, *The Church*, 303.
[213] Ibid., 310.

up positively, then these movements of reform will assume new breadth and depth.²¹⁴

The same mindset informs Dulles's proposition of the ideal Catholicity. He supports a type of Catholicity that is unique in nature—one that is "not the accomplished fact of having many members or a wide geographical distribution, but rather the dynamic catholicity of a love reaching out to all and excluding none."²¹⁵ Volf presents the features of that kind of Catholicity as "unity and multiplicity" without which it cannot be realized.²¹⁶ He contends for a *qualitative* (intensive) rather than a *quantitative* (extensive) view of Catholicity.²¹⁷ Isolated church entities do not meet the specifications of Catholicity, so are detached persons.²¹⁸ Walter Kasper (quoted by Dulles) adds more light to this view as he describes what the "new Catholicism" envisions thus,

> The unity and catholicity of the Church are always and, in every case, still in fieri; they will always remain a task. The solution cannot lie either in mutual absorption or in simple integration of individual ecclesiastical communities, but only in the constant conversion of all—i.e., in the readiness to let the event of unity, already anticipated in grace and sign, occur ever and again in obedience to the one Gospel as the final norm in and over the Church.²¹⁹

The way present-day scholars from the RC wing convey the ultimate Catholicity of faith is something that could be borrowed by the evangelicals in that in the evangelical circles, the term Catholic

---

²¹⁴ Ibid.
²¹⁵ Dulles, *Models of the Church*, 122.
²¹⁶ Volf, *After Our Likeness: The Church as the Image of the Trinity*, 262.
²¹⁷ Ibid., 265, 266–267.
²¹⁸ Ibid., 277, 278–282.
²¹⁹ Dulles, *Models of the Church*, 149–150.

is perceived in terms of opposition to the Gospel while the grasp of its basic or important quality is lost.[220]

2.2 The Greek Orthodox Tradition

The Orthodox Church is made up of fourteen independent entities, also known as autocephalous. The independence exists in organization and liturgy.[221] However, they all share faith and benefit at a higher level from the leadership of the "archbishop of Constantinople, known as the ecumenical patriarch" and regarded as "the first bishop of the Church."[222] The Greek Orthodox (GO) is an "autocephalous" within the Orthodox Church.

There is a significant resemblance of understanding of the church among the GO and the RCs. However, there is another view that the Orthodox share a lot with the "evangelicals" than with the RCs because of their elevation of the Bible.[223] They perceive tradition as the Word of God passed over to the "church" and, as such, the most important thing. Besides, their tradition lays stress on Jesus, his ministry, and "the mystery of his Incarnation and Resurrection."[224] Besides, they refute the overall papal ecclesial authority, claiming that the scope of such authority does not stretch beyond the RCC.[225] In addition to not agreeing on certain matters that are of significance, the GOs claim that they are the only legitimate and "true" church, not the RCC.[226] The deep-seated differences between these ecclesial entities are rooted in historical events.[227]

---

[220] Bloesch, *The Church: Sacraments, Worship, Ministry, Mission*, 102.
[221] Reid et al., in *Dictionary of Christianity in America*.
[222] Ibid.
[223] "An Evangelical Appraisal," *Christian History Magazine*, 54 (1997).
[224] Ibid.
[225] Ibid.
[226] Berkhof, *Systematic Theology*, 563.
[227] Many historical factors contributed to the division between the Church in the East (Orthodox) and the Church in the West (RC). It all started with "the Great Schism of 1054" following the inception of an absolute papal rule over

One of the distinguishing features between the GOs and the RCs is that unlike the latter, the former are open in their cognizance of both the "visible" and "invisible" dimensions of the church.[228]

---

the entire Church. [Sharon Rusten, and Michael Rusten, *The Complete Book of when & where in the Bible and throughout History* (Wheaton, IL: Tyndale House Publishers, Inc., 2005), 164]. Rusten and Rusten recounts that "The Orthodox Church, which had agreed to honor the pope, believed that church matters should be determined by a council of bishops, and would not grant the pope undisputed dominion. The two churches already had very distinct cultures and theologies. The Eastern Church developed into the Eastern, Greek, and Russian Orthodox Churches while the Western Roman Church developed into the Roman Catholic Church. The East and West churches remained on friendly terms until Crusaders of the Fourth Crusade captured Constantinople in 1204." (Ibid.). The division escalated to the point that reuniting has been impossible. (Ibid.). According to Dennis, the other points of departure between these two ecclesiastical realities included "Differences over clerical marriage, the bread used for the Eucharist, days of fasting, and other usages assumed an unprecedented importance." [George Dennis, "The East-West Schism (1054)," *Christian History Magazine* 28 (1990)]. He further says that "The eleventh-century reform in the Western Church called for the strengthening of papal authority, which caused the Church to become more autocratic and centralized. Basing his claims on his succession from St. Peter, the pope asserted his direct jurisdiction over the entire Church, East as well as West. The Byzantines, on the other hand, viewed their Church in the context of the imperial system; their sources of law and unity were the ecumenical councils and the emperor, whom God had placed over all things, spiritual and temporal. They believed that the Eastern churches had always enjoyed autonomy of governance, and they rejected papal claims to absolute rule. But neither side was really listening to the other." (Ibid.). The controversy was also around the inclusion of the *Filioque* in the Nicene Creed. Dennis recounts the situation as follows, "The Western Church, concerned about resurgent Arianism, had, almost inadvertently, added the word to the Nicene Creed, claiming that it made more precise a teaching already in the creed. The Greeks objected to the unilateral addition to the creed, and they strongly disagreed with the theological proposition involved, which seemed to them to diminish the individual properties of the three Persons in the Trinity...Today greater efforts are made to address the issues, but neither side seems willing to make the necessary concessions. As a result, Christians who share a common belief and accept Jesus as head of the Church, feel that they cannot share his Eucharist." (Ibid.).
[228] Berkhof, *Systematic Theology*, 563.

However, preeminence is given to the church as an external entity.[229] While describing the two dimensions of the church, Gavin, who is an insider, argues that "as invisible, she [the Church] is the bearer of divine gifts and powers, and is engaged in transforming mankind into the Kingdom of God. As visible, she is constituted of men professing a common faith, observing common customs, and using visible means of grace."[230] Support is lacking among the GO, though, for the existence of "an invisible and ideal Church, of which the various bodies of Christians formed into distinct organisations and calling themselves 'Churches,' are partial and incomplete embodiments" since the church is viewed as "an actual, tangible, visible entity, not an unrealised and unrealisable ideal."[231] This tradition holds that the church's intrinsic nature is found in its "Episcopal hierarchy" rather than in its being a "community of saints."[232] In this Episcopal structure, the understanding is that at "ordination," the bishop is also enthroned; and as he leads the Eucharist, he is to be seen not only as the image of Christ but also as Christ Himself to the audience since the program he is involved in is the same as that which Christ is involved in "invisibly."[233] However, apart from being the *alter Christus*, the bishop is also the *alter apostolus* as it is through him and his ordination by another bishop in the presence of other bishops that the "local church" finds unity "with all the local churches of the past," thus maintaining the apostolic succession.[234] In this *episcopocentric* system, the bishop is so important that without him, the church cannot meet ecclesial status.[235] The hierarchical system is also reflected in

---

[229] Ibid.
[230] Frank Gavin, *Some Aspects of Contemporary Greek Orthodox Thought* (London: SPCK, 1936), 241–242.
[231] Ibid.
[232] Berkhof, *Systematic Theology*, 563.
[233] John Zizioulas, "La Mystere de l'Eglise Dans La Tradition Orthodoxe," *Irenikon* 60 (1987): 329.
[234] John Zizioulas, "The Bishop in the Theological Doctrine of the Orthodox Church," *Kanon* 7 (1985): 31.
[235] Volf, *After Our Likeness: The Church as the Image of the Trinity*, 130, 131, 223–224.

the way laypeople are regarded. Zizioulas views their baptism as an occasion for their ordination, which puts them in a particular ordo.[236] The responsibility that follows this is the pronouncement of amen in "response to the grace they have received," which is regarded as a "charisma" in itself.[237] The pope is not recognized, though.[238] In connection with this position, while the Greek Orthodox Church (GOC) backs the view of the church as an infallible entity, they hold that this "infallibility" is actually in the prelates "and therefore in the ecclesiastical councils and synods.[239] Zizioulas proposes an understanding of ecclesial unity in Catholic rather than "universal" sense.[240] His position is that Catholicity encourages communing with others rather than allowing the "local church" to exclude or enmesh itself from the rest.[241] Whereas the RC tradition understands universality as "unity in collectivity," Zizioulas view is that it stands for "unity in identity."[242] He contends that "schematically speaking, in the first case the various local churches form parts which are added to one another in order to make up a whole, whereas, in the latter, the local churches are full circles which cannot be added to one another but coincide with one another and finally with the body of Christ and the original apostolic church."[243] The import of this argument is that "the local churches" are equal as none is higher ranking and none lesser.[244]

---

[236] Zizioulas is the main theologian in the GOC.
[237] John Zizioulas, *Being as Communion: Studies in Personhood and the Church* (Crestwood, NY: St. Vladimir's Seminary Press, 1985), 215; Volf, *After Our Likeness: The Church as the Image of the Trinity*, 113–114, 115, 116, 121, 224.
[238] Berkhof, *Systematic Theology*, 563.
[239] Ibid.
[240] Volf, *After Our Likeness: The Church as the Image of the Trinity*, 106.
[241] Zizioulas, *Being as Communion: Studies in Personhood and the Church*, 133.
[242] Volf, *After Our Likeness: The Church as the Image of the Trinity*, 106.
[243] Zizioulas, *Being as Communion: Studies in Personhood and the Church*, 158; C.f. 197, 168.
[244] John Zizioulas, "Episkope and Episkopos in the Early Church: A Brief Survey of the Evidence," in *Episcope and Episcopate in Ecumenical Perspective*, vol. 102,

2.3 The Evangelical Protestant Tradition

The "externalism" of the RCC, especially in connection to the understanding of the church, aroused discontent, which culminated in the Reformation.[245] Through the Reformation, the truth came to the forefront again, basically as it pertains to the intrinsic nature of the church.[246] In Protestantism, there is an endeavor to bring the visible and invisible attributes together, even though it tends to place more importance and prominence on the latter.[247] While the Reformers upheld the oneness of the "invisible" aspect of the church, they rejected the premising of it upon "the ecclesiastical organisation of the Church" but in the right proclamation of God's Word and correct celebration of the "sacraments."[248] The Reformation led to a realization that the church is not "an external organization" in its essence but rather a *communio sanctorum* (the community of the saints).[249] The two prominent reformers, Martin Luther and John Calvin, viewed the church as a fellowship of people who have faith in Christ, receive sanctification in their lives, and are united to Christ, who is "their Head."[250] A similar view is affirmed "in the Reformed confessional standards." In the Belgic Confession, this position is stated thus: "We believe and profess one catholic or universal Church, which is a holy congregation of true Christian believers, all expecting their salvation in Jesus Christ, being washed by His blood, sanctified and sealed by the Holy Spirit."[251] The marks setting apart the genuine church from the spurious one are articulated:

Faith and Order Papers (Geneva: World Council of Churches, 1980), 33; Daniel Jenkins, *The Nature of Catholicity* (London: Faber and Faber, 1941),104.
[245] Berkhof, *Systematic Theology*, 563–564.
[246] Ibid., 564.
[247] Pope, *A Compendium of Christian Theology: Being Analytical Outlines of a Course of Theological Study, Biblical, Dogmatic, Historical*, 3:281.
[248] Berkhof, *Systematic Theology*, 573.
[249] Ibid., 564.
[250] Ibid.
[251] The Belgic Confession, Art. XXVII (Ibid).

If the pure doctrine of the Gospel is preached therein; if it maintains the pure administration of the sacraments as instituted by Christ; if Church discipline is exercised in punishing sin; in short, if all things are managed according to the pure Word of God; all things contrary thereto rejected, and Jesus Christ acknowledged as the only Head of the Church. Hereby the true Church may certainly be known, from which no man has a right to separate himself.[252]

In the Second Helvetic Confession, the point is reiterated: "A company of the faithful, called and gathered out of the world; a communion of all saints, that is, of them who truly know and rightly worship and serve the true God, in Jesus Christ the Saviour, by the word of the Holy Spirit, and who by faith are partakers of all those good graces which are freely offered through Christ."[253] In the Westminster Confession, the same thought is conveyed in light of "election": "The catholic or universal Church, which is invisible, consists of the whole number of the elect, that have been, are, or shall be gathered into one, under Christ the head thereof; and is the spouse, the body, the fullness of Him that filleth all in all."[254] The Westminster Confession reflects in the Reformed tradition whereby the "doctrine of election" informs the understanding and position about visible and invisible aspects of the church. The view is that while true communion consists of the elect, the church in its visible form as an entity has holiness as its quality; and in Calvin's words, "to depart from which is to deny Christ."[255] For the Congregationalists, those who are known to be real in their profession constitute the invisible church.[256] They seek to use the "visible" as a determinant

---

[252] Ibid., 573.
[253] The Second Helvetic Confession, Chap. XVII (Ibid., 564).
[254] The Westminster Confession, Chap. XXV (Ibid).
[255] Pope, *A Compendium of Christian Theology: Being Analytical Outlines of a Course of Theological Study, Biblical, Dogmatic, Historical*, 3:282.
[256] Ibid.

of the "invisible" in all places.[257] The consequence of this position is the creation of a dividing line distinguishing "the church and the congregation."[258] It is in its earthly form that the church meets the specifications of "the community of the saints."[259]

Generally, the Evangelical Protestants (EP) widely accepts that by the fact that the church consists of God's people drawn together at all times, oneness amid plurality, which has been the principle of its life and growth, is suggested.[260] In the scripture, that unity since the onset is acknowledged as based on the fact that they share "redemption."[261] A "holy" fellowship of all time has existed in oneness amid numerous expressions, shapes, and displays since the time of the patriarchs to the Christian era.[262] Pope refers to it as "the *Civitas Dei* running its course through all ages."[263] The Scottish theologians, however, believe that such kind of unity should manifest in one church entity. While describing their position, Walker (quoted by Berkhof) says that "true Churches of Christ, side by side with one another, forming separate organisations, with separate governments, seemed to them [Scottish theologians] utterly inadmissible, unless it might be in a very limited way, and for some reason of temporary expediency."[264]

Going by what the various confessions tell us, certain qualities qualify a given entity to be part of God's church. These connect various forms of Christian churches even though they function differently. So long as their teachings and beliefs are predicated upon the scripture, and they administer ordinances rightly, worship God in the right way, and discipline their erring members, among

---

[257] Ibid.
[258] Ibid.
[259] Berkhof, *Systematic Theology*, 564.
[260] Pope, *A Compendium of Christian Theology: Being Analytical Outlines of a Course of Theological Study, Biblical, Dogmatic, Historical*, 3:268.
[261] Ibid.
[262] Ibid.
[263] Ibid.
[264] Berkhof, *Systematic Theology*, 573.

other qualities, they become part of that communio sanctorum and unite in an invisible sense. In its invisible aspect, it is complete and all-encompassing or inclusive, yet as it exhibits God's kingdom here on earth, the visible element comes in.[265] Pope observes that "the entire New Testament goes on to the assumption that every extant community is the earthly embodiment of the kingdom of heaven. In this the servants are faithful to the teaching of their Master, who taught the unity, though not identity, of the visible and the invisible communions."[266] The two ecclesial dimensions will remain until the time of the end when the unseen and seen church will be brought together and blended into a "final and eternal unity" as envisaged in the apocalypse. In that new development, the church will become visible forever.[267] In the meantime, Berkhof's description holds:

> The Church forms a spiritual unity of which Christ is the divine head. It is animated by one Spirit, the Spirit of Christ; it professes one faith, shares one hope, and serves one King. It is the citadel of the truth and God's agency in communicating to believers all spiritual blessings. As the body of Christ [sic] it is destined to reflect the glory of God as manifested in the work of redemption. The Church in its ideal sense, the Church as God intends it to be and as it will once become, is an object of faith rather than of knowledge. Hence the confession: "I believe one holy catholic Church." ... It is the unity of the mystical body of Jesus Christ, of which all believers are members. This body is controlled by one Head, Jesus Christ, who is also the King of the Church, and is animated by one Spirit, the Spirit of Christ. This unity implies that all those who belong to the Church

---

[265] Pope, *A Compendium of Christian Theology: Being Analytical Outlines of a Course of Theological Study, Biblical, Dogmatic, Historical*, 3:230.
[266] Ibid.
[267] Ibid., 3:281.

share in the same faith, are cemented together by the common bond of love, and have the same glorious outlook upon the future. This inner unity seeks and also acquires, relatively speaking, outward expression in the profession and Christian conduct of believers, in their public worship of the same God in Christ, and in their participation in the same sacraments.[268]

According to the Protestant tradition (PT), the church is supposed to experience unity in an "internal and spiritual" sense rather than just "externally."[269] However, the PT does not confine Christian unity to the invisible dimension of the church even though it places significant emphasis on it. It is conscious of the unity within the visible church too.

As in the RCC circles, there is a paradigm shift taking place among the EPs resulting from a realization that preoccupation with the expansion of denominations does not suffice and their energies could be expended in "a united evangelical witness before the world."[270] Speaking of this new development, Bloesch states that "some evangelicals are coming to recognise that unity among ourselves is not enough: we must strive for evangelical-Catholic unity [including unity with the Orthodox churches]."[271] "Organizational unity," though, is a matter that is likely to elicit opposition among the majority of evangelicals who are of the view that it is not a valid objective.[272] However, talks are going on between a section of evangelicals and "renewal-minded Roman Catholics," which have culminated in, among other things, the production of works together.[273] This development, however, is not without censure on

---

[268] Berkhof, *Systematic Theology*, 564–565, 572.
[269] Ibid., 572.
[270] Bloesch, *The Church: Sacraments, Worship, Ministry, Mission*, 41–42.
[271] Ibid., 42.
[272] Ibid., 42.
[273] One of such is "The Gift of Salvation" (The Gift of Salvation," *Christianity Today* 41, no. 14 (December 8, 1997): 35–38; Charles Colson and Richard John

the scholars involved, who seem to ignore critical and considerable distinctions among the entities.[274] Whereas the distinctions are indeed significant, certain aspects of beliefs are similar. The perspective of Timothy George is that the evangelicals do not enjoy "unity of faith with the Church of Rome" but enjoy "unity in Christ" with them.[275] Amid these developments, national churches are firmly settled and enjoy the status given to them by their nations. For instance, while "universal unity" is not anticipated by the Church of England with their Episcopal system and the Lutheran Church, both support the kind of unity that is in keeping with their status as national churches.[276] Churches that are in the same position in different lands are doing the same.[277] Pope describes this situation as "the religious unity of race or nation or territory."[278] The Congregationalists, on their part, favor a willful clustering.[279]

The verbalized need for amalgamation into either the RC or Eastern Orthodox Churches is gaining momentum among ecclesiastical leaders and theologians of Protestant background. For instance, a former Lutheran Richard Neuhaus, who decamped into the RCC, holds that the good news about unwarranted justification revealed to Protestantism could find proper maintenance within the RCC now that the majority of Protestant churches, Lutherans included, are caught up in "moralism and individualism."[280] On his part, Silleck, who is a Lutheran pastor, asserts that "the churches of the reformation are not complete churches in and of themselves, but rather constitute only a confessing movement within the greater

---

Neuhaus, eds., *Evangelicals and Catholics Together: Toward a Common Mission* (Dallas: Word, 1995).

[274] Bloesch, *The Church: Sacraments, Worship, Ministry, Mission*, 42.

[275] Art Moore, "Does 'The Gift of Salvation' Sell Out the Reformation?" *Christianity Today* 42, no. 5 (April 27, 1998): 21.

[276] Pope, *A Compendium of Christian Theology: Being Analytical Outlines of a Course of Theological Study, Biblical, Dogmatic, Historical*, 3:274.

[277] Ibid.

[278] Ibid.

[279] Ibid.

[280] Bloesch, *The Church: Sacraments, Worship, Ministry, Mission*, 42.

Christian family because of an emergency situation within that family."[281] Silleck and a significant number of prominent Lutherans support rejoining the "mother church" as the only way through which the good news of "freedom" that the Reformers advocated for could be a reality.[282] In his own words, he says that "Rome is theologically healthy, missiologically vital, truly catholic, truly diverse and increasingly evangelical."[283] Braaten and Jenson contend for "an evangelical Catholicism," which acknowledges the pope as the leader as well as co-opts the RCC practice of ordaining ministers as successors of the apostles.[284] The notion of an organic union continues to inform ecumenism, as shown in these views. Bruinsma observes that "many church leaders and theologians today ... find it hard to conceive that there are Christian believers who refuse to get involved in ecumenical projects. To them this is disobedience to Christ's command that we all be one."[285]

Voices opposed to the literal aggregation of denominations have always emphasized spiritual unity among believers. Bloesch, being one of them, proposes "an evangelical Catholicism," which is keen on "spiritual" rather than "organizational" unification.[286] The church does not need to conglomerate into a gigantic institution for it to fulfill Christ's prayer (in John 17:20–24) or help itself out of its challenges, for history has shown that this cannot work.[287] Boice articulates the ineptitude:

> In the early days of the Church there was much growth but little organisational unity. Later, as the Church

---

[281] Jeffrey Silleck, "A More Radical Proposal," *Lutheran Forum* 32, no. 1 (Spring 1998): 28–31.
[282] Ibid.
[283] Ibid., 31.
[284] Carl Braaten, *Mother Church: Ecclesiology and Ecumenism* (Minneapolis: Fortress, 1998).
[285] Bruinsma, *The Body of Christ: A Biblical Understanding of the Church*, 62.
[286] Bloesch, *The Church: Sacraments, Worship, Ministry, Mission*, 42.
[287] Boice, *Foundations of the Christian Faith: A Comprehensive & Readable Theology*, 583.

came into governmental favor under Constantine and his successors, the visible Church increasingly centralised until during the Middle Ages when there was literally one united ecclesiastical body covering all Europe. Wherever one went—north, south, east or west—there was one united, interlacing Church with the Pope at its head. Was it a great age? Was there deep unity of faith? Was the Church strong? Was its morality high? Did men and women find themselves increasingly drawn to that faith and come to confess Jesus Christ as their own Savior and Lord? On the contrary, the world believed the opposite.[288]

As we work toward achieving unity among Christians, therefore, we have to shun human feelings and emotions that seem to summon us to go back to "the great tradition" of the single ecclesial entity from the first to the fifth century.[289] Retrogression of such kind would result in the riddance of the achievements of the Protestant Reformation and its elevation of God's word above beliefs generated by the church. Forsyth and Schaff—who are Congregational and Reformed theologians, respectively—are among the scholars who have made significant contributions to the study of Christian unity. The two were not in support of such riddance. For instance, Schaff (d. 1893) perceived the Reformation as a "spiritual fulfilment of Catholicism," whose importance has to be recognized by Christians as they seek unity.[290] For Schaff, it is the "flock" that is supposed to be one rather than the "fold."[291] In other words, unity becomes real

---

[288] Ibid.
[289] James Cutsinger ed., *Reclaiming the Great Tradition* (Downers Grove, Ill.: InterVarsity Press, 1997).
[290] Stephen Graham, *Cosmos in the Chaos: Philip Schaff's Interpretation of Nineteenth-Century American Religion* (Grand Rapids, Mich.: Eerdmans, 1995), 231.
[291] Ibid.

when it is "inward and spiritual" as opposed to when it is, in Bloesch's words, "legal or administrative."[292] Schaff further conveys the idea:

> Union is no monotonous uniformity, but implies variety and full development of all the various types of Christian doctrine and discipline as far as they are founded on constitutional differences, made and intended by God himself, and as far as they are supplementary rather than contradictory. True union is essentially inward and spiritual. It does not require an external amalgamation of existing organisations into one, but may exist with their perfect independence in their own spheres of labor.[293]

The thought is reinforced by Dulles, who maintains that the kind of unity supported by a scripture-based theology "is not the external unity of an organised society but rather the interior unity of mutual charity leading to a communion of friends."[294] Bloesch bolsters this position:

> The one Church exists in its relationship to the one Lord, and this relationship is present to a degree in all the churches that appeal to holy Scripture as their infallible guide and criterion. While there is only one Church, we can speak of remnants of this Church in the diversity of churches. No one church can claim for itself the fullness of the mystical life of Christ, but every Church that confesses Christ as its Lord partakes of this mystical life ... Catholics and Orthodox are right in affirming the existence of only one Church, but they are wrong when they

---

[292] Bloesch, *The Church: Sacraments, Worship, Ministry, Mission*, 43.
[293] Philip Schaff, *Christ and Christianity* (New York: Charles Scribner's Sons, 1885), 16.
[294] Dulles, *Models of the Church*, 122.

identify this one Church with a particular empirical or historical institution.²⁹⁵

Schaff was aware of the fact that the "empirical church" had, in many ways and instances, deviated from the "evangelical and apostolic witness of the New Testament."²⁹⁶ However, he argues that the church remains the "bearer of all God's revelations, the channel of Christianity, the depository of all the life powers of the Redeemer, the habitation of the Holy Ghost."²⁹⁷

Forsyth (d. 1921), on his part, contends for a church that is at all times subservient to the Gospel.²⁹⁸ According to this view, ideal unity does not deliberately or inadvertently set aside the truth to give priority to fellowship.²⁹⁹ He observed that "a Christian optimism has grown up," which aspires for "a speedy unity of the Churches without a prime regard to their belief."³⁰⁰ Ecumenism reflects that optimism when it seeks to establish one huge ecclesiastical institution out of the various church groups that neglect the purity of teachings and spirituality.³⁰¹ Speaking about the relationship between unity and the Gospel, Forsyth points out that the church's unity depends "not in itself but in its message, in the unity of the Gospel that made the Church."³⁰² He contends that ecclesial unity does not reside in the organization of the church or planned series of events but in the Word.³⁰³ Moreover, the basis of ecclesial unity is not statements of beliefs or ceremonies of the church but on Christ alone working

---

²⁹⁵ Bloesch, *The Church: Sacraments, Worship, Ministry, Mission*, 100.
²⁹⁶ Ibid., 43.
²⁹⁷ Graham, *Cosmos in the Chaos: Philip Schaff's Interpretation of Nineteenth-Century American Religion*, 231.
²⁹⁸ Bloesch, *The Church: Sacraments, Worship, Ministry, Mission*, 43.
²⁹⁹ Peter Forsyth, *The Justification of God*, 1948th ed. (London: Independent Press, 1917), 38.
³⁰⁰ Ibid.
³⁰¹ Duffield and Van Cleave, *Foundations of Pentecostal Theology*, 423.
³⁰² Peter Forsyth, *The Church and the Sacraments*, 2nd ed. (London: Independent Press, 1947), 39.
³⁰³ Ibid., 38.

toward the redemption of His children at the cross, His rising from the dead in victory, and reigning through the messages spoken by the people he sends.[304] In support of Forsyth, Bloesch contends that the "apostolic succession" coming in the form of ordinations administered by the right prelates does not guarantee unity within the church.[305] Bloesch umplifies the words enshrined in the Second Helvetic Cofession: "unity consists not in outward rites and ceremonies, but rather in the truth and unity of the catholic faith."[306] The lowering of foundational Christian beliefs destroys unity.[307] A church that refuses to abide by the basic teachings of the Christian faith breaks that unity.[308] Therefore, Bloesch cautions that "in seeking evangelical catholicity we must resist the allurements of a theological liberalism that is interested in forging a new faith rather than recovering the richness of the old faith ... We know too that as trustees of God's revealed truth we cannot embrace any form of doctrinal indifferentism, or relativism, or pluralism by which God's truth is sacrificed for a false peace."[309] The dilemma is pointed out by Pope too as he says that within the Protestant circles, some are impressed or excited by the "hierarchical or high church" and aspire for "a unity which a lineal Apostolical succession of orders gives to Eastern and Western Episcopal communions."[310] Boice's views are the same as he states that while the liberal churches aspire for an institutional unity via ecclesial councils and "denominational mergers," the evangelicals are working toward "an identical pattern of appearance and behavior for its members," which was not Christ's goal.[311] He adds that "on

---

[304] Bloesch, *The Church: Sacraments, Worship, Ministry, Mission*, 43–44, 100.
[305] Ibid., 263.
[306] Ibid., 264.
[307] Ibid., 45.
[308] Pope, *A Compendium of Christian Theology: Being Analytical Outlines of a Course of Theological Study, Biblical, Dogmatic, Historical*, 3:272.
[309] Bloesch, *The Church: Sacraments, Worship, Ministry, Mission*, 45, 300.
[310] Pope, *A Compendium of Christian Theology: Being Analytical Outlines of a Course of Theological Study, Biblical, Dogmatic, Historical*, 3:273.
[311] Boice, *Foundations of the Christian Faith: A Comprehensive & Readable Theology*, 583.

the contrary, there should be diversity among Christians, diversity of personality, interests, lifestyle and even methods of Christian work and evangelism."[312] An accommodation that leads to an attempt to be the same as others is not necessary for the church's unity to be achieved and is a blunder that could be avoided by the evangelicals.

Conclusion

While Christian unity is deemed essential, various ecclesial traditions approach it differently. The stances scholars subscribing to different traditions have taken are informed by the divergent understanding of the church. Some of them perceive the church as an exterior or "visible" entity emphasizing hierarchy. This Episcopalian mindset, for instance, informs the RCC's coalescence around the pope as a central figure within its setting who determines the course of the church. Internal disunity within the RCC manifests in the existing dichotomy between the clergy and the laity, whereby the former is invested with more premium than the latter. There is also external disunity between the RCC and other churches, which is mainly because of the perception of Catholicity. The RCC has adopted an exclusive rather than a "universal" position on Catholicity. In recent times, though, some RC scholars began to advocate for a revised understanding of Catholicity to accommodate the church in its multiple forms. The GO tradition, just like the RC tradition, is also "episcopalcentric" and exclusive as it is opposed to the view of the church as a communio sanctorum. As in the case of the RC, this manifests in internal disunity. In it, the bishop stands in the place of Christ and, therefore, is more important than the members since, in his absence, the church fails to be church. The role of the laity is passive. However, the GOC recognizes other Christian churches save the RCC. The EP tradition acknowledges both the visible and invisible aspects of the church, with more emphasis placed on the latter. This approach favors a communion sanctorum,

---
[312] Ibid.

which is universal in scope over the organizational understanding. It proposes that churches come together to form a single ecclesial outfit. Scripture-based teachings and beliefs, the correct administration of ordinances, the right worship of God, and the disciplining of erring members bring the various forms of the Christian church together and qualify them to be in the communio sanctorum. The EP tradition also stresses unity in the visible aspect of the church. At present, the EPs treat ecclesial unity as an item that requires urgent attention as opposed to the preoccupation with numerical expansions over the years. The EP and RC scholars are talking to each other to find out how they could achieve interdenominational unity, but with some censure. Whereas some of these scholars favor a return to the RCC or an amalgamation into the Eastern Orthodox Churches, other voices continue to emphasize spiritual unity rather than uniformity.

CHAPTER 3
The Notion of Kinship in the African Church

3.1 Previous Scholarship

Scholarly discourses have taken place around African kinship and its potential to inform and shape ecclesiology. This chapter traces the notion of kinship from some of the existing works in the academy.

3.1.1 John Mary Waliggo

In his discussion of the structure of the Ganda clan and how it functions, John Mary Waliggo made a successful attempt to demonstrate the kind of church that could arise out of a clan model. Among the Ganda, the clans are, in most cases, linked through "marriage," which provides an avenue of extension—kingship that, as an institution, brings all clans together, "neighborhood," "friendship," "adoption," "blood pact(s)," "chieftainship," among other factors.[313] Their ancestors intended to ensure a connection among people to the

---

[313] John Mary Waliggo, "The African Clan as the True Model of the African Church," in *The Church in African Christianity: Innovative Essays in Ecclesiology* (Nairobi: Initiatives Publ., 1990), 123–124.

extent that nobody is isolated.³¹⁴ Waliggo says, "This is the wonderful sense of community and communion that the Christian Church must rediscover from African values."³¹⁵

One of the values the clan model enforces is acceptance. Among the Baganda, every person in the clan is accepted and respected regardless of age, gender, and other socioeconomic factors. One remarkable feature of the Baganda clan is that women are also allowed to contribute to society. Waliggo says that even though the perpetuation of the clan occurred through male children because of the patrilineal type of family, female children still belong to their clans even after being married.³¹⁶ As such, they attend clan functions and meetings that are convened from time to time.³¹⁷ Besides, married women are not supposed to take their husbands' names lest they lose their identity.³¹⁸ Furthermore, every individual makes sure that a mutual relationship exists between him or her and other clan members.³¹⁹ Leadership qualities among the clans include wisdom, justice, love and care for people, "kindness, generosity, openness, impartiality," the ability to unite people, and mastery of the cultural heritage.³²⁰ Leadership among the clans is synonymous with service.³²¹ The leaders are not supposed to be money lovers and are expected to be available at any time to attend to the call of duty.³²² Women usually have the most significant say on who is invited to lead in the clan.³²³

Unity among the Baganda is nurtured through joint ventures, "sharing," "respect" for one another, etc.³²⁴ They iron out differences

---

[314] Ibid., 124.
[315] Ibid.
[316] Ibid., 121.
[317] Ibid.
[318] Ibid.
[319] Ibid., 122.
[320] Ibid.
[321] Ibid.
[322] Ibid.
[323] Ibid.
[324] Ibid., 122.

fairly and in a considerate manner, and punishment is meted out to redeem the offenders rather than crush them. One of the things shared among the Ganda is knowledge about their culture. Waliggo points out that the clan is a center of "learning" where people are taught their "history," traditions, good deeds, and "the wisdom of the ancestors."[325] Inclusivity is demonstrated in, among other ways, the recognition and appreciation of skills and talents. A clan is a place where the talents of various members are spotted, nurtured, and used to uplift the whole clan.[326]

Waliggo connected her discussion about the Ganda clan with Israel's society and carried the discussion further to the NT times. She points out that through the covenant, Israel became the people of God in a "communitarian relationship" and that it is made up of twelve clans that provide identity to all Jews.[327] In the NT, Jesus is related to all who believe as a brother.[328] He came to link us with the Father after the fall, and through Him, believers of all ages are related.[329] Koinonia, as was practiced in the apostolic church, promoted the familial relationship in the NT further.[330] According to Waliggo, the clan was the model of the church until later on, when the church was institutionalized.[331] However, Christian groups have seen the need to go back to the "familial model" of the church, as demonstrated in the African clan.[332]

Waliggo's work appeals so much to the church in Africa with its focus on relational dynamics. The Baganda clan structure provides a beautiful model of ecclesiology that is not just in sync with the scripture but could help the church in its broader spectrum to appreciate one another as members of the same family where God is

---

[325] Ibid., 122, 123.
[326] Ibid., 123.
[327] Ibid., 124–125.
[328] Ibid.
[329] Ibid., 125.
[330] Ibid.
[331] Ibid.
[332] Ibid.

the Father, Christ our elder brother, and members are brothers and sisters.

The Baganda clan system enriches various ecclesiological concepts found in the Bible, for instance, what it means to have Jesus as our elder brother and each one of us as members of the family of God. This mindset enforces inclusivity in the Church of God, which is an ingredient of unity. As a result of that understanding, Christians could learn to coexist with one another and avoid feuds. Waliggo's work also tells us something about leadership, which ought to be service rather than lordship. Besides, it fosters positive ecumenism in its presentation of God's people as relatives in a spiritual sense. While enhancing active participation in the church's life by the laity, the consciousness of human dignity and equality of all members, including women, is also aroused.

3.1.2 Agbonkhianmeghe Orobator

For Agbonkhianmeghe Orobator, the African church will be a reality when the sense of community is inculcated among Christians, or else, it remains merely the Western church on African soil. To qualify his argument about an African church, which is yet to appear, Orobator makes some pertinent statements. Firstly, he says that the church in Africa "is saddled with a checkered history of an inherited antiquated ecclesial structure."[333] In line with that, he proposes that this church ought to grow until it transitions into a "church that is full-fledged community of faith adapted to the circumstances of its time and place."[334] However, the appearance and structure of the ideal African church would be determined by scholarly reflections that pay attention to the original ideals of the people living in Africa.[335]

Orobator observes that community fosters involvement, close

---

[333] Agbonkhianmeghe Orobator, "Perspectives and Trends in Contemporary African Ecclesiology," *Studia Missionalia* 45 (1996): 267.
[334] Ibid.
[335] Ibid., 269.

association, connection, and inclusivity in the African context.[336] These qualities have the potential to improve the understanding of the church.[337] In addition, he states that the church has to foster a fellowship resembling that experienced by the Godhead and make it a reality.[338] This approach would have a significant impact on, among other aspects, the ecclesial structure. This is because the ecclesial models of community, extended family, and clan support the decentralization of ecclesiastical authority, which is a departure from structures passed on to the church in Africa by the West. They advocate for equality rather than hierarchies.[339] Orobator articulates the idea further as follows:

> This means that any member of the community on whom the task of leadership devolves is not a "boss" but a son/daughter, brother/sister of the entire community/family, whose role is to build the community in solidarity with all the other members. These other members bear no less a vital responsibility for the edification of the community … Along the same lines of thought the role of the priest appears less as that of an authoritarian father, a chief or a boss, and more as that of a coordinator of charisms, an elder brother who is active on behalf of the parents. Like an elder brother who knows the mind of the parents he serves the needs of the family and works to resolve tension in the family by facilitating reconciliation and healing of divisions.[340]

According to Orobator, the appropriation of African categories on ecclesiology would ensure that ministry is not an exclusive possession

---

[336] Ibid., 267.
[337] Ibid., 270.
[338] Ibid., 273.
[339] Ibid., 274.
[340] Ibid., 275.

of the clergy; that every baptized member has a right to minister in the church of God; that no one overrules others as witnessed in clericalism; and no jostling against one another takes place.[341]

3.1.3 Charles Nyamiti, Bénézet Bujo, and Diane Stinton

Nyamiti and Bujo introduced ancestorship into the ecclesial model of the clan in their respective works. Stinton also connects his Christology to this category. Specifically, Nyamiti argues that "the Church is the continuation of the mystery of Christ in human communities, the Church is destined to be the medium and organ of Christ's ancestorship to humankind."[342] It makes sense to say that as an ancestor, Jesus is the "model for good behaviour."[343] This is a positive attribute of this model. To qualify as an ancestor, a person must have shown a good example in life according to the "standards" of behavior and morality laid out by his society.[344] This perception of ancestors is often the same among most African cultures.[345]

It is worth noting that the model of ancestor itself comes with the "notion of communion with the dead."[346] A selective application of this category is necessary instead of a blind appropriation, for if not critically applied, it could encourage prayers for the dead and extension of the "veneration of the ancestors" within the church.[347] This is attributed to the belief that ancestors are nearer to God and

---

[341] Ibid., 276.
[342] Charles Nyamiti, "The Church as Christ's Ancestral Mediation: An Essay on African Ecclesiology," in *The Church in African Christianity: Innovative Essays in Ecclesiology* (Nairobi: Initiatives Publ., 1990), 132.
[343] Charles Nyamiti, *Christ as Our Ancestor: Christology from an African Perspective* (Gweru, Zimbabwe: Mambo Press, 1984), 15–16.
[344] Diane Stinton, *Jesus of Africa: Voices of Contemporary African Christology* (Nairobi: Paulines Publications Africa, 2004), 135.
[345] Nyamiti, *Christ as Our Ancestor: Christology from an African Perspective*, 15–16.
[346] Bénézet Bujo, *African Theology in Its Social Context*, trans. John O'Donohue (Nairobi: St Paul Communications; Maryknoll, N.Y.:Orbis Books, 1992), 25–26.
[347] Jean-Marc Ela, *My Faith as an African*, trans. John Pairman Brown and Susan Perry (Maryknoll, N.Y.: Orbis Books, 1988), 14.

could mediate between him and the living.³⁴⁸ The RCC has forged a connection between "African ancestors and the Christian doctrine of the communion of the saints." ³⁴⁹ The invitation of ancestors to participate in the mass through the libation poured down to them shows that.³⁵⁰ Gehman rightly contends that 'in biblical perspective these are none other than the unclean spirits, the fallen angels who serve their master, even Satan. Nothing could be plainer in the Bible than the divine abhorrence and active opposition to any contact, communication or relationship with the ancestral spirits, divinities or other spirits."³⁵¹ NT theology treats Jesus as the mediator between God and humans. Unlike the dead human ancestors, he died, rose from the dead, and ascended to heaven, where He plays this role before the Father. Francoise Kabasélé said that "Christ fits the category of Ancestor because, finally, he is the synthesis of all mediations ... for Bantu Christians, Christ performs the role of Ancestor, by the mediation he provides. He is the exemplar, Ancestor, who fulfils in himself the words and deeds of the mediation of our Ancestors."³⁵² However, I posit in this work that Christ is an ancestor in His own right, and His ministry and mediation cannot be reduced to fulfillment or a combination of ancestral mediations. The salient "question" that African ecclesiology seeks to answer is stated by Mugambi and Magesa as follows: "How can the Church be truly African and truly Christian?"³⁵³

According to Stinton, the perception of the church as a clan fosters the priesthood of all believers. Every member has a place and contribution to make in the Christian family (church) as in the clan,

---

³⁴⁸ Stinton, *Jesus of Africa: Voices of Contemporary African Christology*, 135.
³⁴⁹ Ibid., 162.
³⁵⁰ Ibid.
³⁵¹ Richard Gehman, *African Traditional Religion in Biblical Perspective*, (Kijabe, Kenya: Kesho Publications, 1989), 184.
³⁵² Francois Kabasélé, "Christ as Ancestor and Elder Brother," in *Faces of Jesus in Africa*, ed. Robert Schreiter (Maryknoll, N.Y.: Orbis Books, 1991), 117.
³⁵³ Jesse Mugambi and Laurenti Magesa, eds., "Introduction," in *The Church in African Christianity: Innovative Essays in Ecclesiology* (Nairobi: Initiatives Publ., 1990), 1.

where every member plays a role. This model, therefore, challenges obstacles to inclusivity in the form of ecclesial hierarchicalism, "clericalism," "episcopalism," and "sacerdotalism."[354] Therefore, this approach to ecclesial life and leadership is necessary. While commenting on its implication for the RCC ecclesiology, Bujo says that "the pope is not the 'holy father'; he is a brother, the eldest brother, because the Father is Christ … And then at the level of the parish, the priest is not a father for the parish; he is a brother among other brothers and sisters."[355] This sense of equality could reverberate among other ecclesial bodies too. Oduyoye's argument resonates with this view, for she says that through baptism, people join "a new humanity modelled after Christ," which leads to the end of prejudicial treatment of other believers on the grounds of class, race, and gender.[356]

The literature reviewed in this section on kinship focused on the broader aspects of the church. None of them explicitly addressed Christian unity. Therefore, the reader is left to figure out from the values presented how the understanding of Christian unity could be enhanced. Waliggo made a good attempt at demonstrating the link, though in passing as in the other aspects of his work.[357] The study about the concept of jo-kang'ato among the Luo and its implications for Christian unity in the ecclesial life of the church in Africa bridges the gap. The study is dedicated fully to Christian unity.

---

[354] Stinton, *Jesus of Africa: Voices of Contemporary African Christology*, 267.
[355] Bujo, *African Theology in Its Social Context*, 97–98.
[356] Mercy Oduyoye, *Hearing and Knowing: Theological Reflections on Christianity in Africa* (Maryknoll, N.Y.: Orbis Books, 1986), 137.
[357] Waliggo, "The African Clan as the True Model of the African Church," 123–124.

3.2 Kinship as an Aspect of the African Family

It suffices to state that kinship and all it entails is a very potent factor in African society.[358] Mbiti summarizes the dynamics of African kinship as follows:

> The deep sense of kinship, with all it implies, has been one of the strongest forces in traditional African life. Kinship is reckoned through blood and betrothal [engagement and marriage]. It is kinship which controls social relationships between people in a given community: it governs marital customs and regulations [sic], it determines the behaviour of one individual towards another. Indeed, this sense of kinship binds together the entire life of the "tribe," and is even extended to cover animals, plants and non-living objects through the "totemic" system. Almost all the concepts connected with human [sic] relationship can be understood and interpreted through the kinship system. This it is which largely governs the behaviour, thinking and whole life of individual [sic] in the society of which he is a member.[359]

As the product of family whereby the line of descent is traced continuously from an ancestor, kinship helps people to identify the connections among them.[360] Nana Chief Azuma Ndagu Edward (quoted by Nkansah-Obrempong) talks of what constitutes kinship when he states that it is "a social relation derive[d] from consanguinity [blood], relations, marriage, and adoption."[361] Kinship also forms the

---

[358] John Mbiti, *African Religions and Philosophy* (London: Heinemann Educational Books Ltd, 1969), 104.
[359] Mbiti, *African Religions and Philosophy*, 104.
[360] James Nkansah-Obrempong, *Foundations for African Theological Ethics* (Langham Monographs, 2013), 311; Mbiti, *African Religions and Philosophy*, 105.
[361] Mbiti, *African Religions and Philosophy*, 104.

basis of the establishment of a clan. As Mbiti puts it, every clan typically has "totems," which are tokens of "unity, of kinship, of belongingness, of togetherness and common affinity."[362] The people who constitute a clan are considered to be so close that they cannot enter into marital relationships with one another.[363] However, not all clans are "exogamous," as there are "endogamous clans" where marital relationships could occur.[364] Furthermore, kinship stretches to encompass dead relatives and the unborn.[365]

Kinship benefits and affects lives in very many and significant ways. As Nkansah-Obrempong puts it, "this extended family or kinship ties provide intricate networks of social ties. The kinship ties evoke strong bonds of relationships and moral responsibility towards members of the clan … each member of the family is to ensure there is social cohesion between its members."[366] Mbiti enlightens further:

> The kinship system is like a vast network stretching laterally [horizontally] in every direction, to embrace everybody in an any [sic] given local group. This means that each individual is a brother or sister, father or mother, grandmother or grandfather, or cousin, or brother-in-law, uncle or aunt, or something else, to everybody else … a person has literally hundreds of "fathers," hundreds of "mothers," hundreds of "uncles," hundreds of "wives," hundreds of "sons and daughters."[367]

As important as it is among African societies, kinship is experiencing the impact of change, just as is the case generally with

---

[362] Ibid., 105.
[363] Ibid., 105–106.
[364] Ibid., 106.
[365] Ibid., 105.
[366] Nkansah-Obrempong, *Foundations for African Theological Ethics*, 312.
[367] Mbiti, *African Religions and Philosophy*, 104,105.

the family unit. The impact of the change manifests more in urban centers. Mbiti captures the new dynamics:

> In the city the individual is one in a loose conglomeration of men and women from different peoples and languages, races and nationalities. These are joined or related together not by bonds of blood and betrothal, but by professions, places of work, clubs, factories, associations, hobbies, trade unions, sports, political parties, Church denominations and religious ties. That is where the individual now finds himself, and often his loyalties are spread over many of these affiliations. The traditional solidarity in which the individual says "I am because we are, and since we are, therefore I am," is constantly being smashed, undermined and in some respects destroyed. Emphasis is shifting from the "we" of traditional corporate life to the "I" of modern individualism … So then, for example, amidst the many people who live in the cities, the individual discovers that he is alone. When he falls sick, perhaps only one or two other people know about it and come to see him; when he is hungry he finds that begging food from his neighbour is either shameful or unrewarding or both; when he gets bad news from his relatives in the countryside, he cries alone even if hundreds of other people rub shoulders with him in the factory or bus. The masses around the individual are both blind and deaf to him, they are indifferent and do not care about him as a person. Almost at every turn of his life the individual in the city and under modern change discovers constantly that he is alone or even lonely in the midst of large masses of people.[363]

---

[368] Ibid., 224, 225.

Despite the adjustments that take place in African society and affect relations, the Luo people still hold kinship with high regard.

3.3 The Extended Family System among the Luo

Kinship is related to the concept of jo-kang'ato as it stems from the latter. On many occasions, however, the two terms are used interchangeably among the Luo. On this basis, I posit that an understanding of the extended family system, which enshrines kinship, is paramount for a broader insight into the concept of jo-kang'ato to be realized. In this work, that understanding is sought in light of Christian unity.

In the first instance, ecclesial unity could be attributed to respect and love among Christians. These virtues create an atmosphere for carrying out church activities together while also contributing to the growth of the church.[369] The absence of conflict among Christians would boost unity and facilitate an enabling environment for Christians to care for one another. The value of the extended family system among the Luo of Kenya lies in its potential to encourage a more profound sense of love, respect, and care for one another, which are the components of unity.[370]

Moreover, unity among Christians based on the extended family system could enable them to work together toward a common goal as well as share a vision. Ayubu Jalang'o (church elder in the SDA Church) enumerated the consequences of disunity among Christians in the church as follows: "Loss of focus on mission, derailment of the church agenda, loss of prayer power, disintegration, loss of a sense of belonging hence low potentiality, and finally, the collapse of the group."[371] In the words of Johana Openda (church elder of Legio Maria Church), "worship services could be hampered as

---

[369] Gordon Oguro, interview by the research assistant, Homa Bay, July 20.
[370] Carmila Achieng, interview by the research assistant, Siaya, July 18, 2020.
[371] Ayubu Jalang'o, interview by the author, Holo in Kisumu County, July 10, 2020.

some members defect to other churches; enmity among Christians; separation; lack of assistance for each other in difficult moments; lack of growth in all its spheres" [which includes spiritual growth] would be experienced.[372] These developments arise because the clergy and laity expend most of their energy and time in politics and wrangles rather than in the execution of the church's divinely assigned mandate. Julieta Opiyo stated that "The Church may fall apart due to divisions, hatred, and misunderstandings amongst its members. At the interdenominational level, negative attitudes towards other denominations, quarrels and fights, and competition among the churches arise."[373] The other characteristics could be scrambling for members by Christian denominations. In the course of these developments, the loss of respect among parties involved, especially leaders, becomes the experience.[374] The Luos' extended family system condemns these habits and proposes a mutual relationship.

Some of the features of the Luos' extended family system are cooperation and teamwork, which happen to be among the ways of demonstrating unity among Christians. These could manifest in pooling resources together to finance church projects and support the needy within their midst.[375] Besides, they are also critical in ensuring success in the church's evangelistic program, for more souls are won when Christians are united.[376] As we go by the views of the respondents who were interviewed during field research, the kind of relationship prescribed by the Luos' extended family system could play a significant role in building unity among Christians. It could enhance cooperation and uphold togetherness among members.

The Luos' extended family system proposes the kind of relationship that, if replicated among Christians and in the church, could increase

---

[372] John Openda, interview by the research assistant, Koru in Kisumu County, July 10, 2020.
[373] Julieta Opiyo, interview by the research assistant, Holo in Kisumu County, July 11, 2020.
[374] Achieng.
[375] Benard Okuku, interview by the research assistant, Siaya, July 18, 2020.
[376] Lilian Ong'ow, interview by the research assistant, Migori, August 12, 2020.

comprehension of ecclesial unity. One of the things about it is that in it disagreements are anticipated, and robust measures are put in place beforehand to settle them when they arise.[377] The process often involves sitting down and having meaningful and genuine conversations among the parties concerned.[378]

Christian unity could be attained through dialogue as a way of solving the relational problems that arise among church members from time to time. This approach presents a better way of dealing with impasses and sorting out stalemates within the ecclesial setting. As a mechanism, dialogue facilitates the mitigation of the causes of disunity among Christians.[379] At the local church level, the catalysts of disunity include misunderstandings among church members, envy and jealousy among members and clergy, pride manifested in the feelings of superiority over other members, discrimination, lack of transparency in handling church funds, sexual immorality, discrimination based on ethnicity and kinship, abuse of spiritual gifts, lack of cooperation in performing church duties, and poor or centralization of management.[380] Failure to handle arising disputes in a timely, judicious, and amicable manner results in leadership wrangles, atrophy, hemorrhage in membership, and retardation of growth and development in all forms.[381]

As a matter of priority, the church's leaders and governing bodies could create forums where unity would not only be discussed but also sensitized and nurtured. Worship services, for instance, provide an opportunity through sermons and presentations that could be

---

[377] Leonard Opiyo, interview by the research assistant, Homa Bay, July 20.
[378] Ibid.
[379] Valentine Mondo, interview by the research assistant, Koru in Kisumu County, July 10, 2020; Peterson Jaoko, interview by the research assistant, Holo in Kisumu County, July 11, 2020; Rocky Migoma, interview by the research assistant, Uyoma in Siaya County, July 18, 2020; William Otieno, interview by the research assistant, Kisumu, August 10, 2020; Julieta Opiyo, interview by the research assistant, Holo in Kisumu County, July 11, 2020.
[380] Ibid.
[381] Ibid.

tuned around the theme of unity or at least touch on it.[382] However, it is through prayers and faithfulness to the Gospel that Christians receive spiritual uplifting, which in turn impacts their relationships with one another and strengthens unity. The Luos' extended family system creates an environment within which all these are possible. At the interdenominational level, it could contribute to an elimination of competition for membership and differences based on doctrinal subscriptions.[383] The outcome would be improved relationships among Christians despite affiliation to different denominations.

3.4 The Luos' Perspective of Community

The communal aspect of life continues to be prominent among the Luo of Kenya, even in this era. The community among the Luo people is made up of extended family and immigrants from other places. Herbich attributed the cause of immigration into different communities to disagreements and conflicts. A complete failure to resolve disputes amicably caused division, "migration," and physical violence in the past.[384] To date, migration is preferred, for it is deemed better for jo-kang'ato to stay apart than to fight and destroy one another. Many Luos buy land far away from their kin and settle in other communities. Following the arrival into the receiving community, the *jadak* (immigrant or tenant), whether a Luo or someone from another tribe or nationality, becomes part of the new community and forges a mutual relationship with the *weg piny* (hosting community), which would see him or her practically working together with the latter for the common good of the society, which could include defense from external aggression.[385] They also team up together with them in other areas of communal life. With

---

[382] Ibid.
[383] George Othuon, interview by the research assistant, Siaya, July 18, 2020.
[384] Ingrid Herbich, "Luo," Encyclopedia of World Cultures Supplement, 2002, accessed August 24, 2020, http://www.encyclopedia.com.
[385] Ibid.

time, the jadak is incorporated to the extent that he or she is treated as family socioeconomic affiliation notwithstanding.[386]

A sense of community informs life among the Luo and reflects in their relationship with one another in many other ways. For instance, one person's mistake can cause trouble for the entire community. On the other hand, the right behavior is for the good of the entire community. As such, an individual is not supposed to do anything that could jeopardize the community's well-being.

The other point is a sense of belonging, which the Luos' perspective of community inculcates among its members. For instance, it is understood that women are married to the community rather than to individuals. However, this does not imply that any male member of the community could do as they wish with them. As part of an introduction exercise, Luo women are usually asked as follows: "Itedo kanye [Where are you married]?" "In chi kanye [To which people are you married]?" and "Imako lowo kanye [Where are you holding land]?" Culturally, a married woman moves to her husband's home and could stake a claim to land there rather than in her father's home.[387] Rarely is a married woman asked, "In chi ng'a [Whose wife are you]?" Children too belong to the community and could be sent and disciplined by any member. This sense of belonging extends to adult members of all ages, as demonstrated in the familiarization exercises through the following questions: "In wuod kanye [To which people are you a son]?" The response would be "An wuod Kano [I am the son of the people of Kano (Kano is the name of a place)]." In the case where the person is a woman, she could be asked, "In nya kanye [To which people are you a daughter]?" which could be responded to as follows: "An nya Kisumo [I am the daughter of the people of Kisumu. (Kisumu too is the name of a place)]." This sense of belonging stretches to the ethnic level where a person could

---

[386] Peter Firstbrook, *The Obamas: The Untold Story of an African Family* (London, Great Britain: Preface Publishing, 2010), 32–33, 35, 47.
[387] Gumbo Ka'Gori, interview by the author, Ahero in Kisumu County, August 10, 2020.

be referred to as wuod Luo or nya Luo (the son of the Luo people or the daughter of the Luo people).

The Luo people's perspective of community is in tandem with the scripture, which addresses life in the Christian community and spells out the behavior that contributes to harmony and unity among members as well as what contributes to conflicts. The kind of relationship enforced by the Luo people's understanding of community is so deep and could be applied among Christians to inculcate a sense of belonging and enrich the understanding of Christian unity in the ecclesial life of the church at all levels.

Conclusion

Kinship among the Luo creates an environment that is permeated with meaningful respect, love and care for one another, cooperation, and a spirit of teamwork. These are the components of unity without which meaningful participation in the life of the church and solidarity among members become elusive. Moreover, without these virtues, Christians can never grow their churches as it proves difficult to work toward a common goal and vision. Besides, in the absence of these virtues within the church setting, hemorrhage in membership and dismal attendance set in as the conditions become unfavorable for the survival of some members. The Luos' extended family system and perspective of community disapprove of the anti-unity behaviors, hence its potential to contribute toward the understanding of Christian unity.

CHAPTER 4

The Concept of Jo-kang'ato among the Luo of Kenya

Jo-kang'ato is a compound word formed by *joka* (the people of) and *ng'ato* (a person). *Jo-kang'ato* refers to people who share a common descent in terms of a grandfather, lineage, or parentage.[388] Members of a common lineage are understood by the Luo as "a people of one person" (*jokang'at achiel*).[389] Its synonyms are *jokakwaro* (descendants of a common progenitor), and *anyuola* (clan). The other Luo concepts that are linked to *jo-kang'ato* are *dhoot* (a unit of people who trace their origin from the same "agnatic ancestor," which governs itself through a "council of elders"); *gweng'* (the geographical location of a given dhoot); *libamba* (each dhoot refers to another as such); and *anyuola* (clan, which could include the libamba when they come together for a common purpose—for instance, to offer sacrifice to avert a calamity—despite their rivalry).[390] Jo-kang'ato signifies a people who are connected by common ancestry or have close blood relations. Blood ties apply rather than geographical factors since members "may

---

[388] Aidan Southall, *Lineage Formation Among the Luo* (London, New York, Toronto: Oxford University Press, 1952), 6, 35.
[389] Ibid., 29.
[390] Ibid., 27, 25, 28–29.

or may not live close to one another."[391] On many occasions, though, the jo-kang'ato are connected geographically in the sense of sharing space. In any case, no marriage takes place between them since they are from the same lineage.

The concept of jo-kang'ato is the cord that binds or holds together various social units and relations that exist among the Luo people. This manifests in various levels of social relations, one of which is the household, whereby in a polygamous family setting, uterine siblings show closeness to one another and form a protective bond against other family members whom they share a father and home with.[392] The concept of jo-kang'ato also binds families together. Family members are expected to remain together no matter what happens. In the past, the head of a homestead (*wuon dala* or *wuon pacho*) was especially bound to his family and could not leave under any circumstance lest he dies upon coming back into the home.[393] Marriage is a relationship that is binding and permanent and can only be dissolved as a result of "ritual offenses" and not even by marital unfaithfulness.[394] The inability to produce children with one's spouse could cause divorce, but this anomaly could be sorted out by soliciting support from the husband's brother to fertilize or give pleasure to one's wife (but with the highest level of respect and confidentiality) or the marriage of another wife in addition to the existing one when the problem lies with the woman.[395] The concept of jo-kang'ato is also the basis of unity and solidarity among the Luo people. Jo-kang'ato could be extended to include enemies, thus becoming a panacea for handling feuds and disputes. It has always been unconsciously stretched to include tribes in Kenya who are perceived as the Luo people's perennial enemies and manifests in intermarriages and political pacts. It is a concept laden with great

---

[391] Ogwel Menga, interview by the research assistant, Oneno Nam in Kisumu County, August 16, 2020.
[392] Southall, *Lineage Formation Among the Luo*, 12, 18, 20..
[393] Ibid., 16.
[394] Ibid., 23.
[395] Mbiti, African *Religions and Philosophy*, 145.

potential to unite. For instance, over the years, rival clans among the Luo have been getting into marriages to become part of the adversary's family and stop fighting since the *wasigu* (enemies) would turn into *oche* (in-laws).³⁹⁶

To date, life among the Luo people is guided by the concept of jo-kang'ato, the application of which in the corporate sense manifests in various ways. One of its features is the reckoning of one another as people from the same family related by blood and ancestry, even when they are from different places and unrelated. The term is often stretched to encompass work colleagues and even people from foreign lands. As articulated by Chief Awiko K'obondo, "even at workplaces and in the diaspora, Luos still consider each other as of the same family, for instance, *Jo-Ugenya* [people of Ugenya], *Jo-Seme* [people of Seme], *Jo-Milambo* [people from South Nyanza], and etcetera."³⁹⁷ According to Onyango KaBoma, the scope extends to include those who share "church, denomination, school, profession, and business since these bring a sense of belonging in people."³⁹⁸ It is a familiar concept that the Luo people have been using through the years to guide relationships among them as a people.

4.1 The Origin of the Concept of Jo-kang'ato

The main factor that prompted the origin of the concept of jo-kang'ato among the Luo was the need to foster unity and oneness within the clan or community. The Luo people sensed the need to be there for one another to protect and help. Dickson Omodho indicated that they needed "to organise themselves into a society that spoke with one voice and did their activities together."³⁹⁹ The concept

---

³⁹⁶ Ibid., 22.
³⁹⁷ Awiko K'Obondo, interview by the research assistant, Kadongo in Homa Bay County, July 15, 2020.
³⁹⁸ Onyango KaBoma, interview by the author, Oyugis in Homa Bay County, August 12, 2020.
³⁹⁹ Dickson Omodho, interview by the author, Kisumu, August 16, 2020.

of jo-kang'ato ensured the corporate responsibility of community members to one another. Furthermore, it mobilized them to be able to defend and protect the interests of the community to ensure their safety and prosperity. The latter case is a reality that the Luo have had to live with throughout their existence. As jo-kang'ato, people could defend one another from interclan wars and external aggression from other tribes. The occurrences of misfortunes and calamities of various forms also informed the development of the concept within the Luo community.

4.2 The Impact of the Colonial and Western Missionaries' Activities on the Luo Unity

Unity existed among the Luo people to a greater degree before the coming of the colonialists and Western missionaries. They lived and worked together and even supported one another as was necessary. Odwogo Semo articulated the experience as follows,

> The Luo were united as *nyikwa Ramogi* [Ramogi's descendants] and *Joka Nyanam* [all belonging to the daughter of the lake]. They had traditions and cultures which identified them as *jo-Luo* like the removal of six lower teeth, and etcetera. They could gather and drink or eat according to generations. The *jodongo* [elders] met together for drinks and sacrifice while the young gathered over wrestling tussles and invited their peers for the eating of *azoko* [part of an animal's body which was preserved for boys whenever an animal was slaughtered]. Girls met for stories at their grandmothers' houses.[400]

Birigita Ragar, on her part, said that the relationship among the people then was "fairly good since one person's problem was

---

[400] Odwogo Semo, interview by the research assistant, Migori, August 11, 2020.

everybody's concern and nobody elevated themselves above others."⁴⁰¹ The sense of belonging, which informed this egalitarian approach to life, did not allow them to fight with one another, as there were channels of dispute resolution based on the spirit of jo-kang'ato.

With the arrival of the colonialists and Western missionaries and their activities among the Luo people, divisions emerged. Their divide-and-rule policy and the capitalistic economic style brought a lifestyle that almost eroded jo-kang'ato.⁴⁰² While describing the situation, Ng'iela K'Otieno said as follows: "Jo-wagunda noketo jo-dini otelo mondo giboo ogandawa mondo jo-wagunda oyak mwanduwa kendo giroch kit chike mane oritowa kod achiel marwa [The colonialists sent missionaries ahead of them to pacify our people and make it possible for them to grab our wealth and destroy our customs and unity]."⁴⁰³ The divisive activities of the colonialists and Western missionaries compelled the Africans to unite and fight back. Through the enlightenment received in the schools set up by them, Luos teamed up together with Kenyans from other tribes to agitate and fight for independence.⁴⁰⁴ In this, an extension of the concept of jo-kang'ato beyond the Luo community is manifested as they were able to embrace people from other ethnic groups to fight for a cause.

4.3 The Ideals Embedded in the Concept of Jo-kang'ato

The concept of jo-kang'ato among the Luo of Kenya gives life to the familial and communal ecclesial models and clarifies Christian unity through various ideals that are embedded in it. As the gems gleaned from it enhance comprehension, the problem of disunity is addressed. Waliggo captures the importance of understanding

---

[401] Birigita Ragar, interview by the research assistant, Homa Bay, July 20, 2020.
[402] Magero Kungu, interview by the research assistant, Koru in Kisumu County, August 16, 2020.
[403] Ng'iela K'Otieno, interview by the author, Oyugis in Homa Bay County, August 13, 2020.
[404] Odongo Nyasuna, interview by the research assistant, Migori, August 16, 2020.

Christian unity in sibling terms when he says that "there is need for the creation of a deeper sense of brotherhood and sisterhood as was found in African traditional society, a spirit of togetherness and concern."[405] Overall, its concern is social relations. The concept sets out values that spur positive relationships.

4.3.1 Solidarity and Support for One Another

Over the years, the Luo people have shown solidarity with one another through their generous acts and support. For instance, there is an interfamilial support system demonstrated in, among other areas, the raising of the bride price to help their members marry and working together in the farms through the *saga* (pooling together) arrangement during plowing, sowing, weeding, harvesting seasons, and in other areas.[406] Amid the adjustments that take place in the African society that affect relations, as well as past attempts by Western missionaries to detach them from these practices, the Luos' egalitarian approach to life continues to be demonstrated. *Winjruok* (understanding) and *romruok* (equality) are understood as cardinal features of egalitarianism as they stress oneness and "solidarity."[407] In the precolonial times, their communal life manifested in the collective ownership of land, livestock, children, and wives represented this view of life.[408]

Support is shown among the Luo people in many other ways; for instance, during childbirth, plenty of food is made available for the new mother, who is referred to as the *ondiek* (hyena). At the *goyo dala* (building a new home) or *goyo ligala* (cutting a new foundation) too, support is readily provided as people come together to help a

---

[405] Waliggo, "The African Clan as the True Model of the African Church," 117.
[406] Oginga Odinga, *Not Yet Uhuru: An Autobiography of Oginga Odinga*, African Writers Series 38 (London, United Kingdom: Heinemann, 1967), 13–14, 64.
[407] David Parkin, *The Cultural Definition of Political Response: Lineal Destiny Among the Luo* (London: Academic Press, 1978), 87.
[408] Odinga, *Not Yet Uhuru: An Autobiography of Oginga Odinga*, 13–14, 64.

person to finish working on his new home.[409] Help in various forms is also available in times of disasters of any kind within the clan. For instance, during bereavement, the community takes care of feeding in the deceased's home and pools resources together to give one of their own a befitting send-off.[410] The unity of the community is manifested as people come together to help one another during such moments. If the death occurs in the city or town far away from the deceased's home, monetary contributions are made through the funeral association to help with the transportation of the body to the ancestral home.[411] When there is a need for a bull to be slaughtered during a funeral or other ceremonies, cattle to pay dowry, or money to lend, it is given to the person needing it through the *singo* (a form of promissory note) system.[412]

Furthermore, the Luo people continue to police over one another's wealth. The perfect example adduced by Oyugi Lusi is that "in cases of attack and cattle rustling by the neighbouring tribes, people would raise the alarm and all male members pursue the attackers."[413] The animals are then brought back home.

Support is also extended to a woman who is bereft of her husband through marriage to one of her late husband's brothers or kin coming from within the immediate circle of relatives about

---

[409] Firstbrook, *The Obamas: The Untold Story of an African Family*, 57, 73; David Cohen and E.S. Odhiambo, *Siaya: The Historical Anthropology of an African Landscape*, Eastern African Studies (London; Nairobi; Athens: James Currey; Heinemman Kenya; Ohio University Press, 1989), 87; Parkin, *The Cultural Definition of Political Response: Lineal Destiny Among the Luo*, 15.
[410] Cohen and E.S. Odhiambo, *Siaya: The Historical Anthropology of an African Landscape*, 82, 83.
[411] Cohen and Odhiambo, *Siaya: The Historical Anthropology of an African Landscape*, 87; Parkin, *The Cultural Definition of Political Response: Lineal Destiny Among the Luo*, 168, 233.
[412] Firstbrook, *The Obamas: The Untold Story of an African Family*, 75; Southall, *Lineage Formation Among the Luo*, 38.
[413] Oyugi Lusi, interview by the research assistant, Homa Bay, July 20, 2020.

twelve months following the death.⁴¹⁴ However, a woman is at liberty to choose whom she wants among the available kin and even to reject a proposal.⁴¹⁵ Firstbrook contends that "this tradition of wife inheritance might seem bizarre, but in an environment where survival is tough and tenuous, it does guarantee that any widowed woman and her children will be looked after within an established family unit, and not abandoned."⁴¹⁶ This practice also ensures the perpetuation of the deceased's lineage.⁴¹⁷ A widower is also allowed to take the sister of her deceased wife, who would assume the role of a spouse in a surrogate marital arrangement.⁴¹⁸ The parents of the deceased woman see to it that their son-in-law receives a wife to fill the void left.⁴¹⁹ Childlessness at the time of death aggravates the need for a surrogate marriage.⁴²⁰ However, marriage to the sister of one's wife also takes place in moments of barrenness with a reduction of bride price. Mbiti observes that in this arrangement, "the elaborate kinship system acts like an insurance policy covering both the physical and metaphysical dimensions of human life."⁴²¹

In urban settings, there are other forms of support that are provided. These include the provision of shelter, meals, and even

---

⁴¹⁴ Margaret Ogola, *The River and the Source* (Nairobi, Kenya: Focus Publishers Ltd, 1994), 12–47; Aidan Southall, *Lineage Formation Among the Luo* (London, New York, Toronto: Oxford University Press, 1952), 23.
⁴¹⁵ Southall, *Lineage Formation Among the Luo*, 23; Mbiti, *African Religions and Philosophy*, 144; Firstbrook, *The Obamas: The Untold Story of an African Family*, 83.
⁴¹⁶ Firstbrook, *The Obamas: The Untold Story of an African Family*, 84.
⁴¹⁷ The perpetuation of lineage is of great importance to the Luo people to date.
⁴¹⁸ Southall, *Lineage Formation Among the Luo*, 23; Mbiti, *African Religions and Philosophy*, 144, 145; Mikateko Maluleke, "Culture, Tradition, Custom, Law and Gender Equality," *PER / PELJ* 15, no. 1 (2012): 2.
⁴¹⁹ Nurudeen Alliyu, "Perception of Propertied Women on Marriage Forms, Widowhood and Living Patterns in Southwest, Nigeria," *African Research Review: An International Multidisciplinary Journal* 9, no. 3 (July 2015): 169.
⁴²⁰ Aina Olabisi, Joshua Aransiola, and ClementinaOsezua, "Sexual Health and Sexual Rights within Marriage," *African Research Review: An International Multi-Disciplinary Journal* 3, no. 1 (2009): 30.
⁴²¹ Mbiti, African *Religions and Philosophy*, 145.

monetary assistance to desperate "job seekers."[422] Some "lodgers" are usually "agnates" like sisters and stepsisters who could be there to be seen through education or training; kin like the "matrilateral cousins"; and affines who are female in most cases.[423] Hospitality is often extended beyond kinship affiliations to include friends.[424] Hosting could be very strenuous because of the significant number of people accommodated by one person.[425]

In any case, jo-kang'ato extends support to one another and ensures that they cater to the needy in their society. As Southall puts it, the "*Anyuola* segments within the minimal *dhoot* and *gweng*' also act as mutual assistance groups … They tend to meet for consideration of any matters of common concern."[426] Moreover, as jo-kang'ato, the Luo of Kenya come together in the spirit of *harambee* (pulling together) to raise money to help the less fortunate find a school or pay university fees for their children or offset hospital bills for the sick.[427] To make it easier to offer instant support when and where needed, Luos get into *riwruok* (support group) where some stipulated amount of money is contributed by each member into the *agulu* (pot) at a specified time to help in times of need.[428] Self-help groups also exist in the form of *nyoluoro* (helping one another in turns), also known as merry-go-round. The membership could consist of women who share certain things, such as the place of birth or marriage, business, job, or friendship.[429] Men have emulated the womenfolk in forming their self-help groups. In 2007 and 2008, following the postelection violence in Kenya, the solidarity of the Luo people came to the fore when they came together in the spirit of jo-kang'ato to support the

---

[422] Parkin, *The Cultural Definition of Political Response: Lineal Destiny Among the Luo*, 87, 88, 91, 93, 89.
[423] Ibid., 93–102, 114.
[424] Ibid., 87, 88, 102–104.
[425] Ibid., 88.
[426] Southall, *Lineage Formation Among the Luo*, 38.
[427] Otado Kababa, interview by the research assistant, Siaya, August 14, 2020.
[428] Ochieng Obondi, interview by the research assistant, Siaya, August 14, 2020.
[429] Roslida Akumu, interview by the author, Siaya, August 14, 2020.

victims. Semo said that "the many Luos who were displaced were received back in their clans, given land, and helped to settle down as compared to other communities who had to stay in tents and public institutions for lack of support from their communities."[430]

The Luo also offer support during happy moments like parties where the sharing of food and drinks takes place.[431] They hold parties from time to time, where food and drinks are shared among the members of the anyuola.[432] In the past, during these parties, the *otia* (an alcoholic drink made from ground sorghum) was served in jugs or sipped with the *oseke* (a long wooden straw measuring about three meters in length) from a joint pot according to a prescribed order, beginning with those who stand for the "major segments of superordinate lineage."[433] The concept brings people together during wedding ceremonies too as people support the bride and groom and their families both materially and morally.

Sporting events also present some of the moments for the demonstration of the concept of jo-kang'ato among the Luo people. Football is a perfect example of such moments. Over the years, they have been demonstrating solidarity in sports through their support for Gor Mahia Football Club.

The Luo people's oneness also comes to the fore as they listen to the directives of their elders as well as take a common stance on specific issues when necessary to achieve their goals. In politics, particularly, unity comes to the fore. Chief K'obondo observed that "Luos still organise themselves whenever they have a common goal to achieve. In politics, for example, they still consider voting in one of their own as a priority or voting in a candidate preferred by their elders."[434] Mathayo Gogni said that "in politics, the Luos seek the direction of the kingpin and vote as a block for one of their

---

[430] Semo.
[431] Southall, *Lineage Formation Among the Luo*, 38.
[432] Ibid., 37.
[433] Firstbrook, *The Obamas: The Untold Story of an African Family*, 37, 62.
[434] Awiko K'Obondo, interview by the research assistant, Kadongo in Homa Bay County, July 14, 2020.

own."⁴³⁵ The former prime minister of the Republic of Kenya, who is also the leader of the Orange Democratic Movement (ODM) party and AZIMIO Coalition at the time of writing this book, and the immediate former African Union High representative for Infrastructure Development, Engineer Raila Amollo Odinga has been the Luo kingpin for a long time after assuming that role from his father, Jaramogi Oginga Odinga.⁴³⁶ The latter was the first vice president of the Republic of Kenya and the doyen of multiparty politics. The other political parties that the Luo community has supported over the years are KANU before shifting to KPU in 1966, FORD Kenya, NDP, LDP, and currently ODM.⁴³⁷ Those who decide to go against the community's political position are seen as traitors.⁴³⁸ The Luo have been voting as a block during general elections.

Besides, the Luo people still have respect for their *ker* (leader of the Luo council of elders).⁴³⁹ The Jo-Luo (Luos) are also brought together by their language, *dholuo* (Luo).⁴⁴⁰ Moreover, the concept of jo-kang'ato comes into play in the naming of newborns. As Ragar

---

⁴³⁵ Mathayo Gogni, interview by the research assistant, Bondo in Siaya County, August 8, 2020.

⁴³⁶ Raila Odinga launched a fifth bid for the Presidency of the Republic of Kenya in the year 2022 with support from the then incumbent President Uhuru Muigai Kenyatta (the son of Jaramogi Oginga Odinga's friend and confidant turned fore, the Late first President Jomo Kenyatta). Uhuru Kenyatta had been Raila Odinga's political nemesis and competitor since the year 2013. Usually, the sitting President would not support an opposition candidate. However, Mr Kenyatta backed the bid of Mr Odinga (the leader of the Official opposition party) in the August 2022 General Elections. Mr Kenyatta's support was the aftermath of an historic handshake between them. They shook hands at the steps of Harambee house for peace, bringing the divided country together and the nation's prosperity. Their action was a typical demonstration of the philosophy of *jo-kang'ato*.

⁴³⁷ Over the years, the Luo have also supported political coalitions such as NARC which formed the government in the year 2002, CORD, and NASA.

⁴³⁸ Parkin, *The Cultural Definition of Political Response: Lineal Destiny Among the Luo*, 170.

⁴³⁹ Apolo Omia, interview by the research assistant, Migori, August 16, 2020.

⁴⁴⁰ KaBoma.

puts it, "the newborn babies are given names associated with their clans or inherit their grandparents' names."[441]

Based on the egalitarian feature of the concept of jo-kang'ato, its potential to enrich the understanding of Christian unity within the ecclesial life of the church in Africa comes to the fore. The understanding generated through this concept would encourage Christians to shoulder one another's burdens in a more meaningful way. The mindset inculcated proves to be better than the hypocritical Western missionaries' approach to the relationship among humans, which saw them preach that people should regard one another as brothers, which is "egalitarianism," but at the same time exalted the culture of "individualism."[442]

4.3.2 A Sense of Belonging

The other ideal enforced by the concept of jo-kang'ato is the sense of belonging. Jo-kang'ato are people who belong to one another and are related by blood—in our case, by Christ's blood. It encapsulates other references of one another like "*jowa* [our people], *yawa* [our agnates], *langwa* [our valiant ones], *kothwa* [our seed]."[443] They also understand culture as *timbewa* (our customs).[444] Other terms of identification include *dalawa* (our home) and *thurwa* (where I [or we] hail from).[445] As Cohen and Odhiambo pointed out, with this kind of identification, "you do not in an important sense exist until you reveal your networks … Identity then is the composition of oneself by others in a constellation."[446] This approach is generally consistent with the collective view among the African people to life whereby a person is defined in connection to a group to which he

---

[441] Ragar.
[442] Odinga, *Not Yet Uhuru: An Autobiography of Oginga Odinga*, 65.
[443] Cohen and Odhiambo, *Siaya: The Historical Anthropology of an African Landscape*, 9.
[444] Ibid.
[445] Ibid., 27.
[446] Ibid., 27–28.

or she belongs. Mbiti states that "to be human [as far as the African worldview is concerned] is to belong to the whole community, and to do so involve participating in the beliefs, ceremonies, rituals and festivals of that community."[447]

In conformity with the Luo people's philosophy of belonging, the *biero* (placenta) is buried by the child's mother at birth in a hole dug somewhere within the home to show that the new baby is part of or genuinely belongs to a particular family.[448] Those whose placentas were not buried in their ancestral homes but in other people's territories are known as *jooko* (outsiders).[449] It is in this sense that one's ancestral home remains a place of significance and insistence on interment there at the end of one's life.[450] It is held that when a Luo person is not buried in the ancestral home, his spirit could disturb those he leaves behind.[451] It is held that just before his death, the Luos' ancestor Ramogi Ajwang' also went back to Tororo in Uganda, where his placenta had been buried in the homestead of his father, Ramogi, from his home in Got Ramogi (in Siaya County in Kenya), leaving his fifteen sons.[452] This habit is well captured in the saying "Oyik biecha kaluo kae [My placenta is buried here in Luoland]."[453] In other words, the "ancestral home" is of great significance; and no matter how far someone goes away from it, he or she is bound to come back dead or alive. In cases where in the past a person died away from home, and his identification got complicated, *nak* (the plucking of six "lower teeth" of a young person before they turned twenty), which was also a method of initiation into adulthood (as the Luo do not

---

[447] Mbiti, African *Religions and Philosophy*, 2.
[448] Cohen and Odhiambo, *Siaya: The Historical Anthropology of an African Landscape*, 9, 25; Firstbrook, *The Obamas: The Untold Story of an African Family*, 57.
[449] Cohen and Odhiambo, *Siaya: The Historical Anthropology of an African Landscape*, 25.
[450] Firstbrook, *The Obamas: The Untold Story of an African Family*, 45, 52, 85.
[451] Ibid., 84–85.
[452] Ibid., 45.
[453] Ibid., 52.

circumcise boys or perform clitorectomy to females like other Kenyan tribes), helped with the identification.[454]

Since the ancestral home is the focal point among the Luo, its abandonment and subsequent disappearance into the city or urban centre are often discouraged. However, it is not just a matter of having a house at the rural *dala* (home) that matters but ensuring that it is in a decent condition, for the continued absence from the house could lead to its collapse.[455] Between the 1950s and 1960s, a song was composed to mock those who were migrating to the city of Nairobi to take advantage of the "Africanization policies of the Kenyan government" at the expense of their huts: "Biye onwang'o Od Japango [The white ants have discovered the worker's hut]. Biye teng'o teng' [How they mince it]!"[456] Apuot Ochieng' also captured this in his song:

> Gero gae odi (Build yourself a house)
> Kata otin (Even a small one)
> Gero gae odi (Build yourself a house)
> Kata otin (Even a small one)
> Masira Jamuomre (Calamities strike unannounced)
> Tho onyuolo yuak (Death capitulates mourning)
> Inyalo Kunyi (It's no good our digging your grave)
> To ikunyo ot (As well as your house's foundation)[457]

The attachment to dala (rural home) is also among the reasons why many Luo men practice polygyny. The possession of two wives, for instance, enables a person to straddle between the rural home and city as the women visit both places in turns while the man, in most

---

[454] Ibid., 65, 63, 64; Ingrid Herbich, "Luo," Encyclopedia of World Cultures Supplement.
[455] Cohen and Odhiambo, *Siaya: The Historical Anthropology of an African Landscape*, 57, 5.
[456] Ibid., 57.
[457] Ibid., 58.

cases, concentrates on work and visits the rural home occasionally.[458] Polygyny ensures that the man does not lose touch with his ancestral home and that the ancestral land is tilled and guarded.[459] The "ruralization" of marriage is another factor contributing to the importance of dala, for town dwellers travel to the countryside to marry or prepare for a marriage, which is in the offing.[460]

4.3.3 Meaningful Incorporation

Lack of full and meaningful incorporation and integration is among the factors attributed to divisions that are rocking the church in Africa. The concept of jo-kang'ato would address this issue squarely. Jo-kang'ato seems to have been present in principle even before the arrival of the Luo in Kenya, as manifested in, among other ways, their treatment of tribes subdued during invasions. Firstbrook enlightens:

> The Luo became adept at incorporating captives into their societies, so their numbers increased at an astonishing rate. And as their numbers increased, so their military strength grew … Soon Luo were sending out raiding expeditions from Pubungu, and their warriors brought back plunder and captives from the Madi and other local tribes … Over time, these captives became part of the Luo tribe, and this process of integration was to become a common feature of their society over many centuries.[461]

The former Catholic priest in East Africa Father Joseph Pasquale Crazzolara (cited by Firstbrook) describes the situation as follows:

---

[458] Parkin, *The Cultural Definition of Political Response: Lineal Destiny Among the Luo*, 46, 84.
[459] Ibid., 50, 51, 52, 53.
[460] Ibid., 53, 50, 77.
[461] Firstbrook, *The Obamas: The Untold Story of an African Family*, 32, 35.

JO-KANG'ATO

On the march, as still in big hunts, the tribal, clan and family groups kept closely united. Female prisoners were absorbed and became completely submerged … For male captives [sic] the case was different in theory, but scarcely in practice. Prisoner slaves were allocated to a family or clan-group, and treated as blood relations, and even given wives or cattle as dowry. But with their children and descendants they started their own sub-clans and social life, as a clan segment, related and hence exogamous, to the main Lwoo [sic] clan.[462]

4.3.4 Teamwork

The other message that the concept of jo-kang'ato would send to the church in Africa is that unity is strength. Throughout their existence, the Luo people have lived knowing that unity is their strength. Firstbrook says that "there was recognition that the strength and power of the group grew from their allegiance to the leader, and from cooperation among the people; this strengthened the political union both among the Luo clans and between Luo and non-Luo groups."[463] As time went by, the smaller clans of the Luo metamorphosed from being separate groups into megaunits and singled out people to lead them. The spirit of allegiance to the larger group and teamwork began to manifest in, among other ways, fighting to protect their land from intrusion.[464] As Firstbrook brilliantly puts it, "it was from this process of social assimilation that the concept of a defined Luo tribe began to emerge."[465] The need to form a formidable force before the Pax Britannica also came to play in the settlement arrangement among the Luo. People lived

---

[462] Ibid., 32.
[463] Ibid., 33.
[464] Ibid., 47.
[465] Ibid.

together in the *gundni bur*, whose singular form is *gunda bur* (space accommodating many people at the same time).[466]

4.3.5 Cooperation

One of the benefits of kinship is the "cooperation" that it enhances in moments of necessity.[467] Mbiti describes some of the instances where kinship has proved helpful over the years,

> In case of internal conflict, clan members joined one another to fight their aggressive neighbours, in former years. If a person finds himself in difficulties, it is not unusual for him to call for help from his clan members and other relatives, e.g. [sic] in paying fines caused by an accident [such as accidental wounding or killing of another person or damage to property]; in finding enough goods to exchange for a wife; or today in giving financial support to students studying in institutes of higher education both at home and abroad.[468]

The concept of jo-kang'ato has the potential to encourage cooperation among Christians drawn from various divides. It would widen circles to include "them" in our ranks. It is the basis of the links formed by the Luo people among themselves in the *gwenge* (territories).[469] It was more helpful in the seventeenth and eighteenth centuries when communities were hostile to one another, as it ensured protection against aggression, assistance, and human resources.[470] Cooperation allowed commercial activities to take place between

---

[466] Cohen and Odhiambo, *Siaya: The Historical Anthropology of an African Landscape*, 10.
[467] Mbiti, *African Religions and Philosophy*, 106.
[468] Ibid.
[469] Cohen and Odhiambo, *Siaya: The Historical Anthropology of an African Landscape*, 15.
[470] Ibid.

the *ogendini* (tribes), for people would pass through others' territories without being attacked.[471] In the process, circles of "kinship" were widened to encompass people from other places.[472]

4.3.6 Selflessness

Selflessness is one of the virtues the concept of jo-kang'ato bolsters. One of the areas where it came to play among the Luo people in the past was during the war. It was due to selflessness and the need to provide defense for the community that Luo men delayed marriage until when they were almost thirty.[473] Firstbrook says that "the defence of the clan was a priority and being a warrior was a form of 'national service' expected of all young men [except only sons whose family lineage depended on them producing an heir; such boys might be married as young as fifteen and would not be expected to fight]."[474] Kinship was considered during the times of war. Firstbrook states that "when war was declared, platoons of warriors were organised along family lines, based on the principle that kinship strengthens the bond between combatants."[475]

One of the areas where selflessness needs to be demonstrated in the present times within the church setting is the way finances are handled. The concept of jo-kang'ato discourages runaway greed and materialism, which bedevil the church in Africa and contribute to disunity. This phenomenon is perpetuated in Christian pulpits every other day by the clergy through their gospel of prosperity. Agents of this gospel continue to fleece vulnerable congregants dry while they rise to opulence. One of the concerns of jo-kang'ato is to discourage greed so that no one amasses much wealth at the expense of others except through hard work.

---

[471] Ibid.
[472] Ibid.
[473] Firstbrook, *The Obamas: The Untold Story of an African Family*, 66.
[474] Ibid.
[475] Ibid.

4.3.7 Sound Leadership

The concept of jo-kang'ato has the potential to have a positive impact on ecclesial leadership in Africa. Lack of sound leadership is one of the prominent causes of disunity in the church in Africa. Through jo-kang'ato, a new form of ecclesial leadership that upholds ecclesial unity is prescribed. It injects a new attitude among leaders to discharge the mandate given to them in such a way that the welfare of the church is considered rather than satisfying their selfish and egotistic motives. That kind of leadership has been described by Odinga:

> We were taught that a good statesman would not give precipitate judgement but would defer his decision … Elders were men of substance and integrity, and recognised as outstanding individuals. Even when they came from leading lineages they did not inherit leadership, but had to demonstrate it. Diligence yielded prosperity and brought respect, but riches alone did not count for leadership, and a rich man who was offensive was not respected … the authority of the elders was much respected, [sic] indeed it was never challenged … [Other qualities included] maturity, experience, steadfastness, and wisdom, and a thorough absorption of the teachings of the elders passed on by them or sung by our traditional musicians.[476]

According to Odinga, a lack of expected qualities resulted in disqualification from leadership, even if a person came from the right "lineage."[477] There was no handpicking and imposing of leaders among the Luo until the arrival of the colonialists when

---

[476] Odinga, *Not Yet Uhuru: An Autobiography of Oginga Odinga*, 11–12, 64.
[477] Ibid., 20.

leadership ceased to be local people-centered and became tainted with corruption.[478]

The concept of jo-kang'ato also fosters an all-inclusive leadership, which invites everybody with leadership qualities, including women, to participate in the running of the church. The contribution of women to leadership among the Luo people is well received. Apart from clans being named after them, the persistent, earnest, and hardworking women are usually invited to give their views on various issues affecting the people, and some even lead the council of elders as well as serve in other capacities.[479] At present, we have a Luo woman who is serving as the governor of Homabay County, Her Excellency Gladys Atieno Nyasuna Wanga. Besides, there are Luo women who serve as members of Parliament, senators, cabinet secretaries, ambassadors, parastatal heads, judges, etc.

4.3.8 Intergenerational Connection

Luo kinship could ensure intergenerational connection in several ways, which include but are not limited to the passing of faith along to the next generation. Besides encouraging continuity in Christian heritage, this promotes unity in faith among Christians from the past to present and future. The Luo society has always been keen on the perpetuation of its culture among successive generations, which usually happens as the older generation passes values, traditions, and culture to young people who would also extend them to their posterity. In the past, this took place at a man's *abila* or *duol* (hut) for boys and young men in the form of stories of great men, forefathers, conflicts, acts of courage, and "hunting" narrated by a father to his sons.[480] Odinga says that "the stories of the elders were one of our two sources of education in the village. The other source was the harpists who played an important role in the community. The harpists learnt at the feet of the elders and expressed the peoples'

---

[478] Ibid., 22, 23.
[479] Ibid., 11.
[480] Firstbrook, *The Obamas: The Untold Story of an African Family*, 62.

philosophy in musical and poetic language."[481] The education of girls or young women took place in the *siwindhe* (a communal sleeping hut used by teenage girls) of a *pim* (an older woman).[482] Education on good conduct; the customs and practices of the clan; issues to do with womanhood like sex, marriage, and child-rearing; and responsibilities toward the community were transmitted through stories.[483] The girls left siwindhe only at the time of marriage.[484] As Cohen and Odhiambo put it, "the *pim's* nurturing was the crucible of Luo culture and society in the past."[485]

Mutuality is a significant characteristic of the concept of jo-kang'ato, which fosters sound intergenerational relationships. For instance, among the Luo, children are often very close to their grandparents, whom they find refuge in to evade punishment at home and get food. They can also eat in other homesteads where people are kind and related to them.[486] Relationship between male and female siblings is also characterized by harmony, love, and interdependence, which spreads to children who would refer to their mother's brother as *nera* (uncle) and their father's sister as *waya* (aunt).[487] Relationships between in-laws are also mutual, though restrained to maintain respect and prevent sexual temptation.[488]

The concept of jo-kang'ato could help the church in Africa to achieve unity in the present time and solidarity with the church in all ages—past and future in its visible and invisible dimensions through subscription to the universal principles of the Christian faith. As far as the Luo people's worldview is concerned, jo-kang'ato as a concept

---

[481] Odinga, *Not Yet Uhuru: An Autobiography of Oginga Odinga*, 9.
[482] Southall, *Lineage Formation Among the Luo*, 19.
[483] Firstbrook, *The Obamas: The Untold Story of an African Family*, 61; Southall, *Lineage Formation Among the Luo*, 19; Cohen and Odhiambo, *Siaya: The Historical Anthropology of an African Landscape*, 92, 93–94, 95.
[484] Firstbrook, *The Obamas: The Untold Story of an African Family*, 61.
[485] Cohen and Odhiambo, *Siaya: The Historical Anthropology of an African Landscape*, 95.
[486] Southall, *Lineage Formation Among the Luo*, 19.
[487] Ibid.
[488] Ibid; Mbiti, *African Religions and Philosophy*, 147.

is applicable not only to the living but to the dead as well. It binds the living with the dead or ancestors. For a Luo person, there must be a good relationship not only with the living but with the dead too. In an ecclesial context, Christian believers of various ages are bound together through allegiance to God and His Word.

4.3.9 Dispute Resolution Mechanisms

While aspects of the Luos' dispute resolution mechanism are present among other African cultures, the Luo were singled out in this study.[489] When disputes arise, a meeting is convened, and a "demand for order" is made.[490] Dispute resolution sessions are adjudicated by the *jodong gweng'* (village elders) at the lower level and, on a broader scope, the *ker* (Luo leader), whose role is mediatorial and "conciliatory."[491] The administrative arm of the government of Kenya, represented by the assistant chiefs and chiefs, also plays a crucial role in dispute resolution among the Luo locally.[492] The law courts are resorted to in advanced stages of disputes.[493]

For the sake of avoiding unfair judgments and hasty decisions, a commission would be formed to delve deep into the matter at hand and, upon completion of the investigation, present their findings.[494]

---

[489] The resolution of disputes is approached in the same way among the Tswana of Botswana, in the South Africa's "traditional justice system," by the Karamojong council of elders (*Akiriket*) in Uganda, the Teso's *arriret* (council of elders) in Uganda, the Pokot, Turkana, Marakwet, Samburu, and the *kamasian* council of elders among the Kipsigis in Kenya. A more or less similar approach is taken in Rwanda by the *Gacaca* courts which are mandated by the government to adjudicate some disputes. (Francis Kariuki, "Conflict Resolution by Elders in Africa: Successes, Challenges and Opportunities,"*Alternative Dispute Resolution Journal* 3, no. 2 (2015): 30–53).

[490] Parkin, *The Cultural Definition of Political Response: Lineal Destiny Among the Luo*, 230.

[491] Ibid., 231, 233.

[492] Ingrid Herbich, "Luo," Encyclopedia of World Cultures Supplement.

[493] Ibid.

[494] Parkin, *The Cultural Definition of Political Response: Lineal Destiny Among the Luo*, 230.

There has always been an aspect of restitution too in the dispute resolution among the Luo people. One of the causes of feuds between lineages before the establishment of British rule—and, of course, a serious one—was murder. In the event of such, the victim's kin would take "revenge" by taking away the life of someone belonging to the killer's lineage.[495] However, this could be stopped by the murderer's people, giving a girl for marriage or "twelve heads of cattle" in restitution.[496] In situations where the marriage was not possible because of consanguinity, an elder who is senior in age and enjoys the respect of the groups of people involved convened a council to discuss the matter. If the offender is found guilty, his banishment becomes inevitable.[497] The murder of one's closest kin was dealt with even more seriously.[498]

I now sum up vital elements of the concept of jo-kang'ato that were identified in this work. These are critical for church unity. They include acts of support, which alleviate challenges affecting others, as well as celebrate successes. Such acts are made possible by mutual understanding, the reckoning of one another as equal and worthy members of society, selfless attitudes, and openness. With this approach to the relationship, one person's experience is the business of every member. A sense of belonging, which comes into play in the elaborate networks that Luos subscribe to and enables them to be in touch with one another, is also outstanding. Incorporation and integration were also identified, and the potentials accompanying them were brought to the fore. Teamwork and the achievements accompanying the consolidation of human efforts are also significant

---

[495] Southall, *Lineage Formation Among the Luo*, 22.
[496] Ibid.
[497] Ibid.
[498] "When a man kills a close relative, belonging to his own minimal class A segment of the maximal lineage, it is *masira*—a ritual offence. The murderer must bury his relative and stay by the grave until *chola* (the first mourning period) is finished. He must cohabit with the dead mans wife, if she has borne no children to her husband, so that she may *bear a child to be named after the dead* and to guard his homestead."(Ibid.).

features of jo-kang'ato. The cooperation that plays out in the broader networks of people as they harness human and material resources for the community's well-being is also key. The other elements are selflessness demonstrated in service to others and intergenerational relationships. The unbiased approach to leadership and dispute resolution—which comes with wisdom, respect, truthfulness, and inclusion—is also remarkable.

4.4 The Relationship between the Concept of Jo-kang'ato and Ubuntu

To some extent, the concept of jo-kang'ato stands for ideals that are like those upheld by *ubuntu*. First and foremost, both concepts foster intimate relationships among people, which translates into appropriate regard and treatment of others, including those who are different.[499] This involves standing with one another in times of need and adversity. Such treatment is to the benefit of all who are involved rather than parasitic or lopsided. In both cases too, humanity transcends the immediate circle to embrace the wider group.[500] A person is understood as a social being rather than "individualistically."[501] According to the latter view, which is Western, a person is alone and is given form by reasoning: "I think, therefore I am," as opposed to the African view, "I am because I belong."[502] As

---

[499] Wonke Buqa, "Ubuntu Values in an Emerging Multi-Racial Community: A Narrative Reflection," (PhD diss., University of Pretoria, 2016), 72, 73, 100; Mogobe Ramose, *African Philosophy through Ubuntu* (Harare: Mond Books Publishers, 2002), 155; A. Shute, "Ubuntu as the African Ethical Vision," in *African Ethics - An Anthropology of Comparative and Applied Ethics* (Scottsville: University of KwaZulu Natal Press, 2009), 85.
[500] Nelson Mandela, *Long Walk to Freedom* (New York: Little, Brown & Company, 1995), 624.
[501] Segun Gbadegesin, "An Outline of a Theory of Destiny," in *African Philosophy: New and Traditional Perspectives* (New York: Oxford University Press, 2004), 61.
[502] Gabriel Setiloane, *African Theology: An Introduction* (Cape Town: Lux Verbi, 2000), 20; Puleng LenkaBula, "Beyond Anthropocentricity - Botho/Ubuntu and

Gbadegesin puts it, in the African context, the "community provides its members with meaning."[503]

Moreover, both concepts support productivity amid various distinctions. They emphasize the importance of diversity, the pivotal part it plays among people, and the need to be united despite it. As in ubuntu, the concept of jo-kang'ato challenges Christians to stretch their borders beyond "us" to include "them." Such kind of approach to diversity leaves the society and the church more strengthened than fragmented.[504] Other values of *ubuntu* that are present in *jo-kang'ato* are, according to Buqa, "trust, helpfulness, respect, sharing, caring, interdependence, cooperation, forgiveness, equality, dignity, and unselfishness."[505] Again, in both cases, prejudicial treatment of others is discouraged since every person counts.[506] Jo-kang'ato and ubuntu are also concerned with bringing in or integrating as opposed to sending away and disintegrating.[507] They are also against exploitation of those who cannot stand for themselves, fraudulent conduct, and graft, among other immoral conducts.[508] According to Tutu, when we are nasty to others, we are nasty to ourselves.[509]

Despite the shared features, jo-kang'ato is more intimate than ubuntu. The reason is that whereas jo-kang'ato is rooted in the family; ubuntu is generic in a sense and, therefore, a bit remote. The concept of jo-kang'ato brings in the aspect of kinship and blood ties, among

---

the Quest for Economic and Ecological Justice in Africa," *Religion and Theology* 15 (2008): 383.

[503] Gbadegesin, "An Outline of a Theory of Destiny," 61.

[504] Buqa, "Ubuntu Values in an Emerging Multi-Racial Community: A Narrative Reflection," 73, 52, 53, 76.

[505] Ibid., 88.

[506] Lieze Meiring, "Exploring Ubuntu Language in Bridging Gaps: A Narrative Reflection on Discussions between Members of Two Reformed Churches in a Rural Town of South Africa" (PhD diss., University of Pretoria, 2016), 88.

[507] Setiloane, *African Theology: An Introduction*, 22.

[508] Buqa, "Ubuntu Values in an Emerging Multi-Racial Community: A Narrative Reflection," 224.

[509] Leonard Hulley, Louise Kretzschmar, and Luke Pato, eds., *Archbishop Tutu: Prophetic Witness in South Africa* (Cape Town: Human & Rousseau, 1996), 102.

other benefits, while ubuntu talks about humanity. Jo-kang'ato is richer in implication if extended to include all of God's children. It is an excellent concept with great potential to enrich the understanding of Christian unity. Therefore, this work is needed by the church in Africa as it grapples with polarization.

The utilization of the concept of jo-kang'ato is a response to the yearning for a theology that, according to Moripe, is generated "through the African and for the people of Africa."[510] Idowu buttresses this argument as follows:

> The day of theology in the perspective of Africa is dawning. There are African scholars and men of faith who are finding the prefabricated theology imported into Africa inadequate for her spiritual and academic needs. These are now promoters of the theology which bears the stamp of original thinking and meditation of Africans.[511]

Peter Kasenene (quoted by Ilesanmi) describes such kind of theology as "the expression of Africa's response to God in their context and experience, based on the Scriptures, Christian tradition and the African heritage … the Christian faith as understood, communicated and lived by Africans and applied to issues which concern them profoundly."[512] It has dawned on African scholars that culture is a great asset given to them by God and needs to be explored.[513]

The concept of jo-kang'ato is drawn from the rich heritage of the Luo people. Sources of this heritage, as among other African

---

[510] Moripe, "The Notion of Independence and Rendering of Service to the African Independent/ Indigenous Churches," 866.
[511] Bolaji Idowu, *African Traditional Religion: A Definition* (London, Great Britain: SCM Press, 1973), xi.
[512] Simeon Ilesanmi, "Inculturation and Liberation: Christian Social Ethics and the African Theology Project," *Annual of the Society of Christian Ethics* 15 (1995): 49.
[513] Idowu, *African Traditional Religion: A Definition*, x.

communities, include the Luos' proverbs, sayings, riddles, stories, myths, plays, songs, symbols presented by culture, and experiences in life. Healey and Sybertz point out the goal of utilizing these as the sharing of the "wisdom" present among Africans and their culture with the entire church (world church).[514] However, as the fusing of experiences and wisdom offered by African cultures with Christianity takes place, the audience within also benefits. Whereas to the outsider, this would "awaken theological and pastoral themes that are dormant or latent in world Christianity," Africans will also find "examples of practical evangelisation and functional African Christianity that can be used on the local level."[515] Healey and Sybertz maintain that when the culture of the African person interacts with Christianity, Christianity gets flavor even though this engagement is not about transferring customs of African tradition into Christianity.[516] Moreover, as Ukpong puts it, when Christianity and African theology are allowed to talk to each other, Africans would "live out Christianity authentically within their cultural milieu."[517] All these render the inculturation of Christian teachings necessary. In Chukwu's words, "authentic inculturation begins from the grassroots … renew the impulse of evangelisation, deepen the faith, and inspire an honest response from the culture."[518] Idowu states in support that "the scholar must try and enter into the feelings of the people and see with their eyes in order to grasp and possess the knowledge of what they actually know and believe about the supersensible world."[519] Nkansah-Obrempong buttresses this argument as follows:

---

[514] Joseph Healey and Donald Sybertz, *Towards an African Narrative Theology* (Nairobi, Kenya: Paulines, 1996), 13–61.
[515] Ibid.
[516] Ibid.
[517] Nkansah-Obrempong, *Visual Theology: Some Akan Cultural Symbols, Metaphors, Proverbs, Myths, and Symbols and Their Implications for Doing Christian Theology*, 49.
[518] Donatus Chukwu, *The Church as the Extended Family of God: Toward a New Direction for African Ecclesiology* (Bloomington, Indiana: Xlibris, 2011), 180, 181.
[519] Idowu, *African Traditional Religion: A Definition*, 18.

Culture will have a major role to play in the formulation of a relevant theology for Africa … all theology, for it to be meaningful to any given people, must be contextualised theology; otherwise that theology will be irrelevant, sterile, and dead … All relevant theologies must be done in context … Theological ideas and theological formulation become more fruitful and relevant if they are cast in the thought forms of the recipient's culture. This is true with every theological endeavour. A true theological reflection emerges as we construct theology using the values and ideas that form the central core of values in a culture.[520]

In jo-kang'ato, the modus operandi of the African people is brought to bear.[521] The Western missionaries did not take this into consideration, for their evangelistic approach among the Luo people was too sudden, careless, abrupt, full of disturbance, shocking, and upsetting.[522] Their method showed a keenness to rip the community-focused Luo people out of their everyday lives and the creation of a wedge between them. Their coming into the Luoland saw the introduction of *laini* (church villages) near churches.[523] People were required to come out of their homes and live in the *od kibanda* (rectangular houses) at the laini, thus separating them from their

---

[520] Nkansah-Obrempong, *Visual Theology: Some Akan Cultural Symbols, Metaphors, Proverbs, Myths, and Symbols and Their Implications for Doing Christian Theology*, 15, 32, 33, 40.
[521] Louis Kanayo and Charles Nweke, "The Relevance of the Church in Oppressive Situations: The Praxis of Liberation Theology in Africa," *Ogirisi: A New Journal of African Studies* 10 (2013): 82; Mbiti, *African Religions and Philosophy*, 1969.
[522] Odinga, *Not Yet Uhuru: An Autobiography of Oginga Odinga*, 3, 62, 63, 64, 65.
[523] Cohen and Odhiambo, *Siaya: The Historical Anthropology of an African Landscape*, 115.

normal lives.⁵²⁴ With time, however, the laini proved unsustainable and closed down.⁵²⁵

4.5 Using the Concept of Jo-kang'ato to Solve the Problem of Disunity in the Church

An interview was conducted with church members, Christian groups, and ecclesiastical leaders to find out the potential of the concept of jo-kang'ato to solve the problem of disunity in the church. Following this exercise, 63 percent of the respondents indicated that the application of values that are presented by the concept of jo-kang'ato could play a significant role in solving the problem of disunity among Christians in the ecclesial life of the church. Only 37 percent expressed a contrary view.⁵²⁶

Overall, the analysis established that the concept of jo-kang'ato could be critically applied to solve the problem of disunity among Christians within the ecclesial life of the church, owing to its potential to bring people together.

---

[524] Ibid.

[525] Ibid.

[526] The research took place in four counties within the Republic of Kenya, which are home to the Luo people, namely Migori, Homa Bay, Siaya, and Kisumu. The decision to base the research within this geographical location was because the concept under study is cultural. Their lives are affected by the concept of *jo-kang'ato* daily. The village elders, being familiar with and knowledgeable in the Luo people's history and culture, provided information that is not obtainable through secondary sources for instance, on the origin of the concept of *jo-kang'ato* and whether it helped in bringing the Luo people together in the past or not. The elders have lived with this concept and continue to do so in the present time. Responses from selected Church members helped the researcher to establish the connection between the concept if any at all, with Christian unity.

4.5.1 The Effects of Christians' Engagement and Treatment of One Another as Jo-kang'ato

Lucas Kwogo (Kenya Assemblies of God Church) said that "*jo-kang'ato* believe in themselves and protect their own. Therefore, if Christians treated each other as *jo-kang'ato*, it is likely for the Church to be in unity forever because the bond between the Christians would be more robust. Christians will be more united than divided."[527] Through it, a sense of brotherhood among Christians could be enhanced. The application of the concept could lead Christians to consider themselves united in Christ rather than as enemies. Church members will look at one another as *jo-kaYesu* (all belonging to Jesus) and would be willing to work together to edify one another spiritually.[528] It also emerged from the responses that the concept provides an environment within which Christians could amicably solve their disputes. When the sense of belonging to one God is awakened in Christians, they will replicate the dispute resolution mechanisms provided by the concept of jo-kang'ato within the church setting whenever misunderstandings arise.[529]

4.5.2 The Relationship among Christian Denominations Arising from the Treatment of One Another as Jo-kang'ato

As a result of the application of jo-kang'ato at the interdenominational level, intolerance will give way to respect and acceptance as Christians consider themselves brothers and sisters from the same Father (God) and united by Christ's love as jo-kang'ato.[530] The result would include a positive and constructive ecumenism, which could manifest in interdenominational fellowships, seminars

---

[527] Lucas Kwogo, interview by the author, Siaya, August 3, 2020.
[528] Jacinta Okomo, interview by the research assistant, Homa Bay County, July 20, 2020.
[529] Mondo.
[530] Betha Olang', interview by the author, Oyugis in Homa Bay County, July 29, 2020.

where information is shared, joint prayers for the society, evangelistic meetings, congresses, the formation of interdenominational choirs and participation in joint music festivals and extravaganzas, and the invitation of one another to other churches to worship and participate in activities and sports.[531]

In connection with this, various denominations could still work together while maintaining their diversities rather than dissolving into a single church entity. Churches could be able to minister to their communities together in, among other ways, supporting the development initiatives of their communities through engagement in various projects—for instance, the construction of health facilities, schools, and tertiary institutions—and taking part in community work of any other kind.[532] Their unity could also come to the fore in a joint involvement with charity work through poverty alleviation ventures and offer support for orphans, widows, the homeless, and the elderly within the community.[533] They would sensitize and educate the masses on various issues of importance, which could include offering health education to create awareness on the outbreaks of diseases and their prevention, such as COVID-19, HIV, AIDS, cholera, typhoid, malaria, Ebola, etc., and promoting basic education, environmental conservation, and provision of farming skills.[534] In the words of Maritha Opien (RCC), churches could "come together in education, health, and economic development of different members of the society."[535] They could also be involved in the campaign against antihuman practices like female genital mutilation (FGM), early marriages, and domestic abuse, as well as speak together against other

---

[531] Kwogo; Marikus Dienya, interview by the research assistant, Homa Bay County, July 20, 2020; Micah Onyango, interview by the research assistant, Siaya, July 18, 2020; Chistine Ochieng, interview by the research assistant, Siaya, July 18, 2020.
[532] Onyango.
[533] Marikus Dienya, interview by the research assistant, Homa Bay County, July 20, 2020.
[534] Maritha Opien, interview by the research assistant, Homa Bay County, July 20, 2020; Benjamin Oduor, interview by the author, Siaya, August 3, 2020.
[535] Opien.

societal evils like corruption.[536] Furthermore, they could work together in mediating peace and reconciliation among disputing sections of society.[537] Benta Ochieng (vicar of the Anglican Church of Kenya) cited a typical example of what is taking place under her leadership in Magwar Parish. She said that various denominations could still work together while maintaining their identities "with love and the unity of Christ. A case here is a group called Anglican Development Society, which brings together people from all denominations."[538] They would also offer free guidance and counseling to members of the community.[539] Kapango said that "they will not focus on individual differences or the interdenominational differences, but rather focus on the common goal and the fact that they are all Christians."[540] Apart from Christ's prayer coming to fulfillment through such kind of relationship between Christians drawn from different denominations, the church would have a strong influence.

The diversity of the church in Africa is evident in, among other ways, ecclesial practices and worship styles and modalities. Whereas some churches are stuck in statism and tradition passed on to them by the West, others are dynamic and innovative.[541] The "dominant" churches like the RCs, Anglicans, Lutherans, etc., tend to be conventional in the way they do church.[542] The "popular" ones like the Pentecostals, Assemblies of God, Churches of Christ, Bible Believers, Deliverance, Redeemed Gospel, Full Gospel, and Holiness Churches, on the other hand, encourage inclusivity in worship, charismatic tendencies, and high appeal to people with "emotional

---

[536] Ibid.
[537] Oduor.
[538] Benta Ochieng, interview by the author, Kisumu, August 14, 2020.
[539] Titus Onyango, interview by the research assistant, Homa Bay County, July 20, 2020.
[540] Christopher Kapango, interview by the author, Uriri in Migori County, August 2, 2020.
[541] Waruta, "Towards an African Church: A Critical Assessment of Alternative Forms and Structures," 37.
[542] Ibid., 34.

or physical crises" and emphasize the hereafter.[543] The "distinctive types" of churches, on their part, demonstrate features like wearing "special uniforms" during worship (for instance, the Salvation Army); worshipping on Saturday as the Sabbath as in the case of the Seventh-day Adventist Church (SDA); and baptizing by immersion as seen among the SDAs, Baptists, and the Africa Inland Church.[544] In the "indigenous" ("independent") churches where culture influences ecclesial practices heavily, worship is characterized by charismatic displays in the form of healing, prophesying, glossolalia, etc.[545]

4.5.3 Ways through Which the Concept of Jo-kang'ato Could Address the Generational Gap within the Church

The concept of jo-kang'ato could be effectively applied to address the generational gap and tensions that arise from time to time in the church. Johnson Simbiri (Pentecostal Evangelistic Fellowship of Africa Church) said that "from time immemorial, each age-group has had the responsibility to keep its obligation for the sake of the unity of *jo-kang'ato*. If this is replicated in the Church, the generational gap and tension as currently experienced would be resolved."[546] When the spirit of jo-kang'ato is allowed to reign, the consciousness of Christians' position in the church family as sons and daughters of God is aroused. As articulated by Titus Owino (Baptist Church), "*jo-kang'ato* can also mean one family which is bonded by Jesus Christ hence people can sit and talk together as one family and bring peace amongst themselves."[547] As members of different age groups cultivate respect for one another, barriers give way, and unity is achieved. Ezra Oriko (youth leader at the African Inland

---

[543] Ibid., 35–36.
[544] Ibid., 36.
[545] Allan Anderson, *Zion and Pentecost: The Spirituality and Experience of Pentecostal and Zionist-Apostolic Churches in South Africa* (Pretoria: University of South Africa, 2000), 242.
[546] Johnson Simbiri, interview by the author, Awendo in Migori County, August 4, 2020.
[547] Titus Owino, interview by the research assistant, Homa Bay, July 20, 2020.

Church at the district level) said that through the application of the concept of jo-kang'ato, "the elders would properly guide the youth. Mutual understanding and respect between the two generations would also be enhanced. The youth would look at the elders as their parents while the latter treat them as their children."[548] Obviously, with this approach to Christian relationships, the correction of one another across generations becomes possible and is taken kindly. The approach to the relationship in light of jo-kang'ato would address conflicts between the youth and old in the church as it deals with discrimination and ushers in a peaceful and loving atmosphere, which is the ingredient of unity. The inclusion of young people in the church's life and ministry would be among the benefits. Such nonexclusive involvement would spring from the younger and older generations' free interaction and understanding between themselves as members of the family of God who could work together.[549] As the understanding of each other increases, amicable solutions to emerging problems between them are also found.

When the generational gap is addressed in the church, spiritual nurture and growth among the youth are succored, and the church's future is guaranteed. However, this takes place when barriers are removed. It makes it possible for the elders to educate, mentor, counsel, and guide the youth accordingly, thus preparing them to take over the operations of the church in the future. It would also enable the latter to experience a sense of belonging and freedom to share with the former and consult them.[550] The spirit of teamwork in ministry is also enhanced in the process.[551]

---

[548] Ezra Oriko, interview by the research assistant, Holo in Kisumu County, July 14, 2020.
[549] Lilian Ong'ow, interview by the research assistant, Migori, August 14, 2020.
[550] Ezra Oriko, interview by the research assistant, Holo in Kisumu County, July 14, 2020.
[551] Lilian Ong'ow, interview by the research assistant, Migori, August 14, 2020.

4.6 The Weaknesses and Strengths of Jo-kang'ato

Like any other model, the Luos' concept of jo-kang'ato is not without weaknesses. Dulles articulates this reality:

> Each model of the Church has its weakness; no one should be canonised as the measure of all the rest. Instead of searching for some absolutely best images, it would be advisable to recognise that the manifold images given to us by Scripture and Tradition are mutually complementary. They should be made to interpenetrate and mutually qualify one another. None, therefore, should be interpreted in an exclusive sense, so as to negate what the other approved models have to teach us.[552]

The major loophole in jo-kang'ato is that it becomes ambiguous the moment its inculturation is not appropriately undertaken. As a result, restrictive behaviors, separation, and prejudicial distinctions arise, the consequence of which could be tension among Christians. Moreover, the concept of jo-kang'ato has not succeeded in totally wiping out conflicts in the Luo society. Dissensions and contentions often arise between people or groups of people, as brought to the fore by Apuot's song:

> Ng'ato loso (The one builds),
> To ng'ato ketho (The other destroys),
> Ng'ato sero (The one woos),
> To ng'ato semo (The other dissuades),
> Ng'ato ong'eyo (One knows),
> To ng'ato kia (The other is ignorant),

---

[552] Dulles, *Models of the Church*, 29.

Polo K'larie Ndalo (There are no land disputes in heaven).⁵⁵³

Cohen and Odhiambo express the same reality:

> [The] stories told every day are replete with *nyiego*, the deadly rivalry between co-wives. Twentieth-century lore, even of today, is full of *juok*, the engagement of witchcraft by brother against brother … One hears the subdued discussion concerning a woman deploying *sihoho*, spells, against the children of co-wives. There are whispers about several brothers … hiring a murder squad to liquidate a whole family because of a land dispute.⁵⁵⁴

One reason in an ecclesial context was adduced by Mondo, who cited imperfection since wrangles exist even among the jo-kang'ato.⁵⁵⁵ The potential of the concept to lead to supremacy battles was also brought forward. Gaodensia Milome (Presbyterian Church of East Africa) said that it would "make some Christians feel that they are greater than the rest and as such nothing could move without them. Such Christians behave as if they were the people's voice."⁵⁵⁶ The same view was expressed by Willis Mbeche (Redeemed Gospel Church), who argued that "the concept of *jo-kang'ato* could promote clan affiliations in the Church which is not helpful. It also promotes individualism whereby some members portray themselves as superior to others."⁵⁵⁷ On his part, Pastor Peterson Jaoko (Holo Community Church) said that the concept of "*jo-kang'ato* could encourage

---

⁵⁵³ Cohen and Odhiambo, *Siaya: The Historical Anthropology of an African Landscape*, 120–121.
⁵⁵⁴ Ibid., 125–126.
⁵⁵⁵ Mondo.
⁵⁵⁶ Gaodensia Milome, interview by the author, Suna in Migori County, August 10, 2020.
⁵⁵⁷ Willis Mbeche, interview by the author, Suna in Migori County, August 5, 2020.

favouritism and hence, will not be efficient in solving the problem of disunity in the Church. *Jo-kang'ato* may bring destructive behaviours and squabbles into the Church and force some unpopular decisions on people."558 The other argument against the concept was that it could breed unconstructive attitudes among members of the church and even between the clergy and laity.

The general view was that in cases where the concept of jo-kang'ato is not appropriately applied, an increase in incidents of disunity could be experienced. The possibility of such occurrences was raised. According to Ong'wen Gwako, for instance, the misuse of the concept of jo-kang'ato and negative implications arising from its misapplication could lead to "taking sides and people supporting only their allies while treating others as outsiders or strangers—*ja-mwa* [a derogative term used to refer to someone from a different tribe] or *onyalo biro* [unwanted plants growing on a given surface]."559 In connection with that, Mathayo Bunde (RCC) said that jo-kang'ato "may also refer to a people who have something in common and have isolated themselves from others in the community. It is a form of social segregation which may lead to following a human being rather than Jesus Christ as the leader and the head of the Church."560 The catalysts of division would be personal interests and leadership wrangles. The latter case arises in response to the coalescence of church members around one of their own in leadership positions. Baker K'Onyango (SDA Church) lamented that some members would "not be allowed to participate in or contribute to the leadership and other activities in the Church at all."561

The segregation arising from such misappropriation would hinder some members within the congregation from identifying fully with

---

558 Jaoko.
559 Ong'wen Gwako, interview by the research assistant, Migori, August 13, 2020.
560 Mathayo Bunde, interview by the author, Asumbi in Homa Bay County, August 14, 2020.
561 Baker K'Onyango, interview by the author, Wire in Homa Bay County, July 14, 2020.

the church. Tribalism, regionalism, clanism, nepotism, and other factors, which the concept is likely to catalyze, would not allow Christians to blend. According to Elisaphan Omollo (SDA Church), this could be because of the understanding of the concept that he perceived as "the assumption of ownership or belonging by a clique of people which may be based on clan affiliations, ethnicity, or social status. By ownership, this clique may feel that they are more entitled to some privileges within the Church than the rest, for instance, holding leadership positions. They may feel that they are more highly placed than others based on nothing more than their socio-economic background."[562] Because of that absence of ownership, the relegated Christians could perceive themselves as foreigners. While describing the potential situation, Rosalia Bala (Free Pentecostal Church) stated that jo-kang'ato is likely to "bring a tendency of exclusive ownership of the Church by a section of members which could be based on clan."[563] David Ralik cited the rejection and betrayal of victims of 2007 and 2008 postelection violence in Kenya by some Luos as an example of potential consequences of misuse of the concept.[564] At the interdenominational level, the engagement and sharing would only be to a limit. Some members held that the misapplication of the concept would lead to a rejection of and enmity among Christian denominations. Salome Ng'iela (Church of Christ), for instance, said that "Christians would fail to reach out to each other. The focus should not be on a group, thinkers, or ideology."[565]

However, these developments do not invalidate jo-kang'ato as a concept for theological reflection. Its strengths outweigh the limitations because of the bonding qualities embedded in it. On that account, the respondents did not find reasons to utterly refute its

---

[562] Elisaphan Omollo, interview by the author, Nyang'iela in Homa Bay County, July 14, 2020.
[563] Rosalia Bala, interview by the author, Oyugis in Homa Bay County, July 14, 2020.
[564] David Ralik, interview by the author, Siaya, August 3, 2020.
[565] Salome Ng'iela, interview by the author, Oyugis in Homa Bay County, August 13, 2020.

validity. Pastor Jaoko, for instance, agreed that the concept "could also bring unity and positively influence the church in many other ways."[566] That would manifest in, among other ways, the distribution of ecclesiastical roles according to ability and giftedness.[567] Equitable treatment of Christians both at the local and interdenominational church levels was also adduced.[568] The other one is the adherence to the purpose for which the church exists.[569] The respondents also alluded to focus on shared features of belief, including the eschatological hope of eternal life.[570]

Focus on the universal objectives among Christians was also brought forward. Christopher Kapango (Pentecostal Assemblies of God), for instance, said that "the Church could purpose to unite the members both locally and interdenominationally. However, it is not until we stop focusing on our differences and rather focus on the common objective and the Church's mission when we will fully unite."[571] The application of the concept of jo-kang'ato to the relationship among Christians has the potential to induce both positive and negative effects depending on how it is appropriated. However, the majority of respondents exuded confidence in its potential to influence positive interpersonal relationships.

The overriding view of the responses was that the concept of jo-kang'ato could mitigate the causes of disunity among church members as it is laden with values that enhance the spirit of togetherness and oneness. Jo-kang'ato could enhance an appreciation and treatment of one another as God's children and as belonging to Christ. This approach to relationship is critical in ensuring that unity prevails among Christians. Its attendants would include growth, which is likely to be numerical since more converts would be won, infrastructural,

---

[566] Jaoko.
[567] Ong'ow.
[568] Murdoch Bala, interview by the author, Uriri in Migori County, July 31, 2020.
[569] Christopher Kapango, interview by the author, Uriri in Migori County, July 31, 2020.
[570] Ibid.
[571] Ibid.

and spiritual in form.⁵⁷² Furthermore, the Christians' treatment of one another as jo-kang'ato would improve cohesion in the ministry and the sharing of possessions among church members, like in Acts.

The study has established that treating one another as jo-kang'ato could alleviate disunity and usher in love, togetherness, and peace, irrespective of denominational affiliations. The focus of Christians would be the proclamation of the Gospel. Fellowship, coexistence in unity, the spirit of community, cooperation, selflessness, harmony, and the sharing of ideas would be enhanced among Christian denominations.⁵⁷³

I submit that if the concept of jo-kang'ato is embraced, the ecclesial relationship in its present condition—marred with insincerity for one another, unresolved and long-standing disputes, and partisanship—would be sorted. As a way of understanding the church, it offers a panacea for the superiority and inferiority complexes deeply entrenched within the Christian church.⁵⁷⁴ The characteristics of jo-kang'ato, which enhance this understanding, are mutuality, removal of barriers, resolutions for disputes and grievances, forgiveness, embracing of each other, commensality, etc. As Volf puts it, "the person is not a self-enclosed substantial entity, but open relational entity."⁵⁷⁵ He conveys the idea further as follows:

> A church is a network of relations, and the constitutive presence of Christ is mediated through these relations, that is, through the communal confession of faith … a local church cannot alone, in isolation from all other churches, claim to be a church. It must acknowledge all other churches, in time and space, as churches, and must at least be open to diachronic and synchronic

---

[572] Hezborn Odero, interview by the research assistant, Holo in Kisumu County, July 10, 2020; Simeon Oduor, interview by the research assistant, Uyoma in Siaya County, July 18, 2020.
[573] Mondo.
[574] Volf, *After Our Likeness: The Church as the Image of the Trinity*, 175.
[575] Ibid., 82.

communication with them ... By isolating itself from other churches, a church attests either that it is professing faith in a "different Christ" than do the latter, or is denying in practice the *common* Jesus Christ to whom it professes faith, the Christ who is, after all, the Savior and Lord of *all* churches, indeed, of all the world ... a discriminatory church [is] not merely a bad church, but no church at all; it is unable to do justice to the catholicity of the eschatological people of God. Even if such a church were to assemble in the name of Christ and profess faith in him with its lips, it could expect only rejection from its alleged Lord: "I never knew you" (Matthew 7:21–23).[576]

Through the understanding generated by the rich ideals of the Luos' concept of jo-kang'ato, a sense of respect could be inculcated, and tolerance and harmony are realized among various denominations. It has the potential to help denominations appreciate one another while managing their distinctions in the spirit of kinship. Such is necessary for the quest for unity. As Dexter puts it, churches at the local level "necessarily owe to each other sisterly affection and activity."[577] Its members are both "siblings" and "friends" in the sense that they are cordially related.[578] The idea is expressed further by Volf: "The church is an 'open' fellowship of friends and siblings who are called to summon enemies and strangers to become friends and children of God and to accept them as friends and siblings."[579]

In addition to enhancing kindness and regard for one another, the understanding facilitated by the concept of jo-kang'ato could ensure checks and balances interdenominationally.[580] Besides,

---

[576] Ibid., 156, 157, 158.
[577] Henry Dexter, *The Congregationalism of the Last Three Hundred Years* (London: Hodder & Stoughton, 1980), 523.
[578] Volf, *After Our Likeness: The Church as the Image of the Trinity*, 180, 181.
[579] Ibid., 181.
[580] Leithart, *The End of Protestantism: Pursuing Unity in a Fragmented Church*, 79.

denominations would complement one another as they learn and borrow ideas among themselves. For instance, according to Karkkainen, mainstream churches, especially those that are Episcopal, will borrow elements of the once-trivialized free churches' ecclesiologies to survive extinction.[581] Already, mainline churches have adopted certain aspects of the African independent churches (AICs), which have proved to be enriching to them. However, while the AICs' impact upon the ecclesiologies of other churches is already a reality in Africa and manifests in different ways, there are chances for improvement in many other areas. The concept of jo-kang'ato advocates for genuineness in all engagements in place of plastic and distant relationships witnessed among Christians presently.

Furthermore, the concept of jo-kang'ato harmonizes with various doctrines of the Christian church. This factor ought to be a criterion that a legitimate ecclesiological model meets. It is vital to note that the principles presented in jo-kang'ato reverberate across the fundamental doctrines of Christianity. One of these principles is respect, which accompanies the recognition of shared Christian identity and discourages meanness and prejudice toward one another in a relationship. Others include forgiveness of one another and reconciliation, among others. Rather than the model militating against Christian teachings, it enriches them. One of the areas where this is manifested is the doctrine of God (the Trinity). This doctrine summons humankind to come into a relationship with the Godhead and with fellow beings despite diversity.[582] Furthermore, as Radner says, understanding the unity that exists within the Godhead

---

[581] Karkkainen, *An Introduction to Ecclesiology: Ecumenical, Historical & Global Perspectives*, 59, 60.
[582] Stephanie Lowery, *Identity and Ecclesiology: Their RelationshipAmongSelect African Theologians* (Eugene, Oregon: Pickwick Publications, 2017), 195; Clifford Green, and Michael DeJonge, eds. *The Bonhoeffer Reader* (Minneapolis, MN: Fortress Press, 2013), 154–155; Paul Mbandi, *A Theology of the Unity of the Church in a Multi-Ethnic Context: Toward a Theological Understanding of the Unity of the Church in Relation Ethnic Diversity* (Saarbbrucken: Dr. Muller, 2010), viii; Titre Ande, *Leadershipand Authority: Bula Matari and Life-Community Ecclesiology in Congo. Regnum Studies in Mission* (Oxford: Regnum, 2010), 106; Volf, *After Our*

correctly provides a benchmark for the polity of the church.⁵⁸³ There is also a glaring relationship between the concept of jo-kang'ato and soteriology. Jesus was crucified to bring peace between humanity and God and among people themselves, the result of which is an emergence of a different kind of humanity drawn from every group of humanity, whose feelings of superiority or inferiority on account of race are overshadowed by the Holy Spirit.⁵⁸⁴ There is as well harmony between the concept of jo-kang'ato and anthropology as it elevates and affirms human dignity. Segregation, which is anti-Gospel, sets in when that dignity is lowered.⁵⁸⁵ The concept of jo-kang'ato reinforces eschatology too. When Christians refuse to remove obstructions to unity with one another so that they can be part of a different body, they show opposition to the divine arrangement of raising a people drawn from different divides at the end of time.⁵⁸⁶ The Holy Spirit prepares humanity at present to be part of that new humanity.⁵⁸⁷ As God's people come together presently, they, in a sense, give a hint of the idyllic harmony in the *eschaton*.

Likeness: The Church as the Image of the Trinity, 173, 176–177, 193, 206–207, 213, 217–218.

⁵⁸³ Radner, *A Brutal Unity: The Spiritual Politics of the Christian Church*, 14–15.

⁵⁸⁴ Eduardus Van der Borght, "Unity That Sanctifies Diversity: Cottesloe Revisited," *Acta Theologica* 31, no. 2 (2011): 321.

⁵⁸⁵ Willem Visser't Hooft, ed., *The Evanston Report: The Second Assembly of the World Council of Churches 1954* (London: World Council of Churches, 1955), 158; Walter Hansen, *The Letter to the Philippians* (Grand Rapids, MI; Nottingham, England: William B. Eerdmans Publishing Company, 2009), 26; Lowery, *Identity and Ecclesiology: Their Relationship Among Select African Theologians*, 196.

⁵⁸⁶ Agbonkhianmeghe Orobator, *From Crisis to Kairos: The Mission of the Church in the Time of HIV/AIDS, Refugees, and Poverty* (Nairobi, Kenya: Paulines Publications Africa, 2005), 169,170; Lowery, *Identity and Ecclesiology: Their Relationship Among Select African Theologians*, 196–197; Paul Mbandi, *A Theology of the Unity of the Church in a Multi-Ethnic Context: Toward a Theological Understanding of the Unity of the Church in Relation Ethnic Diversity*, 138–139; Volf, *After Our Likeness: The Church as the Image of the Trinity*, 268–269.

⁵⁸⁷ Ibid.

4.7 Behavioral Symbols Affecting Christian Unity

According to Max Weber's (1864–1920) symbolic interaction theory, life involves that which takes place around people and how they behave toward one another within a given setting: in their groupings, as friends, as members of the family unit, etc. In other words, people are part of what goes on between them and others, with a level of accountability.[588]

The behavior of people toward one another in a group or network is a determining factor in the quality of the relationship that could be achieved among them. While the social aspect of human life dictates that they interact with one another, such engagement must be done responsibly for a healthy relationship to occur; or else, misunderstandings arise.

Acceptable behavior plays a significant role in the realization of a healthy relationship and unity among Christians in the ecclesial life of the church. The symbols of behavior that are destructive to Christian unity in the ecclesial life of the church have, therefore, been identified in this work. Lack of acceptance and inclusivity, which comes in the form of favoritism, is among these. According to John Saoke (Baptist Church), favoritism manifests in, among other ways, "the awarding of Church tenders to people of a given tribe."[589] Besides negative ethnicity, it is shown through nepotism, classism, and other socioeconomic factors. Omolo said as follows,

> Since the guiding principle in the Church ought to be equality, when a group of people start behaving or feeling like they are better than others, that becomes the beginning of animosity in the Church. Churches are supposed to be communal with shared responsibilities, and that is why it would not be right

---

[588] Alex Dennis and Peter Martin, "Symbolic Interactionism and the Concept of Power," *The British Journal of Sociology* 562 (2005): 191–213.

[589] John Saoke, interview by the research assistant, Homa Bay, July 20, 2020.

when a group or a clique is treated better or given an entitlement than others.⁵⁹⁰

The missing sense of belonging and incorporation, which results in some members being strangers, is the other symbol that is detrimental to Christian unity. This is often exhibited in, among other ways, the discrimination against members by the clergy through their refusal to listen to and consult with the laity on various issues, including church projects. In Africa, clericalism manifests in the exclusion of members or some of them in making decisions and forcing them to do certain things.⁵⁹¹ The superiority complex displayed by some members, abuse of members by the leaders, and a refusal to recognize the opinions of others, especially the poor, which triggers feelings of unimportance and resignation among the victims, also demonstrate the lack of belonging and incorporation.⁵⁹² At the interdenominational level, the superiority complex is based on doctrinal ideologies, forms of worship, and connections with the state.⁵⁹³ The skewed appointment of church leaders also falls here.⁵⁹⁴

The other symbols are selfishness and unfriendliness. Selfishness manifests in the scramble for power and leadership wrangles; the scramble for converts at the interdenominational level; materialistic attitudes, which often manifest in disproportional emphasis on money; and too many projects, which are overwhelming to members while neglecting to nurture them spiritually.⁵⁹⁵ The unfriendliness of members toward one another, which is the other destructive symbol, is usually characterized by poor relations within the church,

---

⁵⁹⁰ Elisaphan Omollo, interview by the author, Nyang'iela in Homa Bay County, July 28, 2020.
⁵⁹¹ Manase Obilo, interview by the research assistant, Homa Bay, July 26, 2020; Mark Ouma, interview by the author, Awendo in Migori County, July 31, 2020.
⁵⁹² Mark Ouma, interview by the author, Awendo in Migori County, July 31, 2020.
⁵⁹³ Ibid.
⁵⁹⁴ Ibid.
⁵⁹⁵ Ibid.

unnecessary and endless disagreements in opinion, jealousy, envy, hatred, gossip, and acts of indiscipline.[596]

The concept of jo-kang'ato fosters harmony among the Luo people. It is characterized by mutuality in all aspects of social life arising from the perception that being descendants of a particular ancestor makes them related. The circle of relationship widens to incorporate even those who are not of the same consanguinity.[597] As with the case in other African communities, the Luo believe that human beings are not meant to live in isolation but to interact with, as well as be responsive to, one another. Doing so in a responsible manner contributes to a healthy relationship, while doing it wrongly contributes to tension. The state of ecclesial disunity, as currently witnessed in the continent of Africa, is because of the neglect of the collectivist approach to life and the adoption of the Western people's culture of individualism. God created humans to relate as neighbors and siblings.[598] When the true sense of community is lost, negative ramifications set into relationships. Individualism even deprives churches of the opportunity to benefit from one another in their rich diversity as they eschew, for instance, all that resembles a given denomination.

As stipulated in symbolic interactionism, whose concern is a social relation, humans come to the fore as involved rather than inactive creatures.[599] Therefore, it is important to behave responsibly, considerably, restrained, respectfully, selflessly, and lovingly with a

---

[596] Murdoch Bala, interview by the author, Uriri in Migori County, July 31, 2020.
[597] While this work is focused on the Luo of Kenya, it is worth considering the belief that through the greater ancestor Ramogi Ajwang', Luos are related to each other no matter their geographical locations—they are all part of a larger kinship.
[598] Igor Bahovec, "Christianity in Confrontation with Individualism and Crisis of Western Culture: Person, Community, Dialog, Reflexivity, and Relationship Ethics," *Bogoslovni Vestnik* 75, no. 2 (2015): 341.
[599] Joel Charon, *Symbolic Interactionism: An Introduction, An Interpretation, and Integration*, 6th ed. (Englewood Cliffs, New Jersey: Prentice Hall, 1998), 23; Karen Willis, and et al, "The Essential Role of Social Theory in Qualitative Public Health Research," *Australian and New Zeeland Journal of Public Health* 315 (2007): 438–443; Gabriel Ottah, "African Culture and Communication Systems in the

consciousness of the fact that as we behave, symbols are displayed, which may have far-reaching consequences on relationships. The Bible prescribes the kind of behavior expected of Christians and which determines the relationship among them.

At the next level, the processing of symbols takes place. Members make sense of the behavior displayed toward them through the process of interpretation and come to some conclusions that either enrich or destroy the relationship. These calls for consciousness of the kind of signals conveyed, for people will make sense of what others who are around them do and how they are treated. This would generally be followed by some conclusions. As far as Okafor and Okoye are concerned, "when we engage in interaction with others, we often look for clues about what type of behaviour is appropriate in the context and how to interpret what others intend."[600] However, there are occasions when the interpretation is not made correctly, leading to unfavorable reactions, hence the need for the clarity of symbols cast.

There are times when Christians display certain behaviors that are then misconstrued and generate unintended meaning, which causes adverse reactions. Lack of proper communication is one of the causes of disunity among African Christians in the ecclesial life of the church.[601] Kapango, while describing this reality, said that "poor communication both between the leaders and members as well as between members themselves could lead to a misinterpretation of the intended message whose consequence could be disunity amongst the parties concerned."[602] Oversensitivity is among the things to avoid in the interpretation stage as it is likely to lead to a wrong and unintended meaning.

Coronation of Ata Igala, North Central Nigeria," *International Journal of Arts and Humanities* 4, no.15 (September 2015): 213.

[600] Godson Okafor and Chukwuemeka Okoye, "Social Media Use and Real-Life Social Relationships: A Study of Nnamdi Azikiwe University," *Creative Artist: A Journal of Theatre and Media Studies* 8, no. 2 (2014): 1–14.

[601] Belinda Owiso, interview by the research assistant, Migori, July 31, 2020.

[602] Christopher Kapango, interview by the author, Uriri in Migori County, July 31, 2020.

There is also an aspect of knowledge of other members within the group that a person gains. This could culminate in suspicion of them and the shunning of the existing relationship altogether or the development of trust and faith, which spurs and propels the relationship to another level. It all depends on how the extraction of meaning has been undertaken. Interpretation also leads to personal knowledge as one becomes aware of who he or she is through involvement in the surroundings.[603] This knowledge affects his or her engagement with other members. A feeling of low self-worth arising from the perceived or actual meanness of some members could cause disengagement with the group or generate specific responses. Domination by one party could create a loss of self-esteem as the subdued begin to see themselves as unimportant and useless and, in some cases, withdraw their allegiance to the seemly august community. Christian unity is not supported in such a situation. The level of societal or communal allegiance informs the ability of the group of people a person identifies with to have an impact on his or her conduct.[604] The concept of jo-kang'ato demonstrates consciousness of this fact; therefore, it can help the church to experience unity.

As members of the group react to the behavior displayed toward them, a particular outcome is realized, the climax of which is either Christian unity or its antithesis. This work displays some of the negative and positive reactions that could be anticipated. In the first case, discouragements could result in the aggrieved or disgusted members stopping to attend church services regularly and to participate in its activities.[605] Kapango said that there could be a "boycott of Church services when people with whom they contradict are leading out in the service. When it is their turn to lead, others could reciprocate."[606] There could also be a formation of factions or groups with different opinions within one church. The

---

[603] Ottah, "Social Media Use and Real-Life Social Relationships: A Study of Nnamdi Azikiwe University," 213.
[604] Ibid.
[605] Ong'ow.
[606] Kapango.

disagreement would manifest in pulling toward different directions as members refuse to cooperate. Furthermore, there could be a total withdrawal and formation of splinter groups.[607] Magdalina Oyuga stated that members could feel disconnected and separate to form new denominations.[608] Omollo captured the situation as follows: "Factional fights and wrangles would be witnessed as each faction tries to gain control of the Church. It could, in turn, lead to the disintegration of the Church. Factions that may feel like they have lost in the fight could decide to leave the Church and form their Churches."[609] One of the consequences of these reactions could be impediments to the mission of the church, for potential members would be afraid to join it, and the church's impact on the community would be lost.[610] Lack of progress and growth in various facets of the church could also be experienced because of the loss of focus.[611]

The favorable outcomes that could come out of the positive reactions at the local church level would include love for one another. There would be ownership of the church by all members and motivation to participate in its activities for progress.[612] Moreover, there would be no scramble, wrangles, and conflicts for power since members would view themselves as a family.[613] With this, unity could prevail among Christians, and progress and growth are experienced as members work together as a family.[614]

There is the likelihood of unity, which is the component of a healthy relationship, setting in when the concept of jo-kang'ato is adopted. The jo-kang'ato perceive themselves as having common descent and stock and, as such, treat one another as siblings. They

---

[607] Zechariah Omondi, interview by the research assistant, Migori, August 1, 2020.
[608] Magdalina Oyuga, interview by the author, Uriri in Migori County, August 1, 2020.
[609] Omollo.
[610] Ong'ow.
[611] Ibid.
[612] Milca Gori, interview by the research assistant, Migori, August 14, 2020.
[613] Ibid.
[614] Ibid.

are aware of the possibility of irritation among themselves, and when this happens, it is treated as sibling rivalry and resolved in a loving and redemptive manner. The scripture provides the blueprint to help Christians deal with relational issues. Disunity sets in when members put other factors ahead of common descent in God and Christ.

Conclusion

The study has established the importance of an African solution to the problem of disunity among Christians in the ecclesial life of the church through an extension of the familial and communitarian models in a way that captures the African people's modus operandi. The Luos' concept of jo-kang'ato instills a new sense of understanding of Christian unity. The values drawn from the concept of jo-kang'ato, which is the source of the Luos' extended family system as well as of their community, reveal its compatibility with Christian unity and include a sense of belonging, solidarity, cooperation, acceptance, appreciation, acts of charity, etc. These are realized through blood ties—in the Christian context, the blood of the Lord Jesus Christ. The dynamics allow the sibling relationship to reign and address marginalization in the church. It eradicates the feeling of being unwanted as members accept and embrace one another. On some occasions, the acceptance is accompanied by incorporation into the Luo society. The concept of jo-kang'ato also enforces a spirit of teamwork, which is perceived as the source of strength. The concept also discourages aloneness and summons each member to be cooperative and pull together with others, as this would ensure that he or she does not lack help in times of need. One of the attitudes not compatible with jo-kang'ato is selfishness. Again, being indiscriminative, it invites all with leadership abilities and integrity to make their contributions as they lead in various spheres of society, no matter their age, gender, and other factors. It also draws the younger and older members together and removes generational chasm within the church. At the same time, it ensures a link between the past, the present, and the future. I submit that these principles are essential for ecclesial unity as they gel people together, their sociocultural distinctions notwithstanding. The basis of the relationship promoted is a shared identity through belonging to a common progenitor—in the case of Christians, belonging to God by creation and redemption courtesy of the blood of Jesus Christ. The application of these principles results in accepting and accommodating attitudes that allow a group of people to experience unity. What they share is magnified above what distinguishes them, and as such, they are willing to cultivate inclusivity. Besides the possibility of supporting one another in various ways, they pick up a sense of togetherness, which has positive and far-reaching implications for what they can achieve. In comparison with ubuntu, jo-kang'ato presents a more profound relationship. The themes manifested in the concept of jo-kang'ato have been consistently manifested throughout the existence of the Luo people over the years. These themes could be replicated in the ecclesial life of the church to inform and improve the relationship among Christians, leading to unity among them at all ecclesial levels. The weaknesses of the concept of jo-kang'ato do not overshadow its benefits as it continues to unite the Luo society together to date. One of its strengths lies in the dispute resolution mechanism encouraged by it. It encourages members to talk to one another and sort out their differences whenever they arise. In some cases, these talks could be mediated. The ideals of the concept of jo-kang'ato could be applied in the ecclesial life of the church, and the result would be Christian unity.

CHAPTER 5

The Familial and Communal Ecclesial Models in Light of Selected Passages of the Scripture

This chapter begins with an overview of ecclesial models and then proceeds to discuss the familial and communal models of the church as well as find out the ecclesial relationship presented in selected passages of the scripture, namely, John 17:20–23; 1 Corinthians 12:12–27; and Ephesians 2:12–22. Later, the scripture is compared with what jo-kang'ato offers to find points of contact and reinforcements to the understanding of Christian unity in the ecclesial life of the church.

5.1 An Overview of Ecclesial Models

In the context of the church, a model tells of the church's view and understanding of itself and the way it intends to function.[615] The multiplicity of models deserves appreciation. Some of these were permissible in the past, hence their presence in the NT.[616]

---

[615] Samuel Kunhiyop, *African Christian Theology* (HippoBooks, 2012), 142.
[616] Volf, *After Our Likeness: The Church as the Image of the Trinity*, 21.

Such models have not lost soundness in the present time.[617] The remarkable feature of them is that they are founded in history and culture, thus considering people's experiences and needs, the benefit of which was favorable results in the evangelization of the Western world.[618] Some of the models at present include the church as an institution. Unchecked, this model results in an overestimation of "visible structures and powers."[619] The other model is the church as a mystical communion whose membership consists of both the living and the dead, whose excesses are the creation of leeway to "prayers to and for the dead."[620] The church as a sacrament (an outward and visible sign of God's inward grace) is also a prominent model.[621] There is also a view of the church as a herald, which places more premium on spreading the Word of God as the relationship between its members and "mystical communion" receives less regard.[622] As a servant, the church highlights service to society and not of "its own interests" as the main reason for its existence.[623] The other perception is of the church as a lecture hall, which portrays it as a venue that brings congregants together for the sake of hearing God's message being presented.[624] This model emphasizes the reception of the word at the expense of action on it.[625] Besides, it is perceived as a theater with a focus on dramatic worship; and as a corporation involved in the "business of retailing religion, much as any other commodity is marketed."[626] In the latter view, the church's goal is to

---

[617] Ibid.
[618] Chukwu, *The Church as the Extended Family of God: Toward a New Direction for African Ecclesiology*, 19, 20.
[619] Kunhiyop, *African Christian Theology*, 142.
[620] Ibid., 143.
[621] Ibid.
[622] Dulles, *Models of the Church*, 76.
[623] Kunhiyop, *African Christian Theology*, 143.
[624] Peter Savage and C. Padilla, eds. "The Church and Evangelism, in New Faces," in *New Faces of Evangelism: An International Symposium on the Lausanne Covenant* (Downers Grove: InterVarsity Press, 1976), 106–109.
[625] Ibid.
[626] Ibid., 107.

make the goods and services of religion available to the people.[627] The other perception is the church as a social club that brings together people who associate with specific concerns and serve society in a particular way, and people are admitted into it when they meet specific criteria.[628] Last but not least is the church as a religious shopping mall, where individuals visit to pick whatever they want to pick while leaving that which is inadequate or unacceptable.[629] As pointed out by Chukwu, there is also the church "as a sheepfold, a tract of land to be cultivated, the field of God, the kingdom of God, the edifice of God … the spotless spouse of the spotless lamb, our mother, the temple, the New Jerusalem, the body of Christ … the people of God, and so on."[630] Amid this array of models, only that which enhances the understanding of unity among Christians would be of value. Since the African Christians' perception of the church would be in familial and communal terms, a proper perception of these social units is paramount.[631]

5.2 The Familial Model of the Church

From a sociological angle, the word *family* does not have one definition. Murdock's view, however, advocates for its understanding as "a social group characterised by common residence, economic cooperation and reproduction, including adults of both sexes, at least one of whom maintains a socially approved sexual relationship, and one or more children, own or adopted, of the sexually cohabiting

---

[627] Ibid.
[628] Ibid., 108.
[629] Howard Snyder, *The Community of the King* (Downers Grove: InterVarsity Press, 1977), 34.
[630] Chukwu, *The Church as the Extended Family of God: Toward a New Direction for African Ecclesiology*, 19.
[631] Bénézet Bujo, "On the Road toward an African Ecclesiology: Reflections on the Synod," in *The African Synod: Documents, Reflections, Perspectives*, ed. Maura Browne (New York: Orbis Books, 1996), 140.

adults."[632] In this definition, several aspects of the contemporary family have not been taken into account, some of which include the fact that some couples are without offspring; some are made up of same-sex couples; and in some, only one parent exists. It is not always the case to have family members residing together under one roof and that people could also be family economically and socially because they share "political" views and common faith.[633]

In the African context, the family is not limited to the man, woman, and their children. Rather, the term encompasses a wide range of networks that are formed by people who are related through a common progenitor, unlike in the Western perspective.[634] Mbiti expresses the point as follows:

> In traditional society, the family includes children, parents, grandparents, uncles, aunts, brothers and sisters who may have their own children, and other immediate relatives. In many areas, there are what anthropologists call *extended families*, by which is generally meant that two or more brothers [in the patrilocal societies] or sisters [in the matrilocal societies] establish families in one compound or close to one another. The joint households together are like one large family. In either case, the number of family members may range from ten persons to even a hundred where several wives belonging to one husband may be involved. It is the practice in some societies, to send children to live for some months or years, with relatives, and these children are counted as members of the families where they happen to live

---

[632] George Murdock, *Social Structure* (New York: Macmillan, 1949), 1.
[633] Chukwu, *The Church as the Extended Family of God: Toward a New Direction for African Ecclesiology*, 76–78.
[634] James Nkansah-Obrempong, *Foundations for African Theological Ethics* (Langham Monographs, 2013), 310, 312; Mbiti, *African Religions and Philosophy*, 106.

... The household is the smallest unit of the family, consisting of the children, parents and sometimes the grandparents. It is what one might call "the family at night," for it is generally at night that the household is really itself. At night the parents are with their immediate children in the same house; they discuss private affairs of their household, and the parents educate the children in matters pertaining to domestic relationships. The household in Africa is what in European and American societies would be called "family." If a man has two or more wives, he has as many households since each wife would usually have her own house erected within the same compound where other wives and their households live.[635]

The scope of an African family stretches to encompass the dead who continue to exist in the minds of the people as involved members in family matters.[636] Those who are yet to be born or yet to be conceived also constitute the family.[637]

Based on current realities, the scope of the family stretches to encompass people who are not related by blood, for instance, the church family.[638] In other words, the church, though a spiritual entity, reflects what goes on in the human family, for instance, "nurture, love, caring, support, meeting the needs of the members of the family."[639] Nkansah-Obrempong conveys the point further by saying that "the Church is the family of God with God as the Father ... God as the head of the Church loves, nurtures, provides, disciplines, and cares for the needs of the Church."[640] As Gyekye puts it, "hospitality,

---

[635] Mbiti, *African Religions and Philosophy*, 106–107.
[636] Ibid., 107.
[637] Ibid.
[638] Chukwu, *The Church as the Extended Family of God: Toward a New Direction for African Ecclesiology*, 77.
[639] Nkansah-Obrempong, *Foundations for African Theological Ethics*, 325.
[640] Ibid.

solidarity, mutual helpfulness, interdependence and concern for the wellbeing of every individual member of society, find their highest and most spontaneous expression in the institution of the family."[641]

The ecclesial model of the family receives vast support in Africa on several grounds. Firstly, the family is a place where culture resides, where "humanity" and their communities are founded, and where their heritage is consolidated.[642] The family is also synonymous with togetherness—standing with one another; being accountable; and cultivating an environment for learning, production, and growth— and the source of existence.[643] It is a place where care and respect are offered, where the spiritual and physical worlds coexist, and a social group is characterized by friendship and mutual support for one another.[644] Furthermore, it is an atmosphere of confidence in one another and where peace can be obtained between members ritually.[645] Besides, it is free from prejudice, bias, etc.[646] The familial model has also been applauded because it enhances "dialogue"; it fosters and upholds fairness within and without the church, among other factors.[647] Ezeweke and Ikechukwu are of the view that as an ecclesial model, it would foster love, unobstructed relationship with one another, faithfulness and allegiance to one another, a forgiving spirit, as well as ministry.[648]

One prominent feature of the family, which Christians need among themselves, is togetherness. The sayings that enforce it include the Igbos' "Otu oke osisi onaghi eme ohia [A single tree does not make

---

[641] Kwame Gyekye, *African Cultural Values: An Introduction* (Accra, Ghana: Sankofa Publishing Company, 1996), 75.
[642] Snyder, *The Community of the King*, 34.
[643] Ibid.
[644] Ibid.
[645] Ibid.
[646] Ibid.
[647] Ibid., 31, 32, 35.
[648] Elizabeth Ezeweke, and Anthony Ikechukwu, "The Family, Justice and the Culture of Life: Afro – Christian Perspectives," *AFRREV IJAH: An International Journal of Arts and Humanities Bahir Dar, Ethiopia* 1, no. 2 (May 2012): 31, accessed May 11, 2020, www.afrrevjo.net/afrrevijah.

a forest though huge; a single person does not make a family]."⁶⁴⁹ The individualism that mars the family presently causes it to obscure the meaning of Christian unity when used as an ecclesial model, hence the need for readjustment. Even the prominence that the familial model of the church enjoys fails to mitigate its weaknesses that are so glaring. These often arise from its misappropriation, particularly in its discriminative application. According to Uzukwu, it smacks of autocracy perpetrated by the clergy and elders.⁶⁵⁰ Such kind of dominance begets disunity, animosity, and subjugation.⁶⁵¹ Current dynamics—for instance, globalization—could also be pointed out as causing the gaps. Ndung'u accurately describes globalization's effects on the African society of which the family is a vital component:

> Globalisation with its baggage of rapid social change has impacted rather negatively on the African communities. Individuals are exposed to new world views with strange values, while the youth are torn away from their cultural bonds. In short, people have become lonely - strangers to themselves and living in a morally bankrupt and spiritually confused society. Others have been economically marginalised, resulting in spiralling poverty.⁶⁵²

---

⁶⁴⁹ Emmanuel Chukwu, "Ezi-Na-Ulo: The Extended Family of God Towards an Ecological Theology of Creation" (Sacrae Theologiae Doctor Dissertation, Katholieke Universiteit Leuven, 2002), 39.

⁶⁵⁰ Elochukwu Uzukwu, *A Listening Church: Autonomy and Communion in African Churches* (Eugene, OR: Wipf and Stock, 2006), 121–122; C.f. Karkkainen, *An Introduction to Ecclesiology: Ecumenical, Historical & Global Perspectives*, 29.

⁶⁵¹ Uzukwu, *A Listening Church: Autonomy and Communion in African Churches*, 121–122; Lowery, *Identity and Ecclesiology: Their Relationship Among Select African Theologians*, 163.

⁶⁵² Nahashon Ndung'u, "Persistence of Features of Traditional Healing in the Churches in Africa: The Case of the Akurinu Churches in Kenya Thought and Practice" 1, no. 2, *A Journal of the Philosophical Association of Kenya* (December 2009): 88.

It will also be appreciated that in our time, stepparenting characterizes relationships in many families whereby members do not experience a sense of belonging despite many assurances given. Each of the parents is subconsciously aware that the children brought by their partner into the union do not belong to them despite attempts to unshackle themselves from that reality. An array of consequences accompanies such an approach, ranging from abuse and brutality toward the children and the foster parent. Conflicts also arise between children born into that union and the foster children because of partiality in parental treatment.

The family in Africa is going through some adjustments now that are influenced by an array of factors. Consequently, the scope of the family unit is being scaled down and limited to the father, mother, and children.[653] Nkansah-Obrempong articulates the situation, thus,

> The moral fabrics of African family life are eroding due to several factors. Modernisation, individualism, and urbanisation are weakening the social strings that hold families together ... Traditional African family life is mostly communitarian. However [sic] with modernisation and social, and economic factors facing many Africans there are significant changes taking place in family life. Families in urban cities are becoming nuclear in nature and losing the sense of community and the moral obligation they have previously had toward the extended family. The traditional support systems that gave support and stability to families are crumbling. Family values are being set aside. They are being eroded.[654]

Mbiti describes the crisis as follows:

---

[653] Mbiti, *African Religions and Philosophy*, 225.
[654] Nkansah-Obrempong, *Foundations for African Theological Ethics*, 313, 314.

> In traditional life the family is the nucleus of both individual and corporate existence, the area where a person really experiences personal consciousness of himself and of other members of society. Now, the family is the most severely affected part of African life … The change means that individuals are severed, cut off, pulled out and separated from corporate morality, customs and traditional solidarity. They have no firm roots anymore. They are simply uprooted but not necessarily transplanted. They float in life like a cloud. They live as individuals, but they are dead to the corporate humanity of their forefathers.[655]

Despite the weaknesses, the adequacy of the familial model of the church in addressing poor relationships among the children of God cannot be dismissed. It only needs to be freed from Western perspectives that are laden with elements of isolation, prejudice, and exclusion, as these promote conflicts among parishioners. Again, it needs to be extended to include the "other" despite their social and denominational affiliations. Nkansah-Obrempong presents the kind of relationship that could be born out of an African understanding of family:

> Through the blood of Christ, we have been accepted into the family of God who is the Father of every family. This strong sense of family serves to provide strong social bonds among people who have left their immediate families to have new families in the Christian community. The Church community, therefore, becomes the new extended family. The loyalty and commitment to see the welfare of the people makes the Church grows [sic]. Thus, the new community of Jesus widens its kinship ties and

---

[655] Mbiti, *African Religions and Philosophy*, 218, 219.

obligations to include the larger family of God and not only members of the immediate family.[656]

Bujo shares these sentiments when he says that "it is necessary to underline then the Church as *family*, not in the Euro-American sense of the nuclear family, but rather in the Negro-African sense of the large family which includes even cousins, distant cousins, and can go as far as to integrate friends and acquaintances; yes, even the dead are part of it."[657]

5.3 The Communal Model of the Church

One of the reasons why the ecclesial model of community appeals so much to the African person is that personhood does not preclude community. In that communal setting, people exist and spend their lives together as opposed to being lone rangers.[658] A person finds meaning and worth within his or her community. This is articulately conveyed by Oduyoye as follows,

> Africans recognise life as life-in-community. We can truly know ourselves if we remain true to our community, past and present. The concept of individual success or failure is secondary. The ethnic groups, the village, the locality, are crucial in one's estimation of oneself. Our nature as beings-in-relation is a two-way relation: with God and with our fellow human beings.[659]

---

[656] Nkansah-Obrempong, *Visual Theology: Some Akan Cultural Symbols, Metaphors, Proverbs, Myths, and Symbols and Their Implications for Doing Christian Theology*, 86.
[657] Bénézet Bujo, *Christmas: God Becomes Man in Black Africa* (Nairobi: Paulines, 1995), 52.
[658] Kunhiyop, *African Christian Theology*, 145.
[659] Mercy Oduyoye, "The Value of African Religious Beliefs and Practices for Christian Theology," in *African Theology Enroute*, eds. Kofi Appiah-Kubi, and

Oduyoye's view resonates with Mbiti's phrase "I am because we are, and since we are, therefore I am."[560] Wilbur O'Donovan articulates the point,

> The community is where you get your values and beliefs and your early training in life. It is the community where you establish the deepest and most enduring relationships of life. It is the group of people from which you derive your name and your identity as a person. It is the community in which you find a sense of purpose in life because you help to make it what it is. Likewise, the Church is the community where you are to get your values and beliefs and your early training in the Christian life. It is the community where you will establish the deepest and most enduring relationships in life. It is the group of people from which you derive your name as a Christian and your identity as a child of God.[661]

The community-of-disciples model of the church is scriptural, hence its preference and adoption by the Vatican II.[662] The Vatican resolved to shift from the perception of "the Church as an ecclesiastical hierarchy to a more biblical and ecumenical view of the church as a body of people, with the laity having an important role."[663] This view was also well received among the Protestants as reflected in the Lausanne Covenant of 1974 (quoted by Kunhiyop): "The Church is at the very centre of God's cosmic purpose and is his appointed means of spreading the Gospel. [It] is the community of God's

---

Sergio Torres, (New York: Orbis Books, 1979), 110–111.
[660] Mbiti, *African Religions and Philosophy*, 113.
[661] Wilbur O'Donovan, *Biblical Christianity in African Perspective* (Carlisle: Paternoster, 2000), 155–156.
[662] Dulles, *Models of the Church*, 2–3, 27.
[663] Kunhiyop, *African Christian Theology*, 144.

people rather than an institution."⁶⁶⁴ Snyder contends in favor of this model that "a properly biblical understanding of the Kingdom of God is possible only if the church is understood—predominantly, if not exclusively—as a charismatic community and God's pilgrim people, his Kingdom of priests ... the Messianic community, the community of the King."⁶⁶⁵ Many scholars are in favor of the communal model of the church as indicated in various works.⁶⁶⁶ Mott, for instance, says that "since the Bible shows our basic need for and dependence on community, it is not surprising that God's salvation calls us into a community."⁶⁶⁷ Kunhiyop emphasizes the importance of community by stating that "personal conversion, ethical responsibility and accountability are vital, but they cannot be lived out in isolation from the rest of God's people. This truth is evident in both the Old and New Testaments."⁶⁶⁸

The Western version of the community presents handicaps that render it unhelpful as a model that could evoke clarity on the subject of Christian unity. The underlying assumption is that, in some way, harmony could be achieved among parties opposed to one another even without doing anything about them. Consequently, the parties decide not to be aggressive toward one another but not because issues among them have been resolved. According to Schmitt (cited by Radner), they do so with the consciousness of their misgivings outstanding, but somehow regulated, and as a "community of enemies," or people "who cannot reach agreement on important matters."⁶⁶⁹ The weakness of the model manifests in this.

Moreover, the community, as currently constituted, is deficient of

---

⁶⁶⁴ Ibid.
⁶⁶⁵ Snyder, *The Community of the King*, 40.
⁶⁶⁶ Samuel Waje Kunhiyop, "Towards a Christian Communal Ethics: The African Contribution," *Cultural Encounters* 6, no. 2 (2010); Mark Husbands and Daniel Treier, eds., *The Community of the Word: Toward an Evangelical Ecclesiology* (Downers Grove: InterVarsity Press, 2005); Snyder, *The Community of the King*.
⁶⁶⁷ Stephen Mott, *Biblical Ethics and Social Change* (New York: Oxford University Press, 1982), 129.
⁶⁶⁸ Kunhiyop, *African Christian Theology*, 147.
⁶⁶⁹ Radner, *A Brutal Unity: The Spiritual Politics of the Christian Church*, 454,455.

a sense of belonging. The "alien" tag often remains with new entrants who cannot fully participate in the lives of their hosts. However, among all human communities, this is the reality: boundary lines cannot be crossed without conflict and tension arising. With this understanding of community, it fails as a model to adequately capture the kind of relationship expected of believers in Christ unless it receives a new sense of meaning.

5.4 The Ecclesial Relationship Presented in the Selected Passages of the Scripture

Vymeister and Robertson stated that an exegetical "method assumes the authority and unity of Scripture and seeks to ascertain the meaning of the Bible, both for its original readers or hearers and for my life and the life of the church today."[670] The work took into account the need to demonstrate uncompromising integrity with scripture for it to be legitimate. This involves allowing the Bible to take center stage as theology flows or stems from it.[671] The importance of keeping this in view is that African Christians believe that divine revelation is embedded in the Bible. Martey articulates that they regard it as "the source and norm of all Christian knowledge and the evidence of the divine will toward all humanity ... [And] also as a diving board from which Africans 'jump' into theology—a platform from which they delve deep into the waters of divine truth

---

[670] Nancy Vyhmeister and Terry Robertson, *Your Guide to Writing Quality Research Papers for Students of Religion and Theology*, 3rd ed. (Grand Rapids, Michigan: Zondervan, 2014), 12.

[671] S. Moripe, "The Notion of Independence and Rendering of Service to the African Independent/Indigenous Churches," 800–900; John Mbiti, "African Theology," in *Initiation into Theology: The Rich Variety of Theology and Hermeneutics* (Pretoria: Van Schaik, 1998), 142; Nkansah-Obrempong, *Visual Theology: Some Akan Cultural Symbols, Metaphors, Proverbs, Myths, and Symbols and Their Implications for Doing Christian Theology*, 54.

to search for, experience and celebrate God."[672] The exegetical process has been utilized to facilitate a realization of the fidelity of this work to the scripture. The biblical passages that received attention for exegeses are John 17:20–23, 1 Corinthians 12:12–27, and Ephesians 2:12–22. According to Vanhoozer, "the two definitions of theology—bringing the Bible to bear on all areas of life, and faith seeking understanding—converge, for the way we make sense of everyday life is by reading it in light of the Scripture."[673]

The passages of the scripture selected for the study presented a familial and communitarian relationship that defies the conventional understanding. To understand them correctly is to discover what constitutes ideal Christian unity within the ecclesial life of the church. To an African person, this presents a familiar worldview. Christians in Africa need to understand the church in this context. They need to filter familial and communitarian ideas within the African cultural milieu for doing so brings them to an understanding that is compatible with what the scripture upholds, or at least closer to it.

5.4.1 John 17:20–23

The overall theme of John 17:20–23 is unity among Christians.[674] It is one of the items Jesus asked for in His prayer for the apostles too.[675] In this section, however, unity comes out with a different force. First, it links the church of the past, composed of the apostles, with the future church, constituted by the would-be converts. Secondly, it connects believers, thus enabling them to present a strong and robust witness about Christ to the world of unbelievers. This unity

---

[672] Emmanuel Martey, *African Theology: Inculturation and Liberation* (Eugene, OR: Wipf and Stock Publishers, 2001), 71.
[673] Kevin Vanhoozer, "What Is Everyday Theology? How and Why Christians Should Read Culture," in *Everyday Theology: How to Read Cultural Texts and Interprete Trends* (Grand Rapids, Michigan: Baker Academic, 2007), 16.
[674] D.S. Dockery, ed., *Holman Bible Handbook* (Nashville, TN: Holman Bible Publishers, 1992), 626.
[675] Verse 11.

stems from each believer's relationship with God.[676] Their knowledge of God leads them to oneness among themselves, whose model is the Trinity and is, therefore, spiritual rather than institutional. John 17:20–23 premises unity, the diversity expected of Christian believers, and their communitarian life upon Jesus and the Godhead as its source and pattern.

5.4.1.1 An Ever-Expanding Family (v. 20)

A special kind of family is in view in John 17:20–23. In formation and growth, this family, although spiritually generated, follows the natural trend as it begins on a small, simple, and unsophisticated scale and gradually swells into a vast and complex formation. Christ reveals that this family would leap beyond the disciples' time into the near and further unforeseeable future.[677] Furthermore, it would expand and culminate into a mega community of people drawn from various geographical and sociocultural backgrounds. As Whitacre puts it, that "band of disciples there in the room with him is the nucleus of the one unified humanity."[678]

The fact that the prayer of Jesus is not narrowed down exclusively to the twelve or eleven brings this point to the fore. As shown in verse 20, He expands it to include future believers in the Gospel as transmitted through the agency and ministry of the eleven or twelve (cf. 4:39).[679] The eleven disciples would go with the message of Christ into the world, and as a result of their preaching, conversions would result even amid resistance that they would face.[680] Jesus is aware

---

[676] Pope, *A Compendium of Christian Theology: Being Analytical Outlines of a Course of Theological Study, Biblical, Dogmatic, Historical*, 3:268.
[677] Verse 20.
[678] Rodney Whitacre, *John*, vol. 4 (Downers Grove, IL: InterVarsity Press, 1999), 417.
[679] Jey Kanagaraj, *John*, vol. 4 (Eugene, OR: Cascade Books, 2013), 169; Robert Wilkin, "The Gospel According to John," in *The Grace New Testament Commentary* (Denton, TX: Grace Evangelical Society, 2010), 460.
[680] R.C.H. Lenski, *The Interpretation of St. John's Gospel* (Minneapolis, MN: Augsburg Publishing House, 1961), 1153–1154.

of this, hence the broadening of the scope of his prayer to embrace these would-be converts. These would-be believers (*pisteuontōn*) are the reason for the prayer.[681]

As in the typical situation where families share common values and ideals that are transferrable from one particular period to another, both generations of the family presented in the passage are related and brought together by the Word of God and belief in the Lord Jesus Christ. The Gospel as it is proclaimed and belief are as well the means of the extension and growth.[682] It is through the proclamation (*dia toũ kērygmatos autôn*) that belief would be catapulted among the would-be *pisteuontōn*, for there is a connection between the word and belief whereby the latter is contingent on the former hence the necessity of the *kērygmatos* to produce *pisteuontōn*. Lenski articulates the relationship between the two:

> In the singular "word" all the teaching and the writing of the apostles is summarised as a unit; yet λόγος has the idea of communication. The word communicated by the apostles is the means for producing faith and making believers—note διά. It is "their" word, not as though they originated it but only as being the agents for its dissemination and transmission. In reality, it is God's Word (v. 17), and its substance is "truth." Word and faith are correlative; the one intends to produce the other, and the other has no basis but the one. Apart from the word there is no church, [*sic*] because there is no faith apart from the word; and the Church is constituted out of those and those alone who have faith. The word is the vital means and the root of faith. At once it appears how dangerous it is to be ignorant of the word or to alter and to falsify it in any

---

[681] *Pisteuontōn*, "those who will believe" is a present active participle and is found in most Greek manuscripts. (Wilkin, "The Gospel According to John," 460). As utilised proleptically, πιστευόντων refers to what would happen in the future.
[682] Lenski, *The Interpretation of St. John's Gospel*, 1157.

way. Ephesians 2:20 shows that Jesus considers the word as given to the Church through the apostles the foundation of the Church for all time.[683]

Christ's consecration of the apostles and subsequent commissioning would produce an expansion in His church.[684] The would-be believers meet the specification of the "other sheep not of this fold" (John 10:16) who would join the fold in the future.[685]

5.4.1.2 Closer Ties (vv. 21–23)

Christ is alive to the fact that following the numerical increase and expansion of his movement, divisions would be inevitable based on diversities in the form of the giftedness of persons as well as in their perspectives.[686] The escalation of disunity would put the church in jeopardy, hence His prayer for oneness among the members.[687] While *pantes* (all) suggests that many people would believe, an expansive family whose members include the Godhead as spelled out in the second part of the verse, and the prospective believers is envisaged. However, both *pantes* (all) and *hen* (one) are there to suggest that despite their numerical greatness, there is supposed to be oneness among Christians—"one unit, one body, one spiritual whole."[688] In other words, diversity is not supposed to be the cause of disunity among Christians.

---

[683] Ibid., 1154.
[684] Markus Dods, *The Gospel of St. John* (New York: George H. Doran Company, n.d.), 844–845.
[685] Whitacre, *John*, 4:420.
[686] Kanagaraj, *John*, 4:169; Dods, *The Gospel of St. John*, 845.
[687] Dods, *The Gospel of St. John*, 845; Kanagaraj, *John*, 4:169; John Henry Bernard, *A Critical and Exegetical Commentary on the Gospel According to St. John* (New York: C. Scribner' Sons, 1929), 576.
[688] Lenski, *The Interpretation of St. John's Gospel*, 1155.

5.4.1.2.1 Intra-Trinitarian Unity

The unity and connection Christ enjoys with the Father is the pattern and model for relationships among members of God's family. The Godhead has set a standard for unity among Christians.[689] According to Whitacre, the intra-Trinitarian unity is also "the cause" of oneness among Christians.[690] However, the unity experienced by the Godhead is unique as it is characterized by an extraordinary kind of "interpenetration," which dogmaticians refer to as *perichoresis essentialis* that is unfathomable as it is the most superior kind of unity.[691] This *perichoretical* union is an inexpressible and absolute harmony, which is neither humanly achievable nor duplicable since Christians cannot indwell one another.[692] However, as Lenski puts it, it "is to be the model and pattern for the oneness of believers."[693] The indwelling is only possible within the Trinity and not among humans since the two realities do not precisely synchronize.

One of the features of the oneness exemplified in the Trinity worth emulating is that it accommodates "multiplicity" without squashing personal "identities," thus matching the kind of "relationship" expected among Christians.[694] Volf points out that through perichoresis, the Godhead "mutually permeate one another, though in so doing they do not cease to be distinct persons."[695] The point is buttressed by Whitacre, who says that "this oneness includes both a unity of being and a distinctness of person, and it has been

---

[689] Volf, *After Our Likeness: The Church as the Image of the Trinity*, 80.
[690] Whitacre, *John*, 4:418.
[691] Lenski, *The Interpretation of St. John's Gospel*, 1155.
[692] Volf, *After Our Likeness: The Church as the Image of the Trinity*, 210; Lenski, *The Interpretation of St. John's Gospel*, 1155 - 1156; Ted Cabal et al, eds., *The Apologetics Study Bible: Real Questions, Straight Answers, Stronger Faith* (Nashville, TN: Holman Bible Publishers, 2007), 1607.
[693] Lenski, *The Interpretation of St. John's Gospel*, 1155 - 1156.
[694] Volf, *After Our Likeness: The Church as the Image of the Trinity*, 193, 195, 203, 207.
[695] Ibid., 209; C.f. George Prestige, *God in Patristic Thought* (London: S.P.C.K., 1956), 298.

seen especially as a oneness of will and love. These are also the characteristics of the oneness that Jesus desires for his disciples to have in their relationship with one another in God."[696] The other point to note is that in the Trinity, there is no hierarchy. The Godhead is not made up of the "different modes of being" where "subordination" reigns to warrant a relegation of non-clergy members in the church, as Zizioulas claims.[697] According to Volf, therefore, the "monistic rule" of the church is nontrinitarian.[698] Again, unity in a spiritual rather than institutional sense is in view. As Dods puts it, "this unity is infinitely more than mere unanimity, since it rests upon unity of spirit and life."[699]

5.4.1.2.2 The Unity between Christians and the Trinity

Unity among believers comes in two ways: when they are in Christ and the Father (v. 21) and when Christ and the Father are in them (v. 23). Whitacre conveys the dynamics as follows:

> This oneness is made possible through two types of mutual indwelling—the believers in the Son and the Son in them (14:20; 15:4–5) as well as the Son in the Father and the Father in the Son (10:38; 14:10–11; 17:21). These two types are combined to explain the believers' living in God: on the one hand, the believers are in the Son, who is in the Father (14:20; cf. Colossians 3:3); on the other hand, the Father is in the Son, who is in the believers (John 17:23). The believers' point of contact in both cases is the Son. Nowhere in this Gospel is it said that the Father is

---

[696] Whitacre, *John*, 4:418.
[697] Zizioulas, *Being as Communion: Studies in Personhood and the Church*, 89; John Zizioulas, "Die Pneumatologische Dimension Der Kirche," *Internationale Katholische Zeitschrift* 2, Communio (1973): 41.
[698] Volf, *After Our Likeness: The Church as the Image of the Trinity*, 215–217.
[699] Dods, *The Gospel of St. John*, 845.

in believers or that believers are in the Father. The believers have a mutual indwelling with the Father, but only by the Son, for no one comes to the Father except through the Son (14:6). So the oneness of the Son with the Father is unique (1:14, 18), for Jesus shares in the deity of the Father. But in the Son believers have access to the Father and share in his very life, the eternal life.[700]

The spiritual essence of unity manifests in this passage as it stems from a relationship with the Father and Christ. Believers concretize it within the Christian group. Whitacre describes this aspect as follows:

> Jesus' prayer shows that there can be no oneness apart from him ... This oneness clearly must come from God and is not something people of goodwill can manufacture. It is predicated on sharing in the divine glory (v. 22) and name (v. 26). Oneness can only come through being born from above, hearing the voice of the Good Shepherd and accepting the witness of the Paraclete, thereby revealing the glory of the Father within history.[701]

In verses 21 and 23, God's willingness to allow his children to take part in his "personhood" comes to the fore and affirms the fact that "the Trinity is precisely an open and inviting communion."[702]

One prominent feature in the family of God is that, as in earthly families, it has a family tree and an ancestor whom Jesus refers to as the Father in verse 21. God is the ancestor *par excellence* through whom believers of all ages are connected. The connection with God, the divine ancestor, results in connection with one another despite

---

[700] Whitacre, *John*, 4:418.
[701] Ibid., 421.
[702] Volf, *After Our Likeness: The Church as the Image of the Trinity*, 78, 208.

diversities and produces Christian unity.⁷⁰³ Besides being a common progenitor, God is the head who is to be emulated by His children as they live together in unity. The message relayed by *kathōs* in the pericope is that the Godhead is the root of the relationship prescribed. Moreover, since both the two renderings of *kathōs* (comparison and cause) are applicable here, "the mutual indwelling of the Father and the Son is both the reason that all may be one and the pattern for such oneness."⁷⁰⁴ The crux of the matter is that ecclesial unity hinges on oneness with Christ, which is shared by His followers. He prays for His followers' unity with Him and among themselves (John 17:21). Bernard states that "to be 'in Christ' is to be 'in God.' Those who are thus 'in God' share the Divine life in common, and are therefore *one*."⁷⁰⁵ Lenski's observation is that "this will not be a mere human oneness [national, racial, political, in a society, or the like]. It will bear the divine stamp: a oneness in the true God, in actual spiritual union with him. This is why so high a model and pattern is [*sic*] set for our oneness."⁷⁰⁶ There is in the Trinitarian unity, something that gels God's children.⁷⁰⁷

5.4.1.2.3 Interpersonal Relationships

The interdependence in the Godhead is a feature that could be applied to the relationship between churches and Christians. While they need and cannot do without one another, churches, rather than doing away with features that differentiate them from one another, could reciprocally enhance themselves.⁷⁰⁸ An appreciation of this fact prompts Christians to give themselves to one another willingly. Volf articulates this fact as follows:

---

[703] Ibid., 86.
[704] Whitacre, *John*, 4:417–418.
[705] John Bernard, *A Critical and Exegetical Commentary on the Gospel According to St. John*, 577.
[706] Lenski, *The Interpretation of St. John's Gospel*, 1156.
[707] Dods, *The Gospel of St. John*, 845.
[708] Volf, *After Our Likeness: The Church as the Image of the Trinity*, 201–202, 206–207, 213.

> In personal encounters, that which the other person is flows consciously or unconsciously into that which I am. The reverse is also true. In this mutual giving and receiving, we give to others not only something, but also a piece of ourselves, something of that which we have made of ourselves in communion with others; and from others we take not only something, but also a piece of them. Each person gives of himself or herself to others, and each person in a unique way takes up others into himself or herself. This is the process of the mutual internalisation of personal characteristics occurring in the Church through the Holy Spirit indwelling Christians. The Spirit opens them to one another and allows them to become catholic persons in their uniqueness. It is here that they, in a creaturely way, correspond to the catholicity of the divine persons.[709]

In the latter part of verse 21, progression in the family of God comes to the fore. The proclamation is not the only means of evangelizing the world and expanding the family of God. Unity is another way. Unity among the people of God is "the centripetal force" that leads unbelievers to Christ (10:16).[710] Ecclesial disunity manifests a lack of integrity, which sooner or later cripples the mission of the church. The point is captured well by Bruinsma, who says,

> The divisions in Christianity are often referred to as a stumbling block for unbelievers. And they are. Sinful human beings have time and again chosen to go their own way rather than the way of Christ … it also remains a lamentable reality that the Christian Church becomes a less-credible witness of the reconciliation of people in Christ Jesus to the

---

[709] Ibid., 211–212.
[710] Kanagaraj, *John*, 4:169; Dods, *The Gospel of St. John*, 845.

> extent that the unity of Christ believers is impaired or only realised very imperfectly … Unfortunately, many people have lost their confidence in the institutional Church because of the endless quarrels and bitter controversies among Christian theologians and clergy as well as between denominations.[711]

The passage alludes to a community of people from the world of unbelievers whom Christian unity would impress and attract into it. As they take notice of Christ's existence in Christians through the demonstration of unity and how real they are in manifesting it, an appreciation of Christ's mission as divine and belief occurs. That is, doubts about the fact that Christ was on the Father's errand would be dispelled.[712] Unity among Christians is an avenue through which their task is going to be accomplished.[713] Lincoln states that "in this way in its ongoing mission the life of the community is meant to be an embodied witness to the truth about Jesus."[714] Bernard reiterates that position in a slightly different way as he says that "this unity, however, as appertaining to Christian discipleship, is not invisible; it is to be such as will convince the world of the Divine mission of the common Master of Christians. And He has already explained that the badge of this unity is love, the love of Christian for Christian which all men may see [13:35]."[715] Jesus made the invisible God known through His incarnation (1:14), and the church too, being noticeable, will make the invisible God known together with His

---

[711] Reinder Bruinsma, *The Body of Christ: A Biblical Understanding of the Church*, 62,143.

[712] Bernard, *A Critical and Exegetical Commentary on the Gospel According to St. John.*, 578.

[713] Whitacre, *John*, 4:420.

[714] Lincoln, *Black's New Testament Commentary: The Gospel According to Saint John*, 439.

[715] Bernard, *A Critical and Exegetical Commentary on the Gospel According to St. John.*, 577.

nature of love.⁷¹⁶ Milne adds more force by saying that "while the unity Jesus prays for us is not organizationally produced, it is equally not historically invisible. The world needs to see our unity."⁷¹⁷

While the mission would be enhanced through Christian unity, it is not the sole objective of oneness among Christians. As Christians unite, it will be known to the world that God loves them just as He loves His Son. Whitacre elaborates this point further as follows:

> This oneness flows from a common life that is characterised chiefly by love, and thus the world will see that the Father has loved the disciples as he has loved the Son (v. 23). In other words, the amazing transcendent love evident between the Father and the Son is not an exclusive glory that humans must be content only to admire from afar. The love the Father has for Jesus is the same love he has for believers, indeed for the whole world (3:16) … The believers are to embody this love and thereby provide living proof of God's gracious character, which is his mercy, love and truth. They will be an advertisement, inviting people to join in this union with God. The love of God evident in the Church is a revelation that there is a welcome awaiting those who will quit the rebellion and return home. Here is the missionary strategy of this Gospel—the community of disciples, indwelt with God's life and light and love, witnessing to the Father in the Son by the Spirit by Word and deed, continuing to bear witness as the Son has done.⁷¹⁸

---

[716] Bruce Milne, *The Message of John: Here Is Your King! With Study Guide* (Leicester, England; Downers Grove, IL: InterVarsity Press, 1993), 248.
[717] Ibid.
[718] Whitacre, *John*, 4:420; C.f. Kruse, *John: An Introduction and Commentary*, 4:341–342; Lincoln, *Black's New Testament Commentary: The Gospel According to Saint John*, 439.

Jesus's ministry and its aftermath are a testimony of the love of the Father not just for His Son but also for human beings He embraces.[719]

The desire of God to see Christians connected and united is also manifested in His investment of glory to help them unite. That glory flows from the Father to Christ, who then deposits it in the church.[720] According to Dods, "that the unity of believers in the Father and the Son might be perfect, it was needful that even the glory which Christ possessed by the Father's gift [v. 5] should be given to His people. The perfect tense is used, because the gift had already been determined."[721] Going by the scope of Christ's prayer, the gift is all-inclusive since all believers partake of it, as opposed to being a preserve of a few preselected beneficiaries.

The oneness that accompanies Christ's gift of glory is a complete experience going by the phrase *hina ōsin teteleiōmenoi eis hen* (that they may be perfected into one).[722] The phrase could also be translated as "consummated [or made perfect] in one" or "being brought on to perfect unity."[723] Through the imbuing of the glory upon His disciples, the believers would not only be made one but also achieve total oneness.[724] According to Dods, the perfection of unity is realized by means of "being wrought to a Divine unity."[725] It happens through the indwelling of believers by the Father and the Son, which occurs through the Holy Spirit. The Holy Spirit indwells them, and so are the Father and the Son.[726] Lenski articulates the import:

---

[719] Dods, *The Gospel of St. John*, 845.

[720] Verse 22.

[721] Dods, *The Gospel of St. John*, 845.

[722] C.f. 1 Jn 2:5; 4:12, 17, 18; Phil 3:12.

[723] Johann Bengel, *Gnomon of the New Testament*, vol. 2, trans. A. R. Fausset (Edinburgh: T&T Clark, 1860), 467.

[724] Bernard, *A Critical and Exegetical Commentary on the Gospel According to St. John.*, 578.

[725] Dods, *The Gospel of St. John*, 845.

[726] Colin Kruse, *John: An Introduction and Commentary*, vol. 4 (Downers Grove, IL: InterVarsity Press, 2003), 340.

> Just as the fuller reception of the word completes the oneness of believers more and more by mediating the indwelling of Jesus and the Father in them, so this indwelling in us and the consequent gift of the glory to us constitute our oneness and constitute it as something that has been made complete and now remains thus. The realisation of this purpose, the actual complete oneness, is attained in every age in all those believers who unite in accepting the word as they should. Those who, though they are still believers, in any way deviate from the word hinder the consummation of the oneness and prevent the fulfillment of Jesus' last prayer as far as they are concerned.[727]

As believers share in God's love and extend it to one another, a powerful testimony about Christ ensues. On the other hand, failure to love and live in unity stifles and cripples this witness.[728] Milne relates the message in John 17:20–23 to the church:

> Our churches are to be "love centres" where relationships between members are a persuasive reflection of the mutually supportive, utterly loyal and eternally accepting love of the Father and the Son. This is true whether the relationships are of men with women, young with mature, laity with clergy, new members with long-standing members, rich with poor, cultured with unsophisticated, socially upper with socially lower, leadership with membership, new converts with established Christians, racially other with racially traditional, and whatever other polarities the Church embraces.[729]

---

[727] Lenski, *The Interpretation of St. John's Gospel*, 1162–1163.
[728] Milne, *The Message of John: Here Is Your King!: With Study Guide*, 251.
[729] Ibid., 248.

In John 17:20–23, Christ envisages a church in the unforeseeable future that would expand the apostolic proclamation of the Gospel beyond its small beginnings to encompass the entire world as the unbelievers come to faith in Him. It is these would-be believers whom Christ prays for. With such an expansion of the church, disunity would be inevitable, hence the need to mitigate it and ensure that the ties remain strong amid diversity. The intra-Trinitarian unity exemplifies the relationship expected among its members. However, unity would be elusive without a relationship with the Trinity, which is facilitated by Christ. Interdependence among believers is the feature of the interpersonal relationships ensuing from their connection to the Godhead. Success in the Christian mission would be the benefit of Christian unity as people are attracted and come to belief and knowledge of Christ and His mission.

5.4.2 1 Corinthians 12:12–27

First Corinthians 12:12–27 presents a body with various constitutive elements that cannot survive on their own. A coordinated activity takes place among different organs of that body for the welfare of one another and, on a bigger scale, the whole body. The passage helps us to find out how to handle issues of diversity and the part it plays toward the church's well-being as Christ's body since the inability to handle it proves to be a great challenge among Christians presently just as it has been over the ages. Rather than being a source of blessing to the church, multiplicity continues to be the source of disunity and parsimonious relationships. During AD first century, the Christian church in Corinth suffered division attributed to poor interpersonal skills among its members, and this was the catalyst of Paul's message. Disputes among members had degenerated into the emergence of four groups, each of whom coalesced around either Paul or Peter or Apollos or Jesus Christ as their leaders.[730] The irresponsible use of charismata too was a great dilemma as it resulted

---

[730] 1 Cor 1-4.

in competition and rivalry among members. The conflict was also around socioeconomic status—that is, the well-to-do pitted against the poor or the well-to-do pitted against themselves.[731] Through a metaphor of the human body, Paul impresses upon believers the importance of living in unity despite the variety in the church's composition.

First Corinthians 12:12–27 is very relevant to our study as it touches on the communal aspect of the church. As observed by Prior, it addresses the subjects of "community and individuality."[732] It explains the possibility of being united while retaining individual peculiarities among Christians.[733] Clement of Rome (quoted by Valliant and Fahy), writing to the Church in Corinth around AD 96, states that "even then parties had been formed among you."[734] He points out further that the disunity and contention that plagued the church in Corinth caused a section of insiders to backslide and the outsiders to ridicule it and show contempt for God's reputation.[735] The Muratorian Fragment sheds more light by saying that the reason for the authorship of the epistle included "prohibiting their heretical schism."[736]

---

[731] Gordon Fee, *The First Epistle to the Corinthians: The New International Commentary on the New Testament* (Grand Rapids: Eerdmans, 1987), 1; Gerd Theissen, *The Social Setting of Pauline Christianity: Essays on Corinth*, ed. and trans. J.H. Schutz (Philadelphia: Fortress Press, 1982), 69–174.

[732] David Prior, *The Message of 1 Corinthians: Life in the Local Church* (Leicester, England; Downers Grove, IL: InterVarsity Press, 1985), 213.

[733] Anthony Thiselton, *The First Epistle to the Corinthians: A Commentary on the Greek Text* (Grand Rapids, MI: W.B. Eerdmans, 2000), 1001.

[734] James Valliant and Warren Fahy, *Creating Christ: How Roman Emperors Invented Christianity* (Crossroad Press, 2016).

[735] Wim Dreyer, "Church, Mission and Ethics: Being Church With Integrity," *H.T.S. Teologiese Studies/ Theological Studies* 72, no. 1 (2016): 2.

[736] Bart Ehrman, *Lost Scriptures: Books That Did Not Make It Into the New Testament* (New York: Oxford University Press, 2003), 332; Lee McDonald, *The Biblical Canon: Its Origin, Transmission, and Authority* (Grand Rapids: Baker Academic, n.d.).

5.4.2.1 A Tightly Knit yet All-Inclusive Community (v. 12)

Through this particular metaphorical use of a "body," which brings its various parts (*ta melē tou sōmatos*) together in oneness in verse 12, Paul demonstrates oneness amid multiplicity.[737] The *tertium comparationis* helps him to convey the idea more clearly as he reasons from unity to diversity and then from diversity to unity.[738] In the first case, he says that "the body is one and has many members." He then says that "all the members of the body, being many, are one body." Pope expresses this feature further as follows:

> Unity and Variety are both and alike essential to the idea of the Christian Church; and their sound combination is a test that may be applied to all ecclesiastical systems ... [there exists a] universal Body of Christ of which the Christian Church is the last earthly form ... [and] the Christian Fellowship proper as an institution. As to the first, the note of manifoldness is most conspicuous; as to the second, oneness and multiplicity unite.[739]

A community of close associates comes to the fore in this section. In its nonhomogeneous and nonexclusive nature, it is made of people drawn from various backgrounds who converge to form a single entity. It is these various parts that constitute the "body."[740] The parts are not the same in nature or likeness, yet that does not negate

---

[737] Archibald Robertson and Alfred Plummer, *A Critical and Exegetical Commentary on the First Epistle of St. Paul to the Corinthians* (New York: T&T Clark, 1911), 271.

[738] R.C.H. Lenski, *The Interpretation of St. Paul's First and Second Epistle to the Corinthians* (Minneapolis, MN: Augsburg Publishing House, 1963), 512.

[739] Pope, *A Compendium of Christian Theology: Being Analytical Outlines of a Course of Theological Study, Biblical, Dogmatic, Historical*, 3:267–268.

[740] Leon Morris. *1 Corinthians: An Introduction and Commentary*, vol. 7 (Downers Grove, IL: InterVarsity Press, 1985), 168.

the existence of oneness among them.⁷⁴¹ As Morris puts it, "since all believers are in Christ [*sic*] they are one body."⁷⁴²

5.4.2.2 A Common Experience Despite Diversity (v. 13)

The other characteristic of the community presented in 1 Corinthians 12 is that its members share certain things regardless of their original backgrounds. Firstly, they were baptized by the Holy Spirit at the time of joining it. While lives are born into natural societies, people become part of the church society by way of a new birth.⁷⁴³ As stated by Mott, "the individual act of faith by which we are born anew takes place in the context of the church, which proclaims the gospel, nurtures the converts, and shares the eternal blessings for which it was chosen by God."⁷⁴⁴ Baptism ensures the death of "the individual" and birth or "resurrection" of "the person."⁷⁴⁵ It deals with the "postlapsarian existence," which "is fragmentary existence" whereby "every human being encounters every other human being as a self-enclosed entity."⁷⁴⁶ This birth is the second one after the natural one, and it distinguishes the church from a "club," which those who are interested become part of in that people do not "join" but are reborn into it.⁷⁴⁷ To an extent, though, there are club features in the church as it is "a functional social unit whose members mutually

---

⁷⁴¹ This fact justifies Augustine's statement, *totus Christus caput et corpus est*, "The whole Christ includes both head and body." [Johann Lange, et al, *A Commentary on the Holy Scriptures: 1 Corinthians* (Bellingham, WA: Logos Bible Software, 2008), 253]. Bittlenger (quoted by Prior) on his part says that "In order to accomplish his work on earth, Jesus had a body made of flesh and blood. In order to accomplish his work today, Jesus has a body that consists of living human beings." (Prior, *The Message of 1 Corinthians: Life in the Local Church*, 210).

⁷⁴² Morris, *1 Corinthians: An Introduction and Commentary*, 7:168.

⁷⁴³ Jn 3:3, 5; Ti 3:5.

⁷⁴⁴ Stephen Mott, *Biblical Ethics and Social Change* (New York: Oxford University Press, 1982), 129.

⁷⁴⁵ Volf, *After Our Likeness: The Church as the Image of the Trinity*, 88, 89, 90, 91.

⁷⁴⁶ Ibid., 92.

⁷⁴⁷ Ibid., 180.

support one another in order to pursue their own common goals."[748] It is through that spiritual baptism and nothing else that they can be one body despite their diversities.[749]

The formation into one body, however, does not obliterate the features that make believers distinct from one another. The distinctions continue, though, superseded by the oneness formed of them by the Spirit. As Wiersbe says, since Christians have received spiritual baptism, "race, social status, wealth, or even sex [Galatians 3:28] are neither advantages nor handicaps as we fellowship and serve the Lord."[750] They have obtained a new identity, which supersedes race and social status since joining that body; and as Thisselton puts it, they are the "people of the Spirit."[751] Jamieson, Fausset, and Brown stated that "as the many members of the body compose an organic whole and none can be dispensed with as needless, so those variously gifted by the Spirit, compose a spiritual organic whole, the body of Christ, into which all are baptised by the one Spirit."[752] According to Thisselton, *pantes* (all) is an offensive against "categorisation or elitism within the church."[753] A miraculous union has resulted from the Spirit's baptism, which has removed discrimination within God's community.

In addition to baptism by the Spirit, believers in Corinth had also

---

[748] Ibid.

[749] Prior points out that, "Corinth was a cosmopolitan seaport full of people from many different cultures. That presented difficulties, but it offered immense potential for a full-blooded testimony to Christ. The more we today draw on the richness of the world-wide community of believers, the more pungent and attractive will be our testimony." (Prior, *The Message of 1 Corinthians: Life in the Local Church*, 212).

[750] Warren Wiersbe, *The Bible Exposition Commentary*, vol. 1 (Wheaton, IL: Victor Books, 1996), 609.

[751] Thisselton, *The First Epistle to the Corinthians: A Commentary on the Greek Text*, 997.

[752] Robert Jamieson, Andrew Fausset, and David Brown. *Commentary Critical and Explanatory on the Whole Bible*. vol. 2 (Oak Harbor, WA: Logos Research Systems, Inc., 1997), 287.

[753] Thisselton, *The First Epistle to the Corinthians: A Commentary on the Greek Text*, 998.

been "made to drink of one Spirit." The expression "made to drink of one Spirit" is used in a nonliteral sense to refer to the action of receiving the Holy Spirit.[754] According to Wilson, this refers to the spiritual reality of which their baptism in water was the symbol.[755] In Morris's words, "the Spirit has entered their innermost being."[756] Goodspeed (quoted by Morris) buttresses this point when he says that "we have all been saturated with one Spirit."[757] As in Acts 2, which talks of "the outpouring of the Spirit," the Holy Spirit is "a flowing stream here."[758] Volf articulates the role of the Spirit:

> The Spirit unites the gathered congregation with the triune God and integrates it into a history extending from Christ, indeed, from the Old Testament saints, [sic] to the eschatological new creation. This Spirit-mediated relationship with the triune God and with the entire history of God's people—a history whose center resides in Jesus' own proclamation of the reign of God, in his death and in his resurrection—constitutes an assembly into a Church.[759]

5.4.2.3 A Sense of Belonging (vv. 14–16)

The sense of belonging in the community of Christ manifests in unhindered participation of every single member in its life toward the smooth running and well-being. This constitutes Catholicity,

---

[754] The event took place in the past in every believing person's life as indicated by the aorist (Lenski, *The Interpretation of St. Paul's First and Second Epistle to the Corinthians*, 516). The Word *epotisthēmen* rendered as "made to drink" is a form of *potizein*, a verb whose other meaning is "to irrigate." Therefore, as Morris puts it, "ἐποτίσθημεν could also suggest an 'abundant supply.'" (Morris, *1 Corinthians: An Introduction and Commentary*, 7:169).

[755] Geoffrey Wilson, *1 Corinthians* (Banner of Truth, 1978).

[756] Morris, *1 Corinthians: An Introduction and Commentary*, 7:169.

[757] Ibid.

[758] Lange, et al, *A Commentary on the Holy Scriptures: 1 Corinthians*, 254.

[759] Volf, *After Our Likeness: The Church as the Image of the Trinity*, 129; C.f. 213.

one aspect of which is "the absence of exclusion."⁷⁶⁰ The members of the community presented by Paul, some of whom are less endowed than others, belong on equal footing. As Zizioulas puts it, "the person cannot exist without communion; but every form of communion which denies or suppresses the person, is inadmissible."⁷⁶¹ In support of this view, Volf argues that "the person is not a self-enclosed substantial entity, but rather an open relational entity."⁷⁶² Paul's argument presents an offensive against individualism, which is the greatest hindrance to Christian unity.

Moreover, the apostle uses the body metaphor to pass a message that the failure of various members to play the roles given to them even in their plurality would shatter the body into what Thiselton refers to as a chaotic array of conflicting forces, without focus or coherence.⁷⁶³ The various parts of the Christian body are meant to be complementary and supportive of one another through the charisms endowed upon them.⁷⁶⁴

In verse 15 and several verses following it, the different parts of the body are personified and presented as speaking out their disenchantment. According to Mitchell, this rhetorical device was "a polemic against factionalism."⁷⁶⁵ As the different parts play their distinctive roles, harmony is experienced within the body. On the contrary, slothfulness on any part of the body results in chaos and brings it down.⁷⁶⁶ Paul's message is that members who devalue

---

⁷⁶⁰ Ibid., 104.

⁷⁶¹ Zizioulas, *Being as Communion: Studies in Personhood and the Church*, 18.

⁷⁶² Volf, *After Our Likeness: The Church as the Image of the Trinity*, 82.

⁷⁶³ Thiselton, *The First Epistle to the Corinthians: A Commentary on the Greek Text*, 1002.

⁷⁶⁴ Robert Jamieson, Andrew Fausset, and David Brown, *Commentary Critical and Explanatory on the Whole Bible*, vol. 2 (Oak Harbor, WA: Logos Research Systems, Inc., 1997), 287.

⁷⁶⁵ Margaret Mitchell, *Paul and the Rhetoric of Reconciliation* (Tübingen: Mohr, 1991), 68–83, 157–164.

⁷⁶⁶ It is thought that the imagery of the body is Stoic and was borrowed by Paul, who then adjusted it to explain an "idea." The political entity was equated with the "human body" with parts constituting it. As recounted by Livy and others,

themselves and those who look down upon the rest need to work together for the greater good of the body.⁷⁶⁷ The phrase *ean eipē ho pous* (if the foot should say) *ouk eimi ek tou sōmatos* (I do not belong to the body) shows discontentment.⁷⁶⁸ However, that feeling and the expression of it does not take away the "objective" reality that the foot is indeed part of the body.⁷⁶⁹ The disenchantment expressed here could even be attributed to envy. Chrysostom (cited by Robertson and Plummer) comments that "the foot contrasts itself with the hand rather than with the ear because we do not envy those who are very much higher than ourselves so much as those who have got a little above us."⁷⁷⁰ Deluz relays the argument in another way:

> Christians must give up anxiously comparing themselves with each other … It leads to jealousy [cf. 1:10–12; 3:1–4] and discouragement … They complain that they are not like so-and-so … They develop an inferiority complex and lose all the joy

---

an ancient fictitious tale was used by Menenius Agrippa who was an orator to end the dispute between subjects in the Roman Empire and the authorities. The tale said that different parts of the body launched accusation against the belly for unwillingness to work and waiting to be fed. As a punishment, the hands declined to carry food into the mouth. The mouth as well rejected the food while the teeth were not willing to bite and crush it. Consequently, the whole body got lean and weak due to lack of nourishment. The components of the body learnt that they were wrong in their actions. This allusion could be found not only in the works of Socrates, but of Seneca, Marcus Aurelius, and Marcus Antoninus too (Archibald Robertson, *Word Pictures in the New Testament (1 Co 12:13–27)* (Nashville, TN: Broadman Press, 1933).

⁷⁶⁷ Thiselton, *The First Epistle to the Corinthians: A Commentary on the Greek Text*, 1002.

⁷⁶⁸ While referring to Menenius Agrippa's tale in his works, Socrates said that it would be weird for the feet and the hand to undermine each other bearing in mind that they were created to work jointly towards a common goal (Robertson, *Word Pictures in the New Testament (1 Co 12:13–27)*.

⁷⁶⁹ Thiselton, *The First Epistle to the Corinthians: A Commentary on the Greek Text*, 1002; Morris, *1 Corinthians: An Introduction and Commentary*, 7:169.

⁷⁷⁰ Thiselton, *The First Epistle to the Corinthians: A Commentary on the Greek Text*, 1002.

of salvation. The foot grumbles because it walks in the dust and carries the whole weight of the body … Others would like to be the eye which oversees or [especially!] the mouth which speaks … God knows why he has made each one of us as we are; he knows what use each one of us can be.[771]

The argument in verse 15 continues in verse 16, where the ear too speaks low of itself in comparison to the eye. Thisselton sheds light on the verse as follows:

> Paul primarily addresses those whose gifts have been regarded as "inferior" by others, but his logic equally anticipates his rebuke to the self-sufficient "quasi-gnostics" [who prize "knowledge"], or "spiritual people" [who prize more visible, unusual phenomena of the Spirit], or social patrons [who provide prestige and practical support], who may think [or even implicitly say], "I have no need of you" (v. 21).[772]

The import of both verses is that every believer is part of the body and is there to stay. They cannot jump out of it.[773] Pratt observes that "by analogy, Paul meant that Christians are not cut off from the body of Christ because they think they have no importance or place of service. Each part of the body makes a unique contribution to the whole."[774] They are part of it no matter what happens, no matter their dissatisfaction at times with the arrogance of some of their own who deem them inferior. They know of no other community.

---

[771] Gaston Deluz, *A Companion to 1 Corinthians* (Darton: Longman & Todd, 1963), 179–180.
[772] Thisselton, *The First Epistle to the Corinthians: A Commentary on the Greek Text*, 1003.
[773] Morris, *1 Corinthians: An Introduction and Commentary*, 7:169.
[774] Richard Pratt Jr., *I & II Corinthians*. Vol. 7 (Nashville, TN: Broadman & Holman Publishers, 2000), 218.

5.4.2.4 Members Complementing One Another (vv. 17–19)

The main point in verses 17–19 is that the contribution of every person who is part of the community presented in the passage counts and is of value no matter the degree of such input. Each member plays a pivotal role despite the variance in functionality. Therefore, without any single member, the entire community suffers since each exists for a purpose. No part of the body (ear, eye, nose, etc.) does what the other part is supposed to be doing, yet all their inputs contribute to the well-being of the body.[775] That being the case, a low estimation of a given part and the contribution it makes, or the thought of a given organ allowing itself to be consumed with the desire for what the other member has, ought to be set aside.[776] In verse 17 and the three preceding it, the discriminative attitude of members who deemed themselves superior to others in the church at Corinth has been exposed. As far as Paul was concerned, these hubristic members were not justified in their prejudice against those whom they despised. The apostle was very much alive to the damage inflicted through such haughtiness.[777] He dispels the fears and doubts in the believers whose spiritual gifts were considered lesser and more dispensable by encouraging them and bolstering a sense of belonging in them as vital parts of the whole.

Paul proceeds to verse 18, where the message conveyed is that the diversity present in the body is by divine design. Since it is the work of God, to fault it is tantamount to faulting God.[778] Thiselton relays this argument as follows:

---

[775] Morris, *1 Corinthians: An Introduction and Commentary*, 7:169.
[776] Robertson and Plummer, *A Critical and Exegetical Commentary on the First Epistle of St. Paul to the Corinthians*, 273.
[777] Pratt, *I & II Corinthians*, 7:219.
[778] In the verb *ēthelēsen*, "as He wanted" or "as He chose," divine prerogative or discretion comes to fore. (Thiselton, *The First Epistle to the Corinthians: A Commentary on the Greek Text*, 1003). For Kennedy (cited by Thiselton), *ēthelēsen* as an "aorist of divine sovereignty is reflecting divine decision and decree." (Ibid., 1004). According to Robertson and Plummer, since the root of this verb is *etheto*, its meaning is that God Himself "placed the members" where they are. (Robertson

> To try to rank some gifts as "more essential" than others, let alone as necessary marks of advanced status to which all should aspire, is to offer a blasphemous challenge to God's freedom to choose whatever is his good will for his people both collectively and individually … How dare anyone either boast or exult in his or her own gifts as if these were a status symbol, or devalue other people's gifts, as if God had not chosen them for the other?[779]

The point is that oneness, as opposed to sameness and homogeneity, is God's product. This aspect of the relationship resonates with jo-kang'ato, which also entertains multiplicity in the course of enhancing unity. Moreover, no part of the body exists in a careless, disorganized, and disorderly manner, for they have been neatly placed in various locations by God Himself through His creative act. God attends to them without partiality for parts deemed most significant and exciting to look at.[780] As Morris puts it, "His oversight and creativity extend to every member of the body. He made them all just as he wanted them to be ['just as he willed']."[781] The understanding of divine discretion in this matter results in a cautious approach. Robertson and Plummer articulate it as follows:

> Pride and discontent are quite out of place, for they are not only the outcome of selfishness, but also rebellion against God's will. This has two points: it was not our fellow-men [sic] who placed us in an inferior position, but God; and He did it, not to please us or our fellows, but in accordance with His will, which must be right.

---

and Plummer, *A Critical and Exegetical Commentary on the First Epistle of St. Paul to the Corinthians*, 274).
[779] Thiselton, *The First Epistle to the Corinthians: A Commentary on the Greek Text*, 1004.
[780] Morris, *1 Corinthians: An Introduction and Commentary*, 7:170.
[781] Ibid.

Who is so disloyal as to gainsay what God willed to arrange?⁷⁸²

In his argument, the apostle also rules out self-independence, for he says that one organ does not constitute a body. As Morris puts it, "no matter how important any one member may be, there can be no body formed from it alone. That would be a monster, not a body. But in fact, as things are, there are many parts, and together they make up but one body."⁷⁸³

5.4.2.5 Mutual Interdependence among Members (vv. 20–22)

The other feature that is of equal importance in the community presented by Paul is that its members are so intertwined that it ceases to exist without the participation of each one of them in its life. The members do not just need but are part of one another. This idea underscores the fact that as social beings, God has made each person relate to others within a given network rather than segregate themselves.⁷⁸⁴ However, this does not cause the reduction of a person to a nonentity. Unique features are maintained.⁷⁸⁵ In verse 21, therefore, the independent attitude among certain members at Corinth, who were showing an overly high opinion of themselves and the charisms in their possession, is reproved.⁷⁸⁶ In their estimation, others were less important and somehow not real members.⁷⁸⁷ They could cope even in the absence of the input of such. The attitude stemmed from the perception of being more spiritually gifted.⁷⁸⁸ Paul tells them that the despised members are indispensable. The

---

⁷⁸² Robertson and Plummer, *A Critical and Exegetical Commentary on the First Epistle of St. Paul to the Corinthians*, 274.
⁷⁸³ Morris, *1 Corinthians: An Introduction and Commentary*, 7:170.
⁷⁸⁴ Volf, *After Our Likeness: The Church as the Image of the Trinity*, 183, 185.
⁷⁸⁵ Ibid., 187, 188, 189.
⁷⁸⁶ Thiselton, *The First Epistle to the Corinthians: A Commentary on the Greek Text*, 1005.
⁷⁸⁷ Ibid.
⁷⁸⁸ Morris, *1 Corinthians: An Introduction and Commentary*, 7:170.

eye needs the hand, and the head needs the feet.⁷⁸⁹ The *asthenestera* (weaker members), rather than being subsidiary parts of the body, are the inseparable components who cannot be done away with.⁷⁹⁰ Thiselton further captures the prevailing situation at Corinth:

> It is hardly mere speculation to imagine that those who perceived themselves as possessing the "high-status" gifts of knowledge and wisdom, or of the power to heal or to speak in tongues, could be tempted to think of themselves as *the* inner circle on whom the identity and function of the Church really depended … the passage carries the corollary that no single type of gift or experience should be used as a measure for other believers.⁷⁹¹

5.4.2.6 Care for the Weaker and Vulnerable Members (vv. 23–24)

Care for the weaker and vulnerable members is of utmost importance in the community of Christ. Members recognize that when one of them is weak, all of them are. As such, they act in the best interest of one another. However, those referred to as the less honorable and less respectable parts of the body (v. 23) receive much

---

⁷⁸⁹ Ibid.

⁷⁹⁰ By *asthenestera*, reference is made of those believers who could have been perceived as weak not because they were, but either because the part they played appeared not significant, or due to their personalities and statuses which did not portray them as influential people and keep them at the edge (Thiselton, *The First Epistle to the Corinthians: A Commentary on the Greek Text*, 1007). Thiselton expresses the idea as follows: "The "strong" or the "gifted" perceived them as not providing much effective *weight* or *power* in the Church's mission, and not much *confidence* borne of *status*. They were insufficiently impressive to count for much, either socially or spiritually, within the Church, or in terms of what "contacts" or ability they might show for mission or for speaking with wisdom and knowledge to outsiders. Probably they never did effective mighty works or healing, seldom or never prophesied, and perhaps never spoke in tongues." (Ibid).

⁷⁹¹ Thiselton, *The First Epistle to the Corinthians: A Commentary on the Greek Text*, 1005.

attention.⁷⁹² Paul goes further to suggest that the "more respectable members" ought not to be soliciting for more recognition and acclamation as they already have the charisms: pleasant, meaningful, and smart.⁷⁹³ Paul credits God for the variety in His church manifesting in the presence of the "presentable" and "unpresentable" members.⁷⁹⁴ Thiselton describes the process:

> At all events, it is God who decides what or who forms part of a hidden foundation beneath the earth, or an ornamental spire or tower [more showy, but less fundamental] in the case of a building; which parts of a painting shine and which yield dark shadow; or which parts of a body are on display and which parts perform utterly essential functions for the survival of the whole.⁷⁹⁵

The point driven by Paul is that God has so designed that those members suffering from a sense of unimportance or inadequacy

---

⁷⁹² Whereas in Thiselton's view the weaker parts of the body could include "the private male organ" (Thiselton, *The First Epistle to the Corinthians: A Commentary on the Greek Text*, 1008), Robertson understands them to be the "breasts" of a mother and other female organs" (Robertson, *Word Pictures in the New Testament (1 Co 12:13–27)*, 172). These parts are necessary for reproduction and "nurture" and are usually covered as opposed to other sections of the body (Thiselton, *The First Epistle to the Corinthians: A Commentary on the Greek Text*, 1008).

⁷⁹³ Thiselton, *The First Epistle to the Corinthians: A Commentary on the Greek Text*, 1010.

⁷⁹⁴ Paul uses the verb *synekerasen* which, according to Bauer, Arndt, Gingrich, Danker, and Edwards (cited by Thiselton), is the first aorist indicative form of *synkerannymi*. The word refers to the act of combining colours as done by those who do painting; forming or configuring a congruous piece; or the act of a Supernatural Being of making up a composite whole out of different bits which jointly constitute "human body." (Ibid., 1010). It also gives a portrait of "a musician composing *a harmony.*" (Morris, *1 Corinthians: An Introduction and Commentary*, 7:177; Thiselton, *The First Epistle to the Corinthians: A Commentary on the Greek Text*, 1010).

⁷⁹⁵ Thiselton, *The First Epistle to the Corinthians: A Commentary on the Greek Text*, 1010.

should also be part of His church. Their deficiency is not a state but a perception.[796]

5.4.2.7 A Cohesive Society of Friendship and Solidarity (vv. 25–26)

In verse 25, the apostle states the purpose of God's formation as presented in verse 24, which is the prevention of *schisma* (dissension) among believers.[797] As Morris puts it, "God's arrangement of the members in the body does away with clashing and blends all into one harmonious whole."[798] Instead of dissension, there should be an environment of "care for one another" within the church that follows consciousness of one another's needs and solidarity with one another in bad and good times. The kind of care prescribed for Christians to show one another is a peculiar one, going by the rendition in Greek.[799] As used in verse 25, *merimnōsin* (care or concern) suggests a situation where a problem in one part of the body creates discomfort in the entire body.[800] Equality is a significant characteristic of the concern, which members are called upon to show one another since the care alluded to is one that is devoid of partial treatment.[801] The gist of verse 25 is that when believers within the body of Christ realize that they are not independent of one another, strife will cease as interest in others increases among them, and that is God's wish.[802]

---

[796] Ibid.

[797] The other renditions of *schisma* are "rent," "tear," and "split" - 1:10 (Ibid.).

[798] Morris, *1 Corinthians: An Introduction and Commentary*, 7:171.

[799] As used elsewhere in the New Testament, *merimnáō* whose subjunctive form *merimnōsin* as been employed has a connotation of "anxious care," (Matthew 6:25, 27, 28, and 31), or "a concern which absorbs the attention" (1 Corinthians 7:32, 33, 34; C.f. 7:32–34). (Thiselton, *The First Epistle to the Corinthians: A Commentary on the Greek Text*, 1011). Its other application is "thoughtful trouble." (Robertson and Plummer, *A Critical and Exegetical Commentary on the First Epistle of St. Paul to the Corinthians*, 276).

[800] Robertson, *Word Pictures in the New Testament (1 Co 12:13–27)*.

[801] Morris, *1 Corinthians: An Introduction and Commentary*, 7:171.

[802] Prior, *The Message of 1 Corinthians: Life in the Local Church*, 215.

The mingling of various organs of the body alluded to in verse 24 was to make the bearing of one another's burdens possible.

Paul's proposition of reciprocal attention and sensitivity toward one another's feelings and needs extends into verse 26. Unlike the trend in the West, where every person minds their business, Paul recommends a society where people mind one another's business.[803] The verbs *paschei* and *sympaschei* convey suffering medically.[804] While relating the idea to the church, Thornton says, "It follows that in the Body of Christ there are, strictly speaking, no private sufferings. All are shared because there is one life of the whole. Accordingly, wrong done to one member is wrong done to the whole Church, and therefore to Christ himself."[805] That being the case, members of the church in Corinth who were diminishing their brothers and sisters to increase their standing were, in actuality, reducing rather than ennobling themselves.[806]

---

[803] The phrase "If one member suffers, all suffer together with it" corresponds to what Plato said — that when there is discomfort in the finger, the entire being experiences it. (Thiselton, *The First Epistle to the Corinthians: A Commentary on the Greek Text*, 1011). By the imagery, Plato was emphasising a relationship characterised by the sharing of feelings and experiences. The laws of Plutarch of Solon also help us to understand the solidarity of various parts of the body with the suffering organ. He said (in his "Republic," v., 462 quoted by Vincent) that, "If anyone was (sic) beaten or maimed or suffered any violence, any man that would and was able might prosecute the wrongdoer; intending by this to accustom the citizens, like members of the same body, to resent and be sensible of one another's injuries." (Marvin Vincent, *Word Studies in the New Testament*, Vol. 3 (New York: Charles Scribner's Sons, 1887), 259–260). Chrysostom on his part says that "When a thorn enters the heel, the whole body feels it, and is concerned: the back bends, the belly and thighs contract themselves, the hands come forward and draw out the thorn, the head stoops, and the eyes regard the affected member with intense gaze." (Jamieson, Fausset, and Brown, *Commentary Critical and Explanatory on the Whole Bible*, 2:287–288).

[804] Thiselton, *The First Epistle to the Corinthians: A Commentary on the Greek Text*, 1011.

[805] Lionel Thornton, *The Common Life in the Body of Christ* (Dacre Press, 1942), 36; C.f. 34-65, 156-187.

[806] Thiselton, *The First Epistle to the Corinthians: A Commentary on the Greek Text*, 1012.

Suffering is not the only experience shared by the different parts of the body, however. They also experience the honor received by one of them and "rejoice together." In other words, they are all congratulated.[807] The body accepts all that works toward its well-being and pleasing appearance. As Chrysostom puts it, "the head is crowned, and all the members have a share in the honor; the eyes laugh when the mouth speaks."[808] Best adds that "what affects one member affects all … One member of the Church uses his spiritual gift as God intended its use, and the whole Church rejoices, one member misuses his gift and the whole Church sorrows."[809] Preoccupation with self, often manifesting in feeling discontented or resentful of another member's endowment and putting forward individual welfare and interests ahead of those of others, does not belong in oneness and "interdependence."[810] Oneness in the body manifests during times of adversity as well as exaltation.[811] Its members succeed or fail together.

In verse 27, which is a summary of Paul's argument, the nature of the relationship expected of Christians within the church setting comes out even more forcefully: "Now you are the body of Christ and individually members of it."[812] According to Prior, "on this basis at least three facts are spelt out: we need one another, we differ from one another and we are to care for one another."[813] We belong both to our Lord Jesus Christ as well as to one another. The community is all about this. To appreciate it, though, a "deindividualization" of church members, which happens only by divine means, is necessary as it turns them into "people" who are ready to interact with one another.[814] Whereas people relate with others, individualization

---

[807] Ibid.
[808] Vincent, *Word Studies in the New Testament*, 3:259–260.
[809] Ernest Best, *One Body in Christ* (London: S.P.C.K., 1955), 104.
[810] Deluz, *A Companion to 1 Corinthians*, 182.
[811] Morris, *1 Corinthians: An Introduction and Commentary*, 7:171.
[812] The thought is also captured in the epistle to the Romans where Paul says that "We, though many, are one body in Christ, and individually members one of another." (Rom 12:5).
[813] Prior, *The Message of 1 Corinthians: Life in the Local Church*, 215.
[814] Volf, *After Our Likeness: The Church as the Image of the Trinity*, 83, 86.

does not encourage the relationship, even in the church.[815] In Volf's words, "only in communion with the triune God can human beings become free, 'catholic' persons living in communion. Otherwise, they remain alone with themselves and the world, and for that reason also ensnared in their own individuality and thus ultimately given over to death."[816] The message conveyed is that as individuals, members of the body of Christ contribute to its being.

First Corinthians 12:12–27 aligns with the concept of jo-kang'ato, whose unity-enhancing values include a sense of corporate identity and belonging, which come with recognizing the input of other components of society. While discouraging selfish tendencies, jo-kang'ato also encourages incorporating those who do not look like "us" or possess qualities similar to ours within society. The values presented are necessary because they make interaction among people possible.

5.4.3 Ephesians 2:12–22

Besides being the "body of Christ," the church is also God's family or his "household." In Ephesians 2:12–22, Paul makes it clear that through the cross and the blood of the Lord Jesus Christ, impediments to the oneness between God and humans and human to human are no longer there, and the privilege of sharing God as a Father is enjoyed. The passage is filled with familial overtones, which have been identified in this book.

5.4.3.1 Acceptance in the Family of God (vv. 12–13)

The first characteristic of the family presented in Ephesians 2:12–22 is that its members enjoy full acceptance among themselves and are tolerated despite their peculiarities. This family is extended yet very intimate since members are "near" to one another rather than "far off." The condition of the Gentiles before being drawn to God

---

[815] Ibid., 84.
[816] Ibid.

to be part of His family was pitiable. Stott refers to their dilemma as "Gentile disabilities."[817] Firstly, the Gentiles were "without Christ," a situation aggravated by their not being part of the "commonwealth of Israel."[818] In other words, the Gentiles were not members of Yahweh's nation (Israelites) as well as "his saving purposes."[819] *Apēllotriōmenoi*, from the verb *apallotrioō* (estranged from), properly represents their status. While they could be accommodated into Jewish society through proselytization, the distance between them and the Jews remained palpable.[820]

Furthermore, the Gentiles were "strangers to the covenants of promise" made to the patriarchs of Israel.[821] Best states regarding the promise that "there is a forward look in the covenants relating to the continuance of Israel which could be seen as indicating a promise. Gentiles are strangers with respect of that forward look and so to that promise."[822] O'Brien expresses the idea as follows:

> Being separated from the chosen people of Israel was a serious disadvantage since it meant being outside the sphere of God's election and isolated from

---

[817] John Stott, *God's New Society: The Message of Ephesians* (Downers Grove, IL: InterVarsity Press, 1979), 95.

[818] The latter condition is to be understood in the sense of a literal Israel rather than as the Church [Ernest Best, *A Critical and Exegetical Commentary on Ephesians* (Edinburgh: T&T Clark International, 1998), 241].

[819] Peter O'Brien, *The Letter to the Ephesians* (Grand Rapids, MI: W.B. Eerdmans Publishing Co., 1999), 187.

[820] *Politeias* a form of *politeia* has been used here in the sense of a "theocratic constitution from which they were excluded" as opposed to the contemporary understanding of "citizenship" in the Greco-Roman world which would suggest the act of being kept out of a "commonwealth." [Francis Foulkes, *Ephesians: An Introduction and Commentary*, vol. 10 (Downers Grove, IL: InterVarsity Press, 1989), 87].

[821] The covenants' prominent feature was the "promise" of the anointed one brought to fore in Acts 13:32 [Thomas Abbott, *A Critical and Exegetical Commentary on the Epistles to the Ephesians and to the Colossians* (New York: C. Scribner's Sons, 1909, 58].

[822] Best, *A Critical and Exegetical Commentary on Ephesians*, 242.

any covenant relationship with him. Hence Paul's readers were foreigners to the covenants of promise. The covenants with the patriarchs had held out the promise of great blessing to all nations of the earth, but it was not until the coming of Christ and the open proclamation of the gospel that believing Gentiles could be blessed along with Abraham, the man of faith (Galatians 3:9).[823]

The next predicament among the Gentiles was hopelessness. Their state was a result of being separated from Christ, who happened to be Israel's anointed one.[824] On the other hand, the Jewish people, even in their unbelief and lives lived in exclusion from Jesus, recognized the Messiah and anticipated the fulfillment of the words of the scripture given to them concerning Him (Romans 3:2).[825] In addition to the disadvantages recounted so far, the Gentiles were also "without God." They could have been worshipping other gods apart from the one worshipped by the Israelites, though.[826] As O'Brien puts it, "in contrast to Israel which had a relationship with the true God, [Gentiles] were God-forsaken."[827] It is a condition Meyer (cited by Abbott) describes as "the deepest stage of heathen misery."[828] Hendriksen (quoted by Stott) summarizes the whole situation among the Gentiles as "Christless, stateless, friendless, hopeless and Godless."[829]

The good news of the Gentile people's full acceptance into the

---

[823] O'Brien, *The Letter to the Ephesians*, 189.
[824] The hope alluded to as to be understood in light of the Messiah's work in saving the nation (Ibid., 187, 188).
[825] O'Brien, *The Letter to the Ephesians*, 188.
[826] [826] The phrase, *kai atheoi*, "and without God" denotes inexistent connection with Yahweh as the only genuine deity (Ibid., 190; Best, *A Critical and Exegetical Commentary on Ephesians*, 243.
[827] O'Brien, *The Letter to the Ephesians*, 190.
[828] [828] Abbott, *A Critical and Exegetical Commentary on the Epistles to the Ephesians and to the Colossians*, 59.
[829] Stott, *God's New Society: The Message of Ephesians*, 95–96.

family of God is conveyed in verse 13. The message relayed by Paul is that there has been a bestowal of blessings that non-Jews were previously deficient of.[830] These blessings do not come with incorporation into the literal Israelite society but to a "new Israel" bound by a "covenant," which is different from the Abrahamic one.[831] It is "in Christ Jesus" and on account of his blood that this happened. By the expression "the blood of Christ," the offering of His life on sinners' behalf and death by crucifixion is implied (Ephesians 1:7).[832] It is by this that reconciliation of humanity to the Father and fellow humans occurs.[833] "In Christ Jesus" also denotes being united with Him as an avenue for the reception and appreciation of "reconciliation" brought by Him. As Stott puts it, "the two expressions witness to the two stages by which those 'far off' are 'brought near.' The first is the historical event of the cross, and the second Christian conversion, or the contemporary experience of union with Christ."[834] Bratcher and Nida enlighten that "in Rabbinic teaching, 'to come near' was used of the reception of a Gentile convert into the Jewish faith."[835] O'Brien adds that "in drawing near to the congregation of Israel that person came near to God, who was near his people."[836] However, Paul introduces an exceptional means.

Nearness to Christ sets the stage for reconciliation as it brings people closer to God and fellow human beings. Jesus destroyed the separation between the races mentioned when He died by way of

---

[830] *Nyni de* breaks the monotony introduced in verse 11 by *mnēmoneuete*, "remember." [Johann Lange, et al, *A Commentary on the Holy Scriptures: Ephessians* (Bellingham, WA: Logos Bible Software, 2008), 91].
[831] Best, *A Critical and Exegetical Commentary on Ephesians*, 246.
[832] Stott, *God's New Society: The Message of Ephesians*, 98.
[833] Ibid.
[834] Ibid.
[835] Robert Bratcher, and Eugene Nida, *A Handbook on Paul's Letter to the Ephesians* (New York: United Bible Societies, 1993), 54.
[836] O'Brien, *The Letter to the Ephesians*, 191.

crucifixion.[837] Volf articulates what happens when people embrace God's salvation as follows:

> [They] do not remain alone with their God. By entering into this relation to God, supported by the communion of believers, they are simultaneously constituted into the communion of believers ... To believe means to enjoy communion with God ... Because the Christian God is not a private deity. Communion with this God is at once also communion with those others who have entrusted themselves in faith to the same God. Hence one and the same act of faith places a person into a new relationship both with God and with all others who stand in communion with God ... faith means entering into communion, communion with the triune God and with other Christians.[838]

5.4.3.2 A Peaceful Coexistence (vv. 14–17)

The members of the church family presented in Ephesians are at peace with one another and able to interact freely, as there are no obstacles to communion among them. Peace is of utmost importance to this family than the peculiarities within it. That peaceful environment set in courtesy of the accomplished work of Christ. O'Brien points out that "He is the central figure who effects reconciliation and removes hostility in its various forms."[839]

Peace, as understood in the OT and the Jewish perspective, was widened to mean "well-being" and encompassed "salvation," whose

---

[837] Max Anders, *Galatians, Ephesians, Philippians & Colossians*, vol. 8, Holman New Testament Commentary (Nashville, TN: Broadman & Holman Publishers, 1999), 114; Foulkes, *Ephesians: An Introduction and Commentary*, 10:88, 89.
[838] Volf, *After Our Likeness: The Church as the Image of the Trinity*, 172, 173, 174.
[839] O'Brien, *The Letter to the Ephesians*, 194.

dispenser is none but Yahweh.⁸⁴⁰ However, besides referring to the saving work of the Messiah (Luke 1:79, 2:14, 19:42), it speaks of the absence of conflict among humans (Acts 7:26, Galatians 5:22, Ephesians 4:3, James 3:18).⁸⁴¹ In Best's description, "peace is the end of alienation; people can be alienated from God, from one another or internally alienated; the first two aspects are present here, the third is not. Peace as salvation is God's gift."⁸⁴² It is "in Christ Jesus" (verse 13) that the OT promises of peace came true.⁸⁴³ Best observes that since the meaning of "peace" stretched further than the termination of animosity to the complete welfare of its recipients, "it is not merely, 'I am no longer angry with you,' but more positively, 'I seek your well-being.'"⁸⁴⁴ This understanding is behind the NT's concept of peace too.

It is in Christ and "his flesh" that oneness between the two "groups" has been achieved. Since the Jews and Gentiles came together as believers in Christ Jesus, their way of treating each other has changed, and a new kind of oneness has set in, which supersedes the previous condition.⁸⁴⁵ The Gentiles are no longer "far off" (v. 13) but near enough to enjoy the Messiah together with their Jewish counterparts.⁸⁴⁶ Chrysostom (cited by Abbott) says that Christ has elevated all the sides together to a higher status rather than elevating us to the Jewish people's social rank.⁸⁴⁷ Chrysostom equates the process to the act of liquefying a figure made of silver and another

---

[840] Ibid., 193.

[841] Ibid.

[842] Best, *A Critical and Exegetical Commentary on Ephesians*, 252.

[843] The word "peace" has been used "four times" between verses 14–17 to bring to fore the reconciliatory "work" of Jesus. (O'Brien, *The Letter to the Ephesians*, 193). The reconciliatory tone is manifested in the statements, "he has made both groups into one" (verse 14), "create in himself one new humanity" (verse 15).

[844] Best, *A Critical and Exegetical Commentary on Ephesians*, 270.

[845] O'Brien, *The Letter to the Ephesians*, 194.

[846] Best, *A Critical and Exegetical Commentary on Ephesians*, 251; O'Brien, *The Letter to the Ephesians*, 191.

[847] Abbott, *A Critical and Exegetical Commentary on the Epistles to the Ephesians and to the Colossians*, 61.

one made of lead to form gold.⁸⁴⁸ Before they were drawn to Christ, the relationship between the groups was one of animosity. Lenski describes the situation:

> The Jews utterly despised the goyim or Gentiles; they considered them dogs, vile, unclean (Matthew 15:27; Revelation 22:15). One must know the status of dogs in the Orient. This attitude toward Gentiles is reflected in many New Testament passages and flashes forth in shocking language in rabbinical literature. The Gentiles reciprocated in kind and hated the Jews because of their arrogance, their scornful separatism, their peculiar religious laws and ways. The enmity was mutual. The world of men was actually divided into two classes, Jews and Gentiles; there was a gulf between them so deep and wide that it seemed impossible ever to close it ... Uncompromising rabbis spoke derogatorily even of the proselytes.⁸⁴⁹

The intense hostility and dislike that existed between the Jews and Gentiles resulted in the formation of a barrier that kept them apart. However, through Christ's death, the barrier that made the realization of peace impossible has been brought down. As a result, the two groups have been transformed into one entity in the eyes of God.⁸⁵⁰ The wall existed in the form of ceremonial laws. Jews and Gentiles were at enmity with each other, but after the divisive law had been taken out, there was nothing to keep these two parts of humanity apart.⁸⁵¹

---

[848] Ibid.

[849] R. C. H Lenski, *The Interpretation of St. Paul's Epistles to the Galatians, to the Ephesians and to the Philippians* (Columbus, O.: Lutheran Book Concern, 1937), 440.

[850] Anders, *Galatians-Colossians*, 8:114.

[851] As opposed to *anēr*, which mainly refers to a masculine being, *anthrōpos* has been used to suggest "man" in a collective sense. The inclusive nature of the word is remarkable as it speaks of the "new" formation, that is, *eis hena kainon anthrōpon*,

In verse 16, the elusiveness of peace among humankind without a relationship with God comes to the fore. Each of the separate divides was in the past as a result of their sinfulness estranged from God (vv. 1–3).[852] As such, peace with God was a necessity for both.[853] The Jews, to be specific, had a law that stood not only between them and Gentiles but with God too.[854] Therefore, since sin controlled both the two groups, none of them needed to join the other.[855] There was a need for reconciliation with God, which Christ's death accomplished. Paul refers to the removal of animosity among them and with God as "putting to death that hostility." Robinson states that "Christ in his death was slain, but the slain was a slayer too."[856]

The other step taken by Christ was to ensure peaceful coexistence between the Jews and Gentiles, and humanity was his preaching of peace. Christ might not have done all the preaching in person but through His apostles and others sent by Him with the help of the Holy Spirit following His vicarious death (Matthew 28:20, Luke 10:16, John 13:2).[857] However, even as human agencies did the preaching, Christ was the one doing the evangelism.[858] In His proclamation, He declared as a King the termination of enmity between the two groups

---

"new humanity," "one new humanity" (C.f. Ephesians 4:24) which brings together both men and women (Kenneth Wuest, *Wuest's Word Studies from the Greek New Testament: For the English Reader*, vol. 4 (Grand Rapids: Eerdmans, 1997), 76).

[852] O'Brien, *The Letter to the Ephesians*, 203; C.f. Markus Barth, *The People of God* (Sheffield: JSOT Press, 1983), 45–72.

[853] O'Brien, *The Letter to the Ephesians*, 203.

[854] Ibid., 203.

[855] Bruce Fong, "Addressing the Issue of Racial Reconciliation According to the Principles of Eph 2:11–22," *JETS* 38 (1995): 565–580.

[856] Joseph Robinson, *St. Paul's Epistle to the Ephesians: Translation and Exposition*, 2nd ed. (Macmillan and Co., 1907), 65.

[857] Karl Sandnes, *Paul—One of the Prophets? A Contribution to the Apostle's Self-Understanding* (Tübingen: J. C. Mohr [Paul Siebeck], 1991), 229; Abbott, *A Critical and Exegetical Commentary on the Epistles to the Ephesians and to the Colossians*, 67; Jamieson, Fausset, and Brown, *Commentary Critical and Explanatory on the Whole Bible*, 2:346.

[858] Rudolf Schnackenburg. *Epistle to the Ephesians: A Commentary*, trans. Helen Heron (Edinburgh: T&T Clark, 1991), 118.

following the laying down of His life on the cross and victory.[859] As Foulkes puts it, "through his cross peace was made, and he through his church takes out the message of reconciliation and peace to the world [cf. Acts 10:36, 2 Corinthians 5:18–20]."[860] The verse seems to echo what Yahweh had said through prophet Isaiah that time would come when He would pronounce, "Peace, peace, to the far and to the near."[861] The point presented by the apostle Paul in quoting Isaiah 57:19 is that the Messiah would mediate peace between the Jewish ("those who were near") and Gentile (those "who were far off") people.[862]

5.4.3.3 A Common Descent: One Father (v. 18)

The other important feature of the family presented in Ephesians is that its members have been fathered by one person whom they are free to approach without restrictions. Fee contends that the phrase *both of us* ought to be understood not as "we both alike have access" but as "we both together have access."[863] He continues to say that "Jew and Gentile stand together as one people in God's presence with old distinctions no longer having significance."[864] In other words, together as "one new humanity," they can approach God and refer to Him confidently as Father.[865] No one encroaches upon their inborn right to access Him. The ongoing "relationship" between the two groups with the Father is the consequence of what Christ has done.[866] Chukwu underscores this point as he says that "the church

---

[859] O'Brien, *The Letter to the Ephesians*, 207, 208.
[860] Foulkes, *Ephesians: An Introduction and Commentary*, 10:92.
[861] Is 57:19; C.f. 52:7.
[862] Anders, *Galatians, Ephesians, Philippians & Colossians*, 8:114.
[863] Gordon Fee, *God's Empowering Presence: The Holy Spirit in the Letters of Paul* (Peabody, Mass., 1994), 684.
[864] Ibid.
[865] O'Brien, *The Letter to the Ephesians*, 209.
[866] Ibid., 208–209.

is a community of believers bound together in God by faith in Jesus Christ, through the Holy Spirit."[867]

The relationship enjoyed with the Father within the church family presented by Paul is tight rather than remote. The use of the preposition *pros* in the word *prosagōgēn* brings this fact to the fore.[868] According to O'Brien, in the OT dispensation, the word drew attention to a time when there would be no prohibition of entrance "into the sanctuary as the place of God's presence."[869] At that time, Gentiles would be allowed to go before God to speak to Him as they show reverence and adoration in His house of worship.[870] As rightly conveyed by Lincoln, in the NT dispensation, this access "is not confined to a specific locality such as a temple."[871]

The diversity of the Godhead as a feature, which is prominent in verse 18, establishes further the point about accessibility to God as it rules out human mediation. According to Jamieson, Fausset, and Brown, this is "fatal to the theory of sacerdotal priests in the Gospel through whom alone the people can approach God. All alike, people and ministers, can draw nigh to God through Christ, their ever living Priest."[872] O'Brien points out the connection between the various players as he says that "in this passage also Paul speaks of salvation in trinitarian terms: Christ's peacemaking work has provided access to the Father for both Jews and Gentiles through the one Spirit."[873] Bratcher and Nida describe the part played by each when they say

---

[867] Chukwu, *The Church as the Extended Family of God: Toward a New Direction for African Ecclesiology*, 19.

[868] There is a view that the Apostle's use of *prosagōgēn* figuratively could have been informed by the religious rite of presenting gifts in the temple to be able to appear before God in the Levitical system (C.f. Leviticus 1:3; 3:3; 4:14).[O'Brien, *The Letter to the Ephesians*, 209].

[869] O'Brien, *The Letter to the Ephesians*, 209.

[870] 1 Kgs 8:41–43; C.f. Is 56:6–8; Zec 8:20–23; C.f. Heb 4:16; 7:25; 10:22; 12:22).

[871] Andrew Lincoln, *Word Biblical Commentary*, vol. 42: Ephesians. ed. Ralph Martin (Dallas, Texas: Thomas Nelson, 1990), 149.

[872] Jamieson, Fausset, and Brown, *Commentary Critical and Explanatory on the Whole Bible*, 2:346.

[873] O'Brien, *The Letter to the Ephesians*, 210.

that "Christ provides the means for the access of humanity to God, and the Holy Spirit is the manner, or the circumstances, in which the right of access is exercised."[874] They argue further that this "access" has to do with "our right to enter God's presence in prayer and worship, confident that he will receive us and answer us [3:12]; it does not mean to enter his presence in heaven after death."[875] As Beare (cited by Bratcher and Nida) puts it, the Father is King, and only eligible people are allowed to approach Him.[876]

5.4.3.4 All at Home (v. 19)

The kind of family proposed by Paul is one that attracts homely feelings. No one feels unwanted, unimportant, or even a liability to the family. Instead, each person enjoys the security, protection, care, sympathy, kindness, and support that other members accord them. They experience the warmth associated with a home environment. Furthermore, they enjoy the freedom of expression and participate freely in making their home better for all of them rather than the selected few. This state finds resonance with the African worldview. Within the context of family, life in Africa finds its worth and safeguard, as it is a setting where people feel at home and shoulder one another's burdens.[877]

In their former state, the Gentiles lacked positive qualities as they were mere "strangers and aliens" (v. 19; c.f. v. 12); but since they believed in Christ, their statuses radically changed from being outsiders to insiders.[878] As O'Brien puts it, "they now have a privileged

---

[874] Bratcher and Nida, *A Handbook on Paul's Letter to the Ephesians*, 60.
[875] Ibid.
[876] Ibid.
[877] Elizabeth Ezeweke and Anthony Ikechukwu, "The Family, Justice and the Culture of Life: Afro – Christian Perspectives," *AFRREV IJAH. An International Journal of Arts and Humanities* 1, no. 2 (May 2012): 30.
[878] They have moved from being *xenoi* which as an adjective means "unknown," "unfamiliar" (Acts 17:18; Hebrews 13:9, Ephesians 2:12); and as a noun "stranger," and "foreigner" (Matthew 25:35, 38, 43–44; 27:7; Acts 17:21; Ephesians 2:19; Hebrews 11:13), that is someone coming from a different "tribe or country," and

place in God's new community ... Now they belong in a way they never did before."[879] They have a place to call home and are enjoying full citizenship in their land.[880] Lloyd-Jones says, "We no longer live on a passport, but ... we really have our birth certificates ... we really do belong."[881] Stott articulates the idea as follows:

> To this new international God-ruled community, which had replaced the Old Testament national theocracy, Gentiles and Jews belonged on equal terms ... The words no longer strangers and sojourners but ... citizens emphasise the contrast between the rootlessness of a life outside Christ and the stability of being a part of God's new society.[882]

There are divergent views on the saints Gentile believers share citizenship with. However, as pointed out by Abbott, it describes "membership of the spiritual commonwealth to which Jewish and Gentile Christians alike belong."[883] *Tōn hagiōn*, as used by Paul, encompasses all who believe in God or Christ as opposed to its previous exclusive use to refer to the Jewish people.[884] The message conveyed by the phrase *citizens with the saints* is that there are citizens

---

even a mere traveller (Abbott, *A Critical and Exegetical Commentary on the Epistles to the Ephesians and to the Colossians*, 68; O'Brien, *The Letter to the Ephesians*, 211; Lenski, *The Interpretation of St. Paul's Epistles to the Galatians, to the Ephesians and to the Philippians*, 449). They are also not the πάροικοι, "aliens" anymore (Acts 7:6, 29; 1 Pt 2:11; Eph 2:19).

[879] O'Brien, *The Letter to the Ephesians*, 210, 211.
[880] Lincoln, *Word Biblical Commentary*, 42: Ephesians: 150.
[881] David Lloyd-Jones, *God's Way of Reconciliation: Studies in Eph. 2* (Evangelical Press, 1972), 302.
[882] Stott, *God's New Society: The Message of Ephesians*, 105.
[883] Abbott, *A Critical and Exegetical Commentary on the Epistles to the Ephesians and to the Colossians*, 69).
[884] Going by what *hagioi* means in the rest of the epistle to the Ephesians, everyone who believes is in the mind of Paul, for instance, Ephesians 1:1; 4:12; 5:3; 6:18 (Best, *A Critical and Exegetical Commentary on Ephesians*, 278). *Tōn hagiōn* is to be understood in light of belief in God and does not suggest an individual "holiness."

who came before Paul's Gentile audience whom they are now joining.⁸⁸⁵ These are they who "first hoped in Christ" (Ephesians 1:12).⁸⁸⁶ As O'Brien puts it, "These Gentile Christians now have a homeland or commonwealth. They 'belong' as fellow-citizens with the rest of believers in that heavenly commonwealth ruled by God."⁸⁸⁷

The phrase *citizens with the saints* connects past generations of Christians with the present and future. The would-be believers would form the future.⁸⁸⁸ Christians are part of a vast community. In that community, there is a recognition of the part played by "spiritual ancestors," some of whom are Hebrews and some Christians, as they left us with what to emulate.⁸⁸⁹ These great men and women are in the scripture referred to as "witnesses that surround us" (Hebrews 12:1) and are mentioned by their names (Hebrews 11).⁸⁹⁰ However, biblical ancestors are not the only ancestors, as there are others locally.⁸⁹¹

The status of the believers of Gentile background, however, surpasses mere citizenship, for they have become "members of the household of God." Towner enlightens that in the Roman economy during the times of Paul, being a "member of a household meant refuge and protection, at least as much as the master was able to provide. It also meant identity and gave the security that comes with a sense of belonging."⁸⁹² In the words of Best, "Gentile Christians, once refugees, are now neither homeless nor stateless … Those who

---

(Best, *A Critical and Exegetical Commentary on Ephesians*, 278; Abbott, *A Critical and Exegetical Commentary on the Epistles to the Ephesians and to the Colossians*, 69).
⁸⁸⁵ Frederick Bruce, *The New International Commentary on the New Testament: The Epistles to the Colossians, to Philemon and to the Ephesians* (Grand Rapids, Mich: Wm. B. Eerdmans Publishing Co., 1984), 302–303.
⁸⁸⁶ Ibid.
⁸⁸⁷ O'Brien, *The Letter to the Ephesians*, 211.
⁸⁸⁸ Kunhiyop, *African Christian Theology*, 146.
⁸⁸⁹ Ibid.
⁸⁹⁰ Ibid.
⁸⁹¹ Ibid.
⁸⁹² Philip Towner, "Households and Household Codes," *Dictionary of Paul and His Letters* (Downers Grove, Illinois; Leicester, England: InterVarsity Press, 1993), 417–419.

were once outsiders are now insiders."[893] According to O'Brien, they are "children together [with their Jewish counterparts] in God's own family."[894] As McKelvey puts it, Paul saw "the inclusion of non-Jews in the church as the fulfilment of the great promises that in the eschatological age the nations would be graciously accepted by Yahweh in his house."[895] By "household," a more meaningful relationship between believers and God as well as among themselves is brought to the fore.[896] Through their faith in Christ, they have become God's "children" (2 Corinthians 6:18) through adoption (1:5) and can approach God (2:18) who is "the head of the household."[897] *Oikeioi* is a word that suggests a closely knit relationship.[898] As Eadie (quoted by Best) puts it, Gentile believers are not "guests—here to-day and away to-morrow."[899] The term *household* also rules out the perception of servanthood or slavery among believers as they have transitioned into "children and sons," and God is a Father to all of them.[900] They have become a family whose members in the New Testament refer to one another as "brethren" ("brothers and sisters"), which "expresses a close relationship of affection, care and support."[901]

The expression *members of the household of God* defines the

---

[893] Best, *A Critical and Exegetical Commentary on Ephesians*, 278.

[894] O'Brien, *The Letter to the Ephesians*, 211–212.

[895] R.J. McKelvey, *The New Temple: The Church in the New Testament* (Oxford: Oxford University Press, 1969), 111–112.

[896] Foulkes, *Ephesians: An Introduction and Commentary*, 10:93.

[897] Best, *A Critical and Exegetical Commentary on Ephesians*, 278.

[898] Best describes *oikeioi tou Theou* as "the warmer metaphor." Its use as imagery is significant as it brings to fore a more profound sense of belonging (Best, *A Critical and Exegetical Commentary on Ephesians*, 278). The Gentiles constitute the *oikeioi tou Theou* which is another way of saying that they are "the community of the faithful" (Abbott, *A Critical and Exegetical Commentary on the Epistles to the Ephesians and to the Colossians*, 69). As used by Paul, the phrase has a connotation of "kindred" (Ibid.).

[899] Best, *A Critical and Exegetical Commentary on Ephesians*, 279.

[900] Lenski, *The Interpretation of St. Paul's Epistles to the Galatians, to the Ephesians and to the Philippians*, 449–450.

[901] Stott, *God's New Society: The Message of Ephesians*, 106.

relationship expected of Christians. As in other writings of Paul, it tells with clarity how those who believe in God ought to relate among themselves and to "their Heavenly Father."[902] The state, though, is not realizable in the absence of love. "Brotherly love" (Philadelphia) ought to be a feature among the people of God.[903]

5.4.3.5 Subscription to Common Principles (vv. 20–22)

For a community to be functional, there must be a specific way of perceiving issues and acting shared by its people, the failure of which results in all manner of problems among its members. Lonergan's description is invaluable here:

> Community is not just an aggregate of individuals within a frontier, for that overlooks [sic] its formal constituent, which is common meaning. Such common meaning calls for a common field of experience and, when that is lacking, people get out of touch. It calls for common or complementary ways of understanding and, when they are lacking, people begin to misunderstand, to distrust, to suspect, to fear, to resort to violence. It calls for common judgment and, when they are lacking, people reside in different worlds. It calls for common values, goals, policies and, when they are lacking, people operate at cross-purposes … As common meaning constitutes community, so divergent meanings divides [sic] it … Finally, the divided community, their conflicting actions, and the messy situation are headed for disaster. For the messy situation is diagnosed differently by the divided community; action is ever more at cross-purposes; and the situation becomes still messier to provoke

---

[902] O'Brien, *The Letter to the Ephesians*, 212; Stott, *God's New Society: The Message of Ephesians*, 105.
[903] Stott, *God's New Society: The Message of Ephesians*, 106.

still sharper differences in diagnosis and policy, more radical criticism of one another's actions, and an ever deeper [*sic*] crisis in the situation.[904]

The principles that govern the Ephesian church family are those that were bequeathed by the past generations of believers. These values constitute the norm every member endeavors to adhere to so that they can be "the temple of the Lord." Besides determining conduct, they also inform life in various ways. The principles are part of what makes them into the kind of family that they are. In verse 20, Paul presents what McKelvey refers to as "the bedrock of historic Christianity."[905] As O'Brien puts it, "They [believers] have the right foundation. None may question their membership in God's new community."[906] The twelve or fourteen apostles (inclusive of Paul and Barnabas) spoken of constitute the "foundation" probably not just because they joined the church before anyone else but mainly because it was on account of their efforts of disseminating the Gospel following the event of the "resurrection" that "the church" expanded and received its form.[907] God also revealed his will for his church to the prophets for dissemination. The declaration made in this section that Gentile believers are "built upon the foundation of the apostles and prophets" speaks of their belonging in the community of believers grounded firmly upon established teachings stemming from what God has made known.[908] Christ plays the role of a "cornerstone."[909] Bratcher and Nida say that "Christ is called the most important stone

---

[904] Lonergan, *Method in Theology*, 356–357, 358.
[905] McKelvey, *The New Temple: The Church in the New Testament*, 113.
[906] O'Brien, *The Letter to the Ephesians*, 216.
[907] Best, *A Critical and Exegetical Commentary on Ephesians*, 282.
[908] McKelvey, *The New Temple: The Church in the New Testament*, 113.
[909] In the oriental perspective, a greater significance is attached to the "cornerstone" in comparison to the "foundation" (2 Peter 2:6; C.f. Psalm 118:22; Acts 4:11; Matthew 21:42). (Abbott, *A Critical and Exegetical Commentary on the Epistles to the Ephesians and to the Colossians*, 71). It is through Christ that the entire building with its parts stays joined as per ὄντος ἀκρογωνιαίου αὐτοῦ χριστοῦ Ἰησοῦ, "Christ Jesus himself as the cornerstone" (Ibid).

in the building, the one that provides cohesion and support for the whole structure."⁹¹⁰ To highlight the significance of the metaphor of "cornerstone," Foulkes states that "it denotes primarily the honour of his position in the building, but then also the way in which each stone is fitted into him, and finds its true place and usefulness only in relation to him [c.f. Colossians 2:7, 1 Peter 2:4–5]."⁹¹¹ The building takes place from what God has disclosed "in Christ," as "apostles and prophets" expound "the mystery" the Spirit of God has revealed (3:4–11).⁹¹²

The relationship with Christ is a significant factor as the church strives to be the ideal family, for it is through him as the "the cornerstone" that the joining of building stones with one another takes place. Best observes that "perhaps it is that believers are shaped, smoothed and joined together by their relation to Christ whom they are to resemble [2 Corinthians 3:18, Philippians 3:21]."⁹¹³ Christians, in many cases, are, in reality, not in tune with one another; and as such, *synarmologoumenē* (being fitly joined together) as a present tense presents an ideal that the church strives to achieve (Ephesians 4:25).⁹¹⁴ Best argues that *auxei* (grows) as a present tense "suggests that not all the stones have yet been built in; believers are added daily to the church and the growth is extensive in numbers rather than intensive in love."⁹¹⁵ Foulkes describes the process further as he says that "the work is developing; the Church cannot be described as a complete edifice until the final day of the Lord comes [cf. Revelation 21]. It is growing towards what it is intended to be in the purpose of

---

⁹¹⁰ Bratcher and Nida, *A Handbook on Paul's Letter to the Ephesians*, 63.
⁹¹¹ Foulkes, *Ephesians: An Introduction and Commentary*, 10:94.
⁹¹² O'Brien, *The Letter to the Ephesians*, 218.
⁹¹³ Best, *A Critical and Exegetical Commentary on Ephesians*, 279, 287.
⁹¹⁴ Ibid.
⁹¹⁵ Ibid., 287.

God."⁹¹⁶ The building grows into *naon hagion en Kyriō* (a holy temple [sanctuary] in the Lord).⁹¹⁷

According to the final verse of this passage, the materials used in the construction of God's new "community" are Christians of whom Gentile believers are part of.⁹¹⁸ God brings individuals who believe in Him together with one another and forms them into an entity He indwells by way of His Spirit.⁹¹⁹ Best conveys this idea when he says that "if unbelievers point to their temples as the places where their gods live and ask Christians where theirs are to be found they can respond by saying that God dwells in their community. It is true he may also dwell in individuals and local house churches but the emphasis here is on his dwelling in the community as a whole."⁹²⁰ However, God does not wait for the completion of the building before coming to dwell in it. He does so in its advancing stage.⁹²¹ It is His dwelling in the temple that gives it its characteristic of "holiness."⁹²² Foulkes points out that as far as Paul is concerned, "the community of Christians" is the "temple" or "one organism indwelt by the living Christ."(2 Corinthians 6:16).⁹²³

5.5 A Comparative Analysis of the Concept of Jo-kang'ato and the Scripture

In this work, there has been an endeavor to create an understanding of Christian unity in the ecclesial life of the church in Africa by looking at it comparatively. The approach enabled the dissection of culture and decipherment of selected passages to take place, and

---

⁹¹⁶ Foulkes, *Ephesians: An Introduction and Commentary*, 10:95.
⁹¹⁷ Abbott, *A Critical and Exegetical Commentary on the Epistles to the Ephesians and to the Colossians*, 73.
⁹¹⁸ Best, *A Critical and Exegetical Commentary on Ephesians*, 288.
⁹¹⁹ Ibid., 289–290; 1 Pt 2:4; Rom 12:1; 1 Pt 2:5; Heb 13:15.
⁹²⁰ Best, *A Critical and Exegetical Commentary on Ephesians*, 288.
⁹²¹ O'Brien, *The Letter to the Ephesians*, 219.
⁹²² Ibid.
⁹²³ Foulkes, *Ephesians: An Introduction and Commentary* 10:96.

points of contact between the concept of jo-kang'ato and the scripture were identified. As a result, a new understanding of Christian unity emerged. Moltmann captures the importance of this approach in his argument on the process of doing theology as follows:

> Theology is like a network of rivers, with reciprocal influences and mutual challenges. It is certainly not a desert in which every individual is alone with himself or herself, and with his or her God ... It is communitarian and cooperative. *Theologia viatorum*—the theology of men and women on the way—is an enduring critical conversation with the generations before us and the contemporaries at our side, in expectation of those who will come after us.[924]

Nyamiti points out some of the strengths of the approach as follows: "It will ... awaken dormant themes in the sources of revelation ... Lastly, it will integrate into theology all the theological values in African cultural and religious heritage."[925] However, while it is legitimate to use ideas drawn from the culture and religion of the African people to formulate theology, there is a caveat: only cultural elements that are in harmony with the Christian faith and promise to be a source of enrichment are to be considered and employed. As Nyamiti puts it, "the superstitious or erroneous elements will have to be eliminated."[926] Syncretism, which is an erosion of Christian teachings, sets in when theologians remove this caveat.

A great level of caution was exercised in this work to ensure that only the concepts that deepen understanding in Christian unity

---

[924] Jürgen Moltmann, *Experiences in Theology: Ways and Forms of Christian Theology* (London: SCM Press, 2000), xvii.
[925] Nyamiti, *African Theology: Its Nature, Problems and Methods*, 24.
[926] Ibid.; C.f. Charles Nyamiti, *The Way to Christian Theology in Africa* (Eldoret, Kenya: Gaba Publication, n.d.), 55.

are accommodated.⁹²⁷ The scripture provided the rationale for that cautious approach. The move follows Newbigin's proposition for the interrogation of culture and an appreciation of the fact that God does not foolishly approve all aspects of culture.⁹²⁸ Ukpong (as quoted by Nkansah-Obrempong) articulates:

> The theologian's task consists in re-thinking and re-expressing the original Christian message in an African cultural milieu. It is the task of confronting the Christian faith and African culture. In this process there is inter-penetration of both ... There is integration of faith and culture and from it is born a new theological expression that is African and Christian.⁹²⁹

In this study, a comparison between the concept of jo-kang'ato among the Luo and Christian unity was undertaken. This was followed by the application of the biblical text as a model and objective standard. The endeavor aimed to aid an understanding and enhancement of ecclesial unity through the points of contact not only among Christian believers of Luo origin but also the church in Africa as a whole.

A comparison has been undertaken to find out if the values found in the Luos' concept of jo-kang'ato correspond to the ecclesial relationship presented in the passages of the scripture studied. This exercise was an attempt to enhance the understanding of Christian

---

⁹²⁷ John Dadosky, "Methodological Presuppositions for Engaging the Other in the Post-Vatican II Context: Insights from Ignatius and Lonergan," *JIRD: A forum for Academic, Social, and Timely Issues Affecting Religious Communities Around the World*, 2010, http://irdialogue.org/wp-content/uploads/2010/03/JIRD-3-Dadosky.pdf.

⁹²⁸ Lesslie Newbigin, *The Gospel in a Pluralist Society* (Grand Rapids, Michigan: Eerdmans, 1989), 191, 185; C.f. Idowu, *African Traditional Religion: A Definition*, 106.

⁹²⁹ Nkansah-Obrempong, *Visual Theology: Some Akan Cultural Symbols, Metaphors, Proverbs, Myths, and Symbols and Their Implications for Doing Christian Theology*, 49.

unity in the ecclesial life of the church in Africa. Through this exercise, it has been established that there are indeed values in the Luos' concept of jo-kangato that spur positive relationships. These values corroborate biblical principles on healthy Christian relationships and contribute to a more enriched understanding of ecclesial unity.

In the first place, the interdependence among members comes to the fore in each case. According to Markus and Kitayama, people see themselves either as "independent" or "interdependent" of others. While the former is "egocentric, separate, autonomous, idiocentric [sic], and self-contained," in the latter case, people are "sociocentric [sic], holistic, collective, allocentric [sic], ensembled [sic], constitutive, contextualist [sic], and relational."[930] Interdependence among members is demonstrated in the passages of the scripture studied in this book. In the intra-Trinitarian relationship, for instance, each person in the Godhead shows dependence upon one another.[931] A similar idea runs through the body metaphor, which shows that each part needs the contribution of other parts for its well-being.[932] The familial metaphor follows the same trend as it presents members in their diversities as building blocks brought together by the "cornerstone" and built into the temple of God.[933] The strength of the group comes out as members complement one another.[934] However, the input of each member has to be taken seriously and valued; for while such contributions may appear minimal in the eyes of those who feel independent, in their absence, the success of the entire body is jeopardized since no one else could be available to offer the same kind of contribution to the body. Each member exists for a particular reason and by design. The concept of jo-kang'ato too militates against independence, which is a

---

[930] Hazel Markus and Shinobu Kitayama, "Culture and the Self: Implications for Cognition, Emotion, and Motivation," *Psychological Review* 98, no. 2 (April 1991): 226–227.
[931] Jn 17:20–23.
[932] 1 Cor 12:20–22.
[933] Eph 2:20–22.
[934] 1 Cor 12:17–19.

feature of individualism. It shows dependence upon one another for the well-being of the entire society and each member. Since members need one another, segregationist tendencies are discouraged, and they stand or fall together. Interdependence encapsulates the unity-enhancing values in both cases.

The other point of contact is that the behavior displayed by members toward one another plays a pivotal role as it determines the kind of relationship that could be expected among members. Behavior generates perception in members upon whom such has been shown. Reactions and responses are then emitted, which either jeopardize or foster the relationship. Adverse reactions occur whenever people are not treated well. In the Corinthian church, for instance, there was disenchantment among vulnerable members.[935]

Additionally, solidarity among members is an aspect found in the relationship prescribed in both the scripture and the concept of jo-kang'ato. Solidarity comes to the fore in the form of acts of charity and support of various kinds in times of need. The egalitarian activities are performed to ensure that no one faces his or her struggles alone. In both cases, acts of kindness are extended in times of joy too. Among the Luo, for instance, this manifests during wedding celebrations, childbirth, victory parties, etc. There is a resonance with Paul's words: "If one part suffers, every part suffers with it; if one part is honoured, every part rejoices with it."[936] The duty of care is shown through sensitivity to the needs of one another, especially the underprivileged who are also bona fide members despite their socioeconomic status. This approach to relationship is devoid of partial treatment. Members share the plight or success of one another.

There is a sense of belonging in both cases. Since every person participates in the group's life, they are satisfied and fulfilled by their contribution toward its success. The homely overtones that run through them, are attested to by the fact that each member feels wanted, valued, and an asset. None of them experiences indifference

---

[935] 1 Cor 12:15–16.
[936] 1 Cor 12:26.

or feel insecure, vulnerable, or uncared for; none feel unkindness, hostility, and neglect since they are all insiders. Instead, they feel accepted and enjoy the connection existing among them.[937] The roles played by every one of them toward the well-being of the home are recognized and appreciated. Selfish and individualistic approaches to relationships manifesting in factionalism and the creation of impediments for others are discouraged as they result in disenchantment and withdrawal of the offended and affect success.[938] Since all members are on par, nobody is belittled. Monism and hierarchies are not tolerated either.

Furthermore, in both cases, blood brings people together. Among the jo-kang'ato, this comes into play through a common descent whereby all the members share an ancestor. Likewise, Christians have a Father whom they all share, and the blood of the Lord Jesus Christ brings all of them closer to one another, their socioeconomic background notwithstanding.[939] The consciousness of the blood factor results in the realization of peace among members as it takes away animosity and obstacles to fellowship, which often arise from mismanaged diversities (Ephesians 2:14–17).[940]

In both settings, members can reconcile when their peace comes under threat because they are aware of what brings them together. The bond that exists between them supersedes any difference that could arise, thus making it possible for misunderstandings to be sorted out. One of the Luo sayings that strengthen this approach to relationship is "Remo pek moloyo pi," meaning "When compared to water, blood is thicker," which implies that a person's kin would stand with him or her (even when they have not been in good terms) when all others desert them. The other one is "Aoch wat ilorie mos" which means "Kinship is a river that people are to approach with care." The implication is that one should refrain from inflicting harm on his or her kin no matter how annoyed, irritated, or offended they could be.

---

[937] Eph 2:12–13.
[938] 1 Cor 12:14–16.
[939] Eph 2:18, 13.
[940] Eph 2:14–17.

The importance of kinship is also captured in the saying "Wat imedo gi osiep [Friendship fortifies kinship]."[941]

Moreover, diversity is recognized and tolerated in both realms. However, it is appreciated that failure to handle it properly incurs a curse rather than a blessing to the group as it causes polarity and rivalry. In the church setting, the proper way of handling multiplicity is an appreciation of its nonhomogeneous and inclusive nature as it is made up of people drawn from various backgrounds. The perfect pattern is provided by the Godhead who indwell one another, yet each one of them keeps His uniqueness. While such diversities exist, they are superseded by things shared in common. The church in Corinth, for instance, shared the baptism by the Holy Spirit, whom they also drank.[942] The appreciation of this fact results in the accommodation of all.

Furthermore, there are common principles that members subscribe to in both cases. These principles are those that were handed over to them by their ancestors. Among the Luo of Kenya, these are in the form of customs, which exist to regulate life and conduct. Besides, the contributions of ancestors in the past are recognized, and their lives are recommended as examples to the living. The latter would also pass a heritage to their posterity in the future. Among Christians, the principles are embedded in the scripture handed down by past generations of believers through the proclamation of God's Word.[943] While Christians are to emulate the Godhead in conduct and embrace one another in unity, human examples have also been provided to them.[944]

The other features that are common in both cases are teamwork and cooperation. These values bring members in both settings together and make it possible for them to carry out the group's activities successfully. Incorporation and integration are the other

---

[941] Cohen and Odhiambo, *Siaya: The Historical Anthropology of an African Landscape*, 124.
[942] 1 Cor 12:13.
[943] Jn 17:20; Eph 2:20.
[944] Jn 17:21–22; Eph 2:19.

features that are shared. As the potentials of the new members are unleashed, as a result of meaningful incorporation and integration, growth is experienced, and strength is gained within the group. Selflessness also comes out as an essential virtue toward the realization of unity among the people in both settings. One of its products is sound leadership, which is devoid of greed, egocentrism, imposition, corruption, dictatorship, partiality, discrimination, etc.

Conclusion

While the validity of the age-long ecclesial models of family and community is beyond question, revamping them to adequately clarify Christian unity in the ecclesial life of the church in Africa is necessary. Until this is done, the models will continue to be incapacitated and fail to meet the specifications of the scripture on the kind of relationship expected of Christians. The passages of the scripture studied above have presented a nonstatic family with strong ties: intimate and all-encompassing, diverse yet closely attached. Each member feels wanted and accepted and as an asset allowed to participate fully in the life of the family no matter their weaknesses. Members need and relish the input of one another, mind one another's business, and are warm and friendly toward one another. Members of this community also enjoy a harmonious existence mediated by Christ and unhindered by diversity. The sibling relationship is based on God's spiritual Fatherhood for all of them and the bond of love created by the blood of Christ. Relationship with the Father and with Christ translates into unity among them, not just in a given locality and generation; they are connected to those who went before them and those who would follow them by some age-long principles. All these qualities reside in the Luos' concept of jo-kang'ato.

The ideals found in the concept of jo-kang'ato are not just superior to those provided by the understanding of the family and community within the Western context; they are compatible with the relationship prescribed in the passages of the scripture already studied. Both jo-kang'ato and the passages studied in this section approach relationships in a way that produces bonding, acceptance of one another, a sense of belonging, respect, and involvement.[945] Their other common characteristic is sensitivity to the needs of others and provision of support to those beset by life's challenges as opposed to numbness to their interests. There is also the ability to socialize and an experience of harmony.[946] Besides, in both realities, openness, as opposed to suspicion, is encouraged; selfishness and marginalization as an attendant is removed as they seek the good of all despite their socioeconomic background, and discourage unfairness and partiality among members.[947] The concept could overcome the problem of individualism in the ecclesial models of family and community through its collectivism, which advocates for interdependence among people. On these grounds, it has emerged that the concept of jo-kang'ato could enhance the understanding of Christian unity in the ecclesial life of the church.

---

[945] Uichol Kim, Individualism and Collectivism: A Psychological, Cultural and Ecological Analysis: Nordic Institute of Asian Studies Report Series 21 (Copenhagen:NIAS Press, 1995), 5.
[946] Ibid.
[947] Ibid.

CHAPTER 6

The Implications of the Concept of Jo-kang'ato for Christian Unity in the Ecclesial Life of the Church

The implication of this study to theory is that Christians at all ecclesial levels will be wary of the symbols of behavior emitted toward one another as these could be processed and cause either a good or bad relationship.[948] In the worst-case scenario, enmity would be created as a reaction to actual or perceived offenses. This state would deepen further into disunity. On the other hand, sensible behavior creates a friendly atmosphere where unity can thrive and be sustained. The concept of jo-kang'ato presents symbols that enhance unity as those prescribed by the scripture.

Implications for practice were also drawn from the study, which could shape the understanding of Christian unity in the ecclesial life of the church in Africa. To begin with, the concept of jo-kang'ato challenges us to critique the theology of the church as presented by the West and come up with a different type of leadership "structure," which enhances unity in the church. That kind of structure would allow the laity to participate in the running

---

[948] Ottah, "African Culture and Communication Systems in the Coronation of Ata Igala, North Central Nigeria," 213.

of the church as leaders meaningfully. Consequently, the church will begin to be a real "polycentric community" where all believers, being priests, are accorded the opportunity to contribute toward its well-being as opposed to the divisive "monocentric-bipolar community" inculcated by the Episcopal structure of government where bishops play a dominant role.[949] The lay members would be sensitized in areas of ministry, and they will utilize the charismata bestowed upon them in a "pluriform service" as they participate in the life of the church with the supervision of those who are in leadership positions and "rules" to guard against "pneumatic anarchy."[950] The hierarchical leadership structure is part of the factors that contribute to disunity in churches, hence the need for a different structure that is embracive. As a relational concept, jo-kang'ato encourages listening to one another. Chukwu says that "a church structure and leadership that do not listen to the voices of its members contradicts the image of the church as the family of God."[951] He adds as follows:

> Authority and leadership cannot be restricted to the bishops and priests … The lay faithful are members of the Church; as such, they comprise the Church as much as do bishops and priests … they must play significant roles in the Church … The ancient maxim "Whatever concerns all must be discussed by all" is applicable in this situation … The Church cannot truly be the family of God if most of its members are

---

[949] Dulles, *The Catholicity of the Church*, 126; Welker, *Kirche Im Pluralismus*, 136: 125; Volf, *After Our Likeness: The Church as the Image of the Trinity*, 223–225, 227, 228, 231.

[950] Volf, *After Our Likeness: The Church as the Image of the Trinity*, 226–230, 237–239, 243; Sohm, *Wesen and Ursprung Des Katholizismus*, 54; Brunner, *Das Misverstandnis Der Kirche*, 18; Kraus, *Reich Gottes: Reich Der Freiheit*, Grundriss Systematische Theologie, 376; Pirson, "Communio Als Kirchenrechtliches Leitprinzip," 44; 1 Cor. 14:29, 33, 31.

[951] Chukwu, *The Church as the Extended Family of God: Toward a New Direction for African Ecclesiology*, 144; C.f. 150.

not consulted in matters that concern them and given leadership roles.⁹⁵²

The concept of jo-kang'ato also invites us to revisit the place of women in the church and ministry. In theory, women hold an important place; in practice, the premise is not supported. Women continue to be marginalized not just in the secular society but within the church too. In some ecclesial circles, they continue to be treated as lesser beings and denied full and meaningful participation in the leadership of the church.⁹⁵³ The church in Africa could alter this trend as it is not reflective of the unity expected among Christians. Since the Luos' concept of jo-kang'ato stands for tolerance and accommodative behavior, it summons the church to provide space for all, despite their gender, to make their contributions to the ministry and church's life without being discriminated.

The other message that the concept of jo-kang'ato sends is that the time has come for young people to take their place in the affairs of the church, including leadership since the future of the church lies with them. They are to be prepared for the task ahead through the impressions instilled into them by older leaders by way of good examples and mentorship, as has been the case throughout the church's existence.⁹⁵⁴ The church can tap into its youthful members' strength, vitality, and fervour as it forges ahead into the future. However, the preparation for leadership should not be indefinite. At some point, meaningful incorporation into leadership must take place. The church in Africa needs to take this point into account and find a way to connect with the youth to counteract disinterest toward the church and tensions arising from the generational gaps.⁹⁵⁵

The concept of jo-kang'ato also leads to an understanding of the church as a mega family that defies exclusive parochialism generated by negative ethnicity. Christians in Africa could deal with the

---

⁹⁵² Ibid., 146, 147.
⁹⁵³ Ibid., 153.
⁹⁵⁴ 1 Sam 16:10–13; 17:42; Jer 1:6–7.
⁹⁵⁵ Mal 4:6; Mt 11:13–14.

phenomenon by drawing "them" into "us." As rightly pointed out by Nkansah-Obrempong, ethnocentrism is known for its stress on the peculiar features among the people; the consequence is the relegation of other people's humanness and discrimination of them based on their distinct features and ways of doing things.[956] Through negative ethnicity, others are kept away because of tribal or racial backgrounds. While the church is supposed to provide an atmosphere free from ethnocentrism and the disunity accompanying it, in Africa, ethnic-induced fragmentations are its experience. The concept of jo-kang'ato would facilitate the recovery of the experience of the apostolic church, which functioned as a selfless community whose members catered to one another's needs.[957] Chukwu observes that treating one another as siblings "will help build bridges across races and nations, not only in Africa but all over the world."[958]

The study also has implications for the church's dispute resolution mechanism. The disputes arising among Christians are to be approached prayerfully and resolved in a manner that reflects the principles outlined in the scripture. Christ set a criterion in Matthew, which needs to be followed.[959] As we go by this, an impartial mediation and negotiation process undertaken by the leaders of the church—for instance, the clergy or any other person(s) to whom the task is delegated—takes center stage. In some cases, the disputes could be addressed by the higher administrative levels of the church, such as church boards, committees, and councils. Through it all, a dispute is to be dealt with expeditiously to avoid its acceleration to unmanageable levels. Furthermore, the method requires disputes to be confined to minimal levels as much as possible. Attempts at reconciliation could be made within these levels. The church could explore and exhaust its internal dispute resolution mechanism before any of the warring parties resort to law courts for justice and

---

[956] Nkansah-Obrempong, *Foundations for African Theological Ethics*, 249, 255.
[957] Acts 4:32–34.
[958] Chukwu, *The Church as the Extended Family of God: Toward a New Direction for African Ecclesiology*, 188.
[959] Mt 8:15–17.

fairness.⁹⁶⁰ Throughout the process, the spirit of brotherhood must be allowed to permeate. Since Christians have a common Father in God, they would be willing to listen to and understand one another; bear with one another; and confess, forgive, repent, and make amends. An attitude of love is paramount, and it is to be reflected in the entire process, even when correcting erring members or dispensing discipline.

Lastly, the study has implications on ecumenism, for it tells us that Christian unity is not at all costs as it is contingent on subscription to the truth as lodged in the Scripture. As Wilkin puts it, "Many church people think unity at almost any price should be their aim ... Believers are to be united only with those who are morally and doctrinally sound."⁹⁶¹ As presently undertaken, ecumenism condones religious "subjectivism."⁹⁶² Berkhof cautions that "unless it changes colour and strives for greater unity in the truth, it will not be productive of real unity but only of uniformity, and while it may make the Church more efficient from a business point of view, it will not add to the true spiritual efficiency of the Church."⁹⁶³

The concept of jo-kang'ato could be applied in the church context to effectively address areas of disunity, which are primarily theological and socioeconomic. Current contentious issues in the former case include women's ordination and their general involvement in ministry. In the RCC, the main issue is celibacy among the clergy. The treatment of the LGBTQ+ is a matter that cuts across all denominations; whereas some churches discriminate against them or reject them, other churches are clueless on how to address the issue. At the local church level, forms of worship could also be a source of disunity, especially when parishioners insist on having their varying tastes satisfied within a particular congregation. The interpretation

---

⁹⁶⁰ 1 Cor 6:1–7.
⁹⁶¹ Wilkin, "The Gospel According to John," in *The Grace New Testament Commentary*, 460.
⁹⁶² Berkhof, Systematic Theology, 573–574.
⁹⁶³ Ibid., 574.

of the scripture, which has also proven to be a significant point of disunity, is the catalyst of all contentious theological issues. The main socioeconomic areas of disunity include ethnicity, which often turns to ethnocentricism because of a failure to handle it appropriately. Leadership too attracts conflicts among Christians in the church from time to time.

The concept of jo-kang'ato could facilitate listening and tolerance of one another, respect for divergent views, and dialogue over issues that are posing a threat to the universal doctrines of the Christian faith rather than fighting over the same. In terms of worship, church members could talk and agree to adopt forms of liturgy that are in the best interest of the church and are scriptural. The application of the concept in the socioeconomic dimension makes it possible for Christians to transcend their ethnic affiliations and embrace people from different ethnicities. Besides, jo-kang'ato is a panacea for leadership wrangles as it discourages self-centeredness, which leads to this quagmire. Unhealthy jostling for positions could be avoided as people shelve their ambitions for the sake of the church's well-being. To those in leadership positions, the concept fosters servant leadership as it challenges bossiness.

Conclusion

While the concept of jo-kang'ato is laden with connotations of common descent and blood ties, it emphasizes neither clan affiliations nor lineal leanings among Christians, which could turn prejudicial and discriminative. Instead, the concept of jo-kang'ato establishes a bond that brings people together. Their intimate relationship manifests in solidarity with one another, support for people within its circles, and protection of one another. These qualities are not just necessary but demonstrate unity within the ecclesial life of the church in Africa. The concept of jo-kang'ato would bring Christians together and instil a sense of brotherhood in them. However, disputes are to be anticipated before their arrival. When disputes arrive, measures that are already in place can be used to address them amicably. The church, through its leadership team or board, should be proactive enough to make provisions for mitigating such conditions. As such, jo-kang'ato is an appropriate philosophy for defining relationships among Christians in the ecclesial life of the church in Africa.

The relationship among Christians is defined by a bond created through the blood of Jesus Christ. That relationship is free from coldness and conflicts with one another. To regard others as belonging to God as oneself regardless of their denominational affiliations marks the beginning of that condition. In this sense, the concept of jo-kang'ato facilitates the expansion of relationships beyond immediate to advanced levels. In the face of a relationship, which it informs, the roadblocks and boundaries and "walls of partition" of tribalism, racism, nepotism, regionalism, feminism, patriarchalism, clericalism, and denominationalism give way to acceptance, accommodation, toleration, and incorporation. The concept of jo-kang'ato encourages Christians locally and from various denominational spectrums to come together, exploit diversity, and make their contributions to society.

CONCLUSIONS

The problem this study set out to address is the inappropriate understanding of Christian unity in the ecclesial life of the church in Africa. In their current state, the ecclesial models of family and community do not adequately mitigate this problem. To an extent, they even accelerate it through a selective application by denominations and Christians at the local and higher organisational church levels. This faulty understanding could be seen in the structures and perspectives of Christians for one another at different ecclesial levels. The various traditions that have been discussed brought this fact to the fore. It has emerged that the concept of jo-kang'ato among the Luo of Kenya, through its values, addresses the misunderstanding of ecclesial unity by way of enrichment.

To fulfill the primary purpose of this piece of work, I endeavored to find out if there is any relationship between the Luos' concept of jo-kang'ato and the relationship prescribed for Christians in the scripture. Besides, since the concept of jo-kang'ato belongs to the extended family system among the Luo of Kenya and is the mechanism that binds them together with each other, I sought to find out if the Luos' extended family system synchronizes with the relationships presented in the scripture. Besides, there was an effort to ascertain, if any, the points of contact between the Luos' view and practice of community with the type of communal life expected to enhance Christian unity. The premise of this work is that with an improved understanding of unity arising from the concept of jo-kang'ato, the relationship among Christians is enhanced. This purpose was achieved.

In the first place, it has been established that the values embedded in jo-kang'ato correspond to the relationship expected of Christians in the ecclesial life of the church as presented in passages of the scripture subjected to exegeses. The collectivism it advocates for is not only African but also scriptural. It has also emerged that, indeed, synchrony exists between the Luos' extended family system and the familial model of the church offered in the scripture to inform relationships among Christians and help in the realization of unity within the church.

The relationship prescribed for Christians in the scripture is one of an extended nature. The Luos' extended family system injects into the familial model mutual relationship among members, which is a necessity in the realization of Christian unity. It goes beyond and embraces many people, including those who are not related naturally. The study also found that there are points of contact between the Luos' view and practice of community and the type of communal life, which is expected to enhance Christian unity in the ecclesial life of the church. In the Luos' concept of jo-kang'ato, values are embedded, which are an incentive for a constructive relationship. These values strengthen biblical propositions on the ideal Christian relationships and spur an enriched understanding of ecclesial unity.

The Luo culture has been brought into the conversation and interrogated in light of the scripture to find out if it adds anything to the discussion about ecclesial unity. The fidelity of the concept of jo-kang'ato to the scripture has been noted in the process. Indeed, there are points of contact between the concept of jo-kang'ato and the passages of the scripture studied, which aids in the comprehension of the subject under study. Rather than conflicting with the principles of the Christian faith found in divine revelation, it establishes them. The *posteriori* arrived at through the biblical and cultural exegeses undertaken by the researcher is that the concept of jo-kang'ato is fit and valid for use in a theological discussion. It is a legitimate African concept, and its time of integration into theology has come.

The most important feature found in the concept of jo-kang'ato is that it ensures that the familial and communal models are extended to embrace the "other" and their otherness, which could include social and denominational affiliations. This premise contradicts Murdock's view of the family, which emphasizes its exclusive nuclear aspect. Murdock defines the family in terms of a habitat shared by a husband and wife, the presence of children, and collaboration in handling available resources.[964] This study has found this kind of approach wanting because it is exclusive in nature and because it blurs the meaning of family to an African person and hinders the extension of Christian unity. Africans need an inclusive and all-encompassing understanding of family, which incorporates their kin and connects them to the past, present, and future.[965]

The concept of jo-kang'ato is especially appropriate as it extends its scope beyond natural relations to encompass people who would, in most cases, be considered outsiders. It challenges Christians to come out of the cocoons created by individualism and embrace one another. The study affirms Uzukwu, who pointed out one of the demerits of the ecclesial model of family as the wielding of ecclesial power by the clergy and elders while relegating other members of the church.[966] The contributions of such members could equally be valid. The outcome of the domineering approach is disunity and all that goes with it.[967] This study pumps a new breath into the familial and communal models of the church with a meaning that rids them of individualism and its attendant disunity. While the concept of jo-kang'ato could be abused in terms of misappropriation with negative impacts on relationships arising, its potential to address Christian unity in the ecclesial life of the church stands out as it is a concept

---

[964] Murdock, *Social Structure*, 1.
[965] Mbiti, *African Religions and Philosophy*, 104–107.
[966] Uzukwu, *A Listening Church: Autonomy and Communion in African Churches*, 121–122.
[967] Ibid.; Lowery, *Identity and Ecclesiology: Their Relationship Among Select African Theologians*, 163.

that brings people together and creates a strong bond among them as jo-kaYesu (all belonging to Jesus).

I hold the view that Christians in Africa should not be afraid to apply the principles of family and community in their context as a lens to aid the understanding of what is meant by the ecclesial models of family and community. For instance, as in the case of jo-kang'ato—which embraces the past, present, and future generations—John 17:20 presents an element of connection among different Christian dispensations. The same is true with Ephesians 2:19–20. Here, there is a summons to Christians, urging them that as they live together in unity at present (John 17:21–23), they should not sever themselves from Christians in the past generations. Christians in the present are manifestations of an expansion that has occurred in the family of God over time. Though diverse, they are tied to one another by their ancestor par excellence, God the Father, and are to be understood as jo-kang'ato. Members of the Trinity too experience that bond and belonging to one another. They manifest interdependence.[968]

The other common feature is that of a tightly bonded but all-embracing community whose members are brought together by some common factors despite differing features.[969] Every member counts and is indispensable in that community, as in jo-kang'ato.[970] They contribute to the well-being of one another and the community through various means provided by the father. Domination by a single member within the community and segregation are discouraged while interdependence is emphasized.[971] Moreover, members carry one another's burdens, especially of the vulnerable.[972] It resembles the excellent support system, which the concept of jo-kang'ato encourages. Members relate in a cohesive and friendly manner toward one another and play a vital role in the well-being of the body of

---

[968] Jn 17:20–23.
[969] 1 Cor 12:12–13.
[970] 1 Cor 12:14–16.
[971] 1 Cor 12:17–22.
[972] 1 Cor 12:23–24.

Christ.[973] This view affirms Boice's position, which states that when unity is emptied of love, it produces authoritarianism akin to what the hierarchical churches demonstrate in their governance when the clergy dominate and shows disinterest in the parishioners.[974] The clergy in lower echelons of the hierarchy are also victims in the hands of those senior to them, for instance, bishops.[975] Love generates the consciousness of comradeship arising from the shared life among believers, which has its origin in God.[976] Christian love overshadows socioeconomic factors.

The familial overtones in Ephesians 2:12–22 too are African as much as they are scriptural. They include unconditional acceptance amid plurality in membership (vv. 12–13); the absence of unhealthy conflicts and disagreements and hostility toward one another (vv. 14–17); the possibility of members' treatment of one another with respect because they have a common progenitor (v. 18); and a sense of security attributed to the homely experience of each member (v. 19). These features make reconciliation possible whenever there is conflict.

There are also traditions adhered to by all, which bring the past and the present together.[977] This fact reinforces Schaff's view of the church as the custodian of God's Word.[978] Forsyth is also affirmed as he states that the church will always be subservient to the gospel of which it is a product.[979] As such, an obsession with the fellowship of churches at the expense of truth is not deemed necessary.[980] Subscription to the Word rather than the church's

---

[973] 1 Cor 12:25–27.
[974] Boice, *Foundations of the Christian Faith: A Comprehensive & Readable Theology*, 585.
[975] Berkhof, *Systematic Theology*, 572.
[976] Ibid.
[977] Eph 2:20–22.
[978] Graham, *Cosmos in the Chaos: Philip Schaff's Interpretation of Nineteenth-Century American Religion*, 231.
[979] Bloesch, *The Church: Sacraments, Worship, Ministry, Mission*, 43; P.T. Forsyth, *The Church and the Sacraments*, 39.
[980] Forsyth, *The Justification of God*, 38.

volition is the determinant of its unity.[981] Ecumenism, in its current form, suffers from false optimism manifested in an attempt to gather denominations and forge a single ecclesial entity out of them without due regard for this factor.[982] Subscription to the scripture among the churches is a common feature of their unity.[983] The reduction of the significance of the fundamental teachings of the Christian faith as enshrined in the scripture and the refusal of a given church to abide by the principles of the gospel undermines Christian unity and produces a counterfeit version of peace.[984] Rather than retrogressing to church traditions set in the past, God's Word has to be put in its rightful place of superiority.[985]

Generally, the familial and communal relationships presented in the passages of the scripture that were studied are so African that they challenge the usual understanding of those institutions. Christian unity in the ecclesial life of the church ensues from the relationships presented. God is the Father of all Christians. The blood of the Lord Jesus Christ has created a bond between them.

The position taken in this piece of work is that a deeper understanding of Christian unity results in a deeper and more meaningful relationship among Christians. The concept of jo-kang'ato has contributed to that understanding by discouraging the independent and individualistic approaches to relationships. It predicates the well-being of one another and the entire church upon the interdependence among members. To detach oneself from others spells doom, which in the context of this study is disunity. The dispute resolution mechanism, which emanates from the concept, is among its areas of potency as it persuades the conflicting parties to

---

[981] Forsyth, *The Church and the Sacraments*, 39.
[982] Forsyth, *The Justification of God*, 38; Duffield and Van Cleave, *Foundations of Pentecostal Theology*, 423; Forsyth, *The Church and the Sacraments*, 38.
[983] Bloesch, *The Church: Sacraments, Worship, Ministry, Mission*, 100.
[984] Bloesch, *The Church: Sacraments, Worship, Ministry, Mission*, 45, 300; Pope, *A Compendium of Christian Theology: Being Analytical Outlines of a Course of Theological Study, Biblical, Dogmatic, Historical*, 3:272.
[985] Cutsinger ed., *Reclaiming the Great Tradition*.

discuss and resolve their differences among themselves amicably and, if need be, turn to the channels of mediation. While disagreements are probable, the blood ties among them compel them to make peace with one another rather than hold endless grudges.

The concept of jo-kang'ato also spells out a new engagement among denominations whose characteristics are due regard for one another, acceptance, respect, and friendliness amid differing features. These are necessary components of unity. Accountability for one another and support ensue from such kind of interdenominational relationship as opposed to a competitive spirit. Dulles points out the characteristic of that unity as love and support for one another resulting in a friendly relationship.[986] As various denominations realize that they share God as a Father, a positive and constructive ecumenism is experienced. Such kind of ecumenism could be demonstrated through joint worship, fellowship, and ministry rather than by amalgamation and formation of some mega ecclesial entity.

This position contradicts the RCC's official position, which confines the scope of the church exclusively to themselves and suggests that to be united, Christians have to subscribe to it and its bishops and the institution of the papacy headed by the bishop of Rome. The RCC recognizes the pope as the "one ruler of the visible" church and as "the successor of Saint Peter," who bonds them to one another. The understanding of the church in "visible" terms leads the RCC to assert further that it is the only legitimate church on earth which dispenses salvation.[987]

The understanding arising from the concept of jo-kang'ato is that it is the consciousness of a common Father shared by Christians that brings them together. This work applauds Bloesch when he states that an entity becomes part of a church through its confession of Christ as Lord and that this status is not a preserve of a single entity.[988] It is Christ's achievement at the cross, where He died for

---

[986] Dulles, *Models of the Church*, 122.
[987] Pope, *A Compendium of Christian Theology: Being Analytical Outlines of a Course of Theological Study, Biblical, Dogmatic, Historical*, 3:281, 283.
[988] Bloesch, *The Church: Sacraments, Worship, Ministry, Mission*, 100.

humankind, his resurrection, and reign through the spoken messages that provide the premise of Christian unity as opposed to what various denominations subscribe to in terms of beliefs.[989] This study, however, affirms the present revolutionary scholarship within the RCC, which has come up with a new school of thought that boldly states that the realization of Christian unity is not predicated upon membership to the RCC. These scholars have argued that genuine unity arises from each church's "conversion" to the Lord Jesus Christ and the good news rather than from association with the papacy.[990]

Dulles's views are mostly representative of current developments as he contends for an "interior unity" demonstrated in love and support for one another, which results in a relationship of good-natured recognition and acceptance.[991] This view coheres with the Reformers' view of the church as a *communio sanctorum*, whose membership consists of people who have faith in Christ and are sanctified and enjoy oneness with Christ, who is the indisputable leader of the church.[992] The EP broadens communio sanctorum to encompass and bring Christians to oneness in their plurality in all ages, right from the OT to the present.[993] Berkhof rightly points out that they are all brought together spiritually under Christ, who is their leader and to whom their loyalty goes. Faith, hope, truth, and service to their King are among the things shared in common.[994] This outfit exists in various expressions and defies uniformity in the form of a single visible church entity, which is advocated for by the RCC's official tradition. The study affirmed the views of Schaff, who said

---

[989] Ibid., 43–44, 100.
[990] Ibid., 41.
[991] Dulles, *Models of the Church*, 122.
[992] Berkhof, *Systematic Theology*, 502, 564, 573.
[993] Pope, *A Compendium of Christian Theology: Being Analytical Outlines of a Course of Theological Study, Biblical, Dogmatic, Historical*, 3:268.
[994] Berkhof, *Systematic Theology*, 564–565, 572.

that while one seeks for Christian unity, the reformation must be perceived as the "spiritual fulfillment of Catholicism."[995]

The noninclusive view of Catholicism is the other factor that influences the understanding of Christian unity. While the term Catholicism initially referred to the universality of the church, it came to be used in a biased manner to exclude Christians who are not part of the RCC.[996] Of late, though, the understanding of Catholicity has been adjusted by a new brand of RCC theologians to include Christians from other denominations. Küng, for instance, contends that the term should be applied generally to the whole church while keeping the particularities of each Christian entity intact.[997] He calls upon the "mother church" and "daughter churches" to rediscover this kind of Catholicity by working on their "relationship," by reconciling, and by coming together.[998] In the same vein, Dulles proposes a "dynamic catholicity of a love reaching out to all and excluding none."[999] According to Volf, that state tolerates both "unity and diversity" as it is qualitative (intensive) rather than quantitative (extensive).[1000] A church or person fails to achieve Catholicity when they remain apart from others.[1001]

The study has also revealed that the understanding of the church as a "hierarchically organised ecclesia," whereby unity is achieved through the clergy, is wanting and marginalizing.[1002] The concept of jo-kang'ato prescribes equality among believers, while in hierarchicalism, a view is held that believers are not at par, for there is a dichotomy between those who govern and the people whom

---

[995] Graham, *Cosmos in the Chaos: Philip Schaff's Interpretation of Nineteenth-Century American Religion*, 231.
[996] Pope, *A Compendium of Christian Theology: Being Analytical Outlines of a Course of Theological Study, Biblical, Dogmatic, Historical*, 3:282-284; Volf, *After Our Likeness: The Church as the Image of the Trinity*, 265.
[997] Küng, *The Church*, 303.
[998] Ibid., 310.
[999] Dulles, *Models of the Church*, 122.
[1000] Volf, *After Our Likeness: The Church as the Image of the Trinity*, 262, 265–267.
[1001] Ibid., 277, 278–282.
[1002] Berkhof, *Systematic Theology*, 572.

they govern and even among the former.¹⁰⁰³ In both the RCC and GO circles, this dichotomy exists in the form of active church and passive church. The RCC recognizes an open differentiation and distinction drawn between the *ecclesia docens*, also regarded as the "soul of the church," and the *eecclesia audiens* while the GO practices an Episcopal hierarchy, which requires the laity to take a backseat as their "infallible" prelates make all the decisions.¹⁰⁰⁴

The study has found Zizioulas's views about the laity untenable as he diminishes them to some ordo where the only thing they can do in the church is to pronounce amen upon the reception of graces.¹⁰⁰⁵ However, episcopalism is not exclusively an RCC and GO affair because its features are present in the form of clericalism in churches, which claim to subscribe to different structures. This structure negates the concept of the priesthood of all believers. The study has established that this is among the factors that contribute to disunity among Christians at all church levels. In its relegation of the laity to a position of insignificance and elevation of the clergy to the extent that they have a more significant say in ecclesiastical matters, the hierarchical ecclesial structure deviates from biblical principles of Christian relationship that discourage the treatment of any believer as a stranger and nonentity.

The concept of jo-kang'ato enforces parity through the sibling relationship embedded in it. It corroborates the scripture with its features, which include intimacy, inclusivity, openness, a sense of belonging, acceptance, incorporation, involvement, solidarity, friendliness, respect, fairness, teamwork, cooperation, etc. These constitute behavioral symbols, which, when interpreted, result in a positive reaction, which produces unity among Christians. It also advocates for interdependence whereby all members depend on one

---

¹⁰⁰³ Ibid, 562, 572.
¹⁰⁰⁴ Ibid., 562; Dulles, *Models of the Church*, 31; Volf, *After Our Likeness: The Church as the Image of the Trinity*, 130, 131, 223–224.
¹⁰⁰⁵ Zizioulas, *Being as Communion: Studies in Personhood and the Church*, 215; Volf, *After Our Likeness: The Church as the Image of the Trinity*, 113–114, 115, 116, 121, 224.

another for the progress of their society, charismatic endowments notwithstanding. The supposed giftedness of the ecclesia docens forms the basis of the existing dichotomy between them and the ecclesia audiens in the RCC.[1006] The same applies to the GO's investment of immense powers in the bishop who enjoys an *alter Christus* and *alter apostolus* statuses.[1007] The concept of jo-kang'ato enforces service for others rather than superiority, elitism, and domination.

The study also addressed marginalization in other forms within the ecclesial context. The concept of jo-kang'ato has values that could address patriarchalism and ensure meaningful involvement of the youth in the life of the church as well as deal with the strained relationship between the younger and older members of the church. It invites all members to take their rightful positions in the church as children of God, gender and age notwithstanding. This condition comes with respect for others and unhindered opportunities in ministry and leadership. The other manifestations of marginalization are negative ethnicity, nepotism, and other socioeconomic factors. The familial and communal models of the church, as they stand, now create leeway for marginalization since they lack inclusivity, and that is why they needed to be revised.

It is also held in this work that the conglomeration of denominations advocated for by some EP scholars is not necessary for Christian unity to happen. Silleck is among the scholars whose views were contradicted in my study, for he argues that "the churches of the reformation are not complete churches in and of themselves," as they are "a confessing movement within the greater Christian family," which has risen as a result of some unexpected and challenging situation in the Christian church.[1008] He argues further that since the good news about "freedom," which the churches of the Reformation advocated for, could only be achieved within the RCC circles, such

---

[1006] Berkhof, *Systematic Theology*, 562.
[1007] Zizioulas, "La Mystere de l'Eglise Dans La Tradition Orthodoxe," 329; Zizioulas, "The Bishop in the Theological Doctrine of the Orthodox Church," 31; Volf, *After Our Likeness: The Church as the Image of the Trinity*, 119, 122, 131.
[1008] Silleck, "A More Radical Proposal," 28–31.

churches could rejoin the latter for "Rome is theologically healthy, missiologically vital, truly catholic, truly diverse and increasingly evangelical."[1009] This view displays a lack of recognition for the said churches. Braaten and Jenson go even further to propose "an evangelical Catholicism," which accepts, among other things, the leadership of the pope.[1010] While these views have continued to shape ecumenism, this work found them inadequate and did not support them. The study supports Bloesch's "evangelical Catholicism," which has to do with a spiritual rather than an organizational unification.[1011] As Schaff puts it, Christians are members of the same "flock" but multiple folds.[1012] This kind of unity has nothing to do with the formation of one ecclesial organization.[1013]

The contribution of the study to scholarship has occurred through the blending of nonconflicting elements of culture with the scripture. This exercise has generated a special kind of sense of the Christian faith, which is accompanied by a certain level of authenticity. Since the philosophy of jo-kang'ato is African, it has a tremendous potential to appeal to African Christians, mainly because it advocates for a collective view of human relationships. The correspondence between this perspective of relationship and the scripture makes it possible for the church to benefit globally through it. I submit that if the concept of jo-kang'ato addresses unity among the Luo people and has values and ideals that cohere with the scripture, then there is no reason why it should not be used to improve the understanding of Christian unity in the ecclesial life of the church in Africa and beyond. Its practicality makes it even more appealing. Jo-kang'ato qualifies to be a pattern for Christian relationships in the ecclesial life of the church.

This study contributes to the mission of the church too. In the first instance, it maintains that the success of the mission lies in

---

[1009] Ibid.
[1010] Braaten, *Mother Church: Ecclesiology and Ecumenism.*
[1011] Bloesch, *The Church: Sacraments, Worship, Ministry, Mission*, 42.
[1012] Graham, *Cosmos in the Chaos: Philip Schaff's Interpretation of Nineteenth-Century American Religion*, 231.
[1013] Schaff, *Christ and Christianity*, 16.

the integrity of Christians, which manifests in meaningful unity as generated by the concept of jo-kang'ato.[1014] The study has challenged all Christians at all ecclesial levels to set aside their differences so that they can cooperate and exert a united effort in mission, for this would enable them to unleash their full potential and influence their societies for good. Souls are won for the kingdom when Christians are united. The study has also shown that the mission of the church will be enhanced when the targets realize that they can live their faith within their cultural milieu.[1015] The kind of mission informed by the adoption of jo-kang'ato is characterized by respect and sensitivity to the African people's way of life.

The need to enhance the understanding of unity among Christians in the ecclesial life of the church in Africa is urgent. This study is necessary as it promises to generate a more in-depth and meaningful relationship among Christians. The utilization of the concept of jo-kang'ato makes the reinforcement of meaning a reality through its unity-enhancing values, which could have a positive bearing on the ecclesial relationship and translate into the general well-being of the church. With a persistent misunderstanding, however, disunity is perpetuated, and the mission of the church is jeopardized.

[1014] Onwubiko, *Building Unity Together in the Mission of the Church: A Theology of Ecumenism*, 35; Lonergan, *Method in Theology*, 362.

[1015] Moripe, "The Notion of Independence and Rendering of Service to the African Independent/ Indigenous Churches," 866.

BIBLIOGRAPHY

Abbott, Thomas. *A Critical and Exegetical Commentary on the Epistles to the Ephesians and to the Colossians*. New York: C. Scribner's Sons, 1909.

Alliyu, Nurudeen. "Perception of Propertied Women on Marriage Forms, Widowhood and Living Patterns in Southwest, Nigeria." *African Research Review: An International Multidisciplinary Journal* 9, no. 3 (July 2015): 157–173.

Anders, Max. *Galatians, Ephesians, Philippians & Colossians*, vol. 8, Holman New Testament Commentary. Nashville, TN: Broadman & Holman Publishers, 1999.

Anderson, Allan. *Zion and Pentecost: The Spirituality and Experience of Pentecostal and Zionist-Apostolic Churches in South Africa*. Pretoria: University of South Africa, 2000.

Ande, Titre. *Leadership and Authority: Bula Matari and Life-Community Ecclesiology in Congo*. Regnum Studies in Mission. Oxford: Regnum, 2010.

Aquinas, Thomas. *Summa Theologica*. Translated by Fathers of the English Dominican Province. London: Burns Oates & Washbourne, n.d.

Awad, Najib. "What Has the Jerusalem of Dogmatic to Do with the Athens of Context, or How Should One Do Contextual Theology?" *PLURA: Revista de Estudos de Religião* 3, no. 2 (n.d.): 198–221.

Ayayo, Ocholla. *Traditional Ideology and Ethics Among the Southern Luo*. Uppsala Sweden: The Scandinavian Institute of African Studies, 1976.

Ayres, Lewis. "The Final Act." *Christian History Magazine*, 2004.

Babbie, Earl, and Johann Mouton. *The Practice of Social Research*. Cape Town: Oxford University Press, 2001.

Bahovec, Igor. "Christianity in Confrontation with Individualism and Crisis of Western Culture: Person, Community, Dialog, Reflexivity, and Relationship Ethics." *Bogoslovni Vestnik* 75, no. 2 (2015): 341.

Barnes, Michel. "Timeline." *Christian History Magazine*, 2004.

Barrett, Charles. *A Critical and Exegetical Commentary on the Acts of the Apostles* Edinburgh: T&T Clark, 2004.

———. *The First Epistle to the Corinthians*, BNTC. Peabody: Hendrickson, 1996.

Barth, Karl. *Church Dogmatics*.Vol. IV/1. Edinburgh: Clark, 1956.

Barth, Markus. *The Anchor Yale Bible: Ephesians 1–3*, vol. 34. New Haven and London: Yale University Press, 1974.

———. *The Broken Wall: A Study of the Epistle to the Ephesians*. Chicago: Judson, 1959.

———. *The People of God*. Sheffield: JSOT Press, 1983.

Bazeley, Patricia. *Qualitative Data Analysis With NVivo*. London: Sage Publications Ltd, 2007.

Bediako, Kwame. *Theology of Identity: The Impact of Culture Upon Christian Thought in the Second Century and in Modern Africa*. 1992nd ed. Oxford: Regnum Books, 1992.

Bengel, Johann. *Gnomon of the New Testament*. Translated by A. R. Fausset. Vol. 2. 1–5 vols. Edinburgh: T&T Clark, 1860.

Berkhof, Louis. *Systematic Theology*. Grand Rapids, MI: Wm. B. Eerdmans Publishing Co., 1938.

Bernard, John. *A Critical and Exegetical Commentary on the Gospel According to St John*. New York: C. Scribner' Sons, 1929.

Babbie, Earl, and Johann Mouton. *The Practice of Social Research*. Cape Town: Oxford University Press, 2001.

Best, Ernest. *A Critical and Exegetical Commentary on Ephesians*. Edinburgh: T&T Clark International, 1998.

———. *One Body in Christ*. London: SPCK, 1955.

Bishwende, Augustin. *Eglise – Famille de Dieu Dans La Mondialisation: Theologie D'une Nouvelle Voie Africaine D'evangelisation*.Paris: L'Harmattan, 2006.

Bloesch, Donald. *The Church: Sacraments, Worship, Ministry, Mission*. Downers Grove, IL: InterVarsity Press, 2002.

Blum, Edwin. "John." In *The Bible Knowledge Commentary: An Exposition of the Scriptures*. Vol. 2., 333–334. Wheaton, IL: Victor Books, 1985.

Blumer, Herbert. *Symbolic Interactionism: Perspective and Method.* Englewood Cliffs, New Jersey: Prentice Hall, 1969.

Boice, James. *Foundations of the Christian Faith: A Comprehensive & Readable Theology.* Downers Grove, IL: InterVarsity Press, 1986.

Braaten, Carl. *Mother Church: Ecclesiology and Ecumenism.* Minneapolis: Fortress, 1998.

Bratcher, Robert, and Eugene Nida. *A Handbook on Paul's Letter to the Ephesians.* New York: United Bible Societies, 1993.

Bruce, Frederick. *The New International Commentary on the New Testament: The Epistles to the Colossians, to Philemon and to the Ephesians,* Grand Rapids, Mich: Wm. B. Eerdmans Publishing Co., 1984.

Bruinsma, Reinder. *The Body of Christ: A Biblical Understanding of the Church.* Hagerstown, MD: Review and Herald® Publishing Association, 2009.

Brunner, Emil. *Das Misverstandnis Der Kirche,* 2nd ed. Zurich: Zwingli, 1939.

Bujo, Bénézet. *African Theology in Its Social Context.* Translated by John O'Donohue. Nairobi: St Paul Communications; Maryknoll, NY: Orbis Books, 1992.

———. *Christmas: God Becomes Man in Black Africa.* Nairobi: Paulines, 1995.

———. "On the Road Toward an African Ecclesiology: Reflections on the Synod." In *The African Synod: Documents, Reflections, Perspectives,* 140. Edited by Browne Maura. New York: Orbis Books, 1996.

Buqa, Wonke. "Ubuntu Values in an Emerging Multi-Racial Community: A Narrative Reflection." PhD Diss., University of Pretoria, 2016.

Cabal, Ted, et al, eds. *The Apologetics Study Bible: Real Questions, Straight Answers, Stronger Faith*. Nashville, TN: Holman Bible Publishers, 2007.

Calvin, John. *Institutes of the Christian Religion*. Edited by J. T. McNeill. Translated by F. L. Battles. Vol. 1. Louisville, KY: Westminster John Knox Press, 2011.

Campbell, Jonathan. "Releasing the Gospel from Western Bondage." *International Journal of Frontier Missions* 16 (Winter/2000 1999): 168–170.

Charon, Joel. *Symbolic Interactionism: An Introduction, An Interpretation, and Integration*. 6th ed. Englewood Cliffs, New Jersey: Prentice Hall, 1998.

Chukwu, Donatus. *The Church as the Extended Family of God: Toward a New Direction for African Ecclesiology*. Bloomington, Indiana: Xlibris, 2011.

Chukwu, Emmanuel. "Ezi-Na-Ulo: The Extended Family of God: Towards an Ecological Theology of Creation." Sacrae Theologiae Doctor Diss., Katholieke Universiteit Leuven, 2002.

Cleveland, Christena. *Disunity in Christ: Uncovering the Hidden Forces That Keep Us Apart*. Downers Grove, IL: InterVarsity Press, 2013.

Coffman, Elesha, and Patrick Rardon. "Saints and Heretics." *Christian History Magazine*, 2004.

Cohen, David, and E.S. Odhiambo. *Siaya: The Historical Anthropology of an African Landscape*. Eastern African Studies.

London; Nairobi; Athens: James Currey; Heinemman Keya; Ohio University Press, 1989.

Collins, Raymond. *Sacra Pagina: First Corinthians*. Vol. 7. Edited by Daniel J. Harrington, S.J. Collegeville, Minnesota: Liturgical Press, 1935.

Cone, James. *God of the Oppressed*. New York: Seabury Press, 1975.

Conzelmann, Hans. *1 Corinthians: A Commentary on the First Epistle to the Corinthians*. Philadelphia: Fortress, 1975.

Cullmann, Oscar. *Baptism in the New Testament*. Translated by J. K. S. Reid. London: SCM, 1951.

Cutsinger, James, ed. *Reclaiming the Great Tradition*. Downers Grove, Ill.: InterVarsity Press, 1997.

Dadosky, John. "Methodological Presuppositions for Engaging the Other in the Post-Vatican II Context: Insights from Ignatius and Lonergan." *JIRD: A forum for Academic, Social, and Timely Issues Affecting Religious Communities Around the World*, 2010. Accessed May 10, 2015. http://irdialogue.org/wp-content/uploads/2010/03/JIRD-3-Dadosky. pdf.

Deluz, Gaston. *A Companion to 1 Corinthians*. Darton: Longman & Todd, 1963.

Dennis, Alex, and Peter Martin. "Symbolic Interactionism and the Concept of Power." *The British Journal of Sociology* 562 (2005): 191–213.

Dennis, George. "The East-West Schism (1054)." *Christian History Magazine*, 1990.

Devine, Arthur. *The Creed Explained, Or, an Exposition of Catholic Doctrine*. Hardpress Publishing, 2012.

Dexter, Henry. *The Congregationalism of the Last Three Hundred Years*. London: Hodder & Stoughton, 1980.

Dockery, D.S. ed. *Holman Bible Handbook*. Nashville, TN: Holman Bible Publishers, 1992.

Dods, Markus. *The Gospel of St. John*. New York: George H. Doran Company, n.d.

Doerries, Hermann *Constantine the Great*. New York: Harper&Row, 1972.

Dreyer, Wim. "Church, Mission and Ethics: Being Church With Integrity." *HTS Teologiese Studies/ Theological Studies* 72, no.1 (2016): 1–5.

———. "The Real Crisis of the Church." *HTS Teologiese Studies/ Theological Studies* 73, no. 3 (2015): 1–5.

Duffield, Guy, and Nathaniel Van Cleave. *Foundations of Pentecostal Theology*. Los Angeles, CA: L.I.F.E. Bible College, 1983.

Dulles, Avery. *Models of the Church*. New York: Doubleday, 1974.

———. *The Catholicity of the Church*. Oxford: Clarendon, 1985.

Ehrman, Bart. *Lost Scriptures: Books That Did Not Make It Into the New Testament*. New York: Oxford University Press, 2003.

Ela, Jean-Marc. *My Faith as an African*. Translated by John Pairman Brown and Susan Perry. Maryknoll, N.Y.: Orbis Books, 1988.

Ezeweke, Elizabeth, and Anthony Ikechukwu. "The Family, Justice and the Culture of Life: Afro-Christian Perspectives." *AFRREV IJAH: An International Journal of Arts and Humanities Bahir Dar, Ethiopia* 1, no. 2 (May 2012): 28–40.

Farrar, Frederic. *Lives of the Fathers: Sketches of Church History in Biography*. vol. 1. Edinburgh: Adam and Charles Black, 1889.

Fee, Gordon. *God's Empowering Presence: The Holy Spirit in the Letters of Paul*. Peabody, Mass., 1994.

———. *New Testament Exegesis: A Handbook for Students and Pastors*. Philadelphia: Westminster Press, 1983.

———. *The First Epistle to the Corinthians: The New International Commentary on the New Testament*. Grand Rapids: Eerdmans, 1987.

Fiorenza, Francis. "Systematic Theology: Task and Methods." In *Systematic Theology: Roman Catholic Perspectives*. Vol. 1, 1–89. Minneapolis: Fortress Press, 1991.

Firstbrook, Peter. *The Obamas: The Untold Story of an African Family*. London, Great Britain: Preface Publishing, 2010.

Flemington, W.F. *The NT Doctrine of Baptism*. London: SPCK, 1957.

Folarin, George, Olusegun Oladosu, and Stephen Baba. "Re-Interpreting the ΥΔΩΡ ΖΑΩ ('Living Water') Metaphor in John 4 & 7 in the Context of the South Western Yoruba in Nigeria." *Ijourels* 2, no. 2 (2012): 15–36.

Fong, Bruce. "Addressing the Issue of Racial Reconciliation According to the Principles of Eph 2:11–22." *JETS* 38, (1995): 565–580.

Forsyth, Peter. *The Church and the Sacraments*. 2nd ed. London: Independent Press, 1947.

———. *The Justification of God*. 1948th ed. London: Independent Press, 1917.

———. *The Person and Place of Jesus Christ*. Philadelphia: Westminster Press, 1910.

Foulkes, Francis. *Ephesians: An Introduction and Commentary*, vol. 10. Downers Grove, IL: InterVarsity Press, 1989.

Frend, William. *The Donatist Church: A Movement of Protest in Roman North Africa*. Oxford: Clarendon, 1952.

Frost, Michael, and Alan Hirsch. *The Shaping of Things to Come: Innovation and Mission for the 21st-Century Church*. Peabody: Hendrickson, 2013.

Gavin, Frank. *Some Aspects of Contemporary Greek Orthodox Thought*. London: SPCK, 1936.

Gbadegesin, Segun. "An Outline of a Theory of Destiny." In *African Philosophy: New and Traditional Perspectives*. New York: Oxford University Press, 2004.

Gehman, Richard. *African Traditional Religion in Biblical Perspective*. Kijabe, Kenya: Kesho Publications, 1989.

Geisler, Norman. *Baker Encyclopedia of Christian Apologetics*. Grand Rapids, MI: Baker Books, 1999.

Giles, Kevin. *What on Earth is the Church? A Biblical and Theological Inquiry*. London: SPCK, 1995.

Gonzalez, Justo. *The Story of Christianity: The Early Church to the Dawn of the Reformation*. Vol. 1. Massachusetts: Prince Press, 1984.

Graham, Stephen. *Cosmos in the Chaos: Philip Schaff's Interpretation of Nineteenth-Century American Religion*. Grand Rapids, Mich.: Eerdmans, 1995.

Green, Clifford, and Michael DeJonge, eds. *The Bonhoeffer Reader*. Minneapolis, MN: Fortress Press, 2013.

Gyekye, Kwame. *African Cultural Values: An Introduction*. Accra, Ghana: Sankofa Publishing Company, 1996.

Hansen, Walter. *The Letter to the Philippians*. Grand Rapids, MI; Nottingham, England: William B. Eerdmans Publishing Company, 2009.

Hart, Trevor, ed. *Justice the True and Only Mercy*. Edinburgh: T. & T. Clark, 1995.

Healey, Joseph, and Donald Sybertz. *Towards an African Narrative Theology*. 1996th ed. Nairobi, Kenya: Paulines, 1996.

Herbich, Ingrid. "Luo." Encyclopedia of World Cultures Supplement. 2002. Accessed August 24, 2020. http://www.encyclopedia.com.

Héring, Jean. *The First Epistle of Saint Paul to the Corinthians*. Translated by A.W.

Heathcote and P.J. Allcock. Wipf and Stock Publishers, 2008.

Hiebert, Paul. "Critical Contextualization." *International Bulletin of Missionary Research* (July 1987): 104–105.

Hirsch, Alan. *The Forgotten Ways: Reactivating the Missional Church*. Grand Rapids: Brazos Press, 2006.

Hodge, Charles. *Systematic Theology*. Vol. 1. Oak Harbor, WA: Logos Research Systems, Inc., 1997.

———. *Systematic Theology*. Vol. 2. Oak Harbor, WA: Logos Research Systems, Inc., 1997.

Hodgson, Leonard, ed. *The Second World Conference on Faith and Order Held at Edinburgh, August 3–18, 1937, London*. London, August 3, 1937.

Horton, Michael. *We Believe*. Nashville: Word, 1998.

Hulley, Leonard, Louise Kretzschmar, and Luke Pato, eds. *Archbishop Tutu:*

Prophetic Witness in South Africa. Cape Town: Human & Rousseau, 1996.

Husbands, Mark and Daniel Treier, eds. *The Community of the Word: Toward an Evangelical Ecclesiology*. Downers Grove: InterVarsity Press, 2005.

Idowu, Bolaji. *African Traditional Religion: A Definition*. London, Great Britain: SCM Press Ltd, 1973.

Ilesanmi, Simeon. "Inculturation and Liberation: Christian Social Ethics and the African Theology Project." *Annual of the Society of Christian Ethics* 15 (1995): 49–73.

Ilo, Stan Chu. *The Church and Development in Africa: Aid and Development from the Perspective of Catholic Social Ethics*. African Christian Studies 2. Eugene, OR: Pickwick, 2011.

Jamieson, Robert, Andrew Fausset, and David Brown. *Commentary Critical and Explanatory on the Whole Bible.* Vol. 2. Oak Harbor, WA: Logos Research Systems, Inc., 1997.

Jay, Eric. *The Church: Its Changing Image through the Twenty Century.* Vol. 1. Atlanta: John Knox Press, 1980.

Jeffers, James. *The Greco-Roman World of the New Testament Era: Exploring the Background of Early Christianity.* Downers Grove, Illinois: InterVarsity Press, 1999.

Jenkins, Daniel. *The Nature of Catholicity.* London: Faber and Faber, 1941.

Jonas, Hans. *The Gnostic Religion.* Boston: Beacon Press, 1958.

Kabasélé, Francois. "Christ as Ancestor and Elder Brother." In *Faces of Jesus in Africa.* Edited by Robert Schreiter. Maryknoll, N.Y.: Orbis Books, 1991.

Kanagaraj, Jey. *John.* Vol. 4. Eugene, OR: Cascade Books, 2013.

Kanayo, Louis, and Charles Nweke. "The Relevance of the Church in Oppressive Situations: The Praxis of Liberation Theology in Africa." *Ogirisi: A New Journal of African Studies* 10 (2013): 1–100.

Kariuki, Francis. "Conflict Resolution by Elders in Africa: Successes, Challenges and Opportunities." *Alternative Dispute Resolution Journal* 3, no. 2 (2015): 30–53.

Karkkainen, Veli-Matti. *An Introduction to Ecclesiology: Ecumenical, Historical & Global Perspectives.* Downers Grove, Illinois: InterVarsity Press, 2002.

Käsemann, E. "The Theological Problem Presented by the Motif of the Body of Christ." In *Perspectives on Paul, 102–121*. London: SCM, 1971.

Kim, Uichol. Individualism and Collectivism: A Psychological, Cultural and Ecological Analysis. Nordic Institute of Asian Studies Report Series 21. Copenhagen: NIAS Press, 1995.

Kinnaman, David. *Unchristian: What a New Generation Really Thinks About Christianity*. Grand Rapids, MI.: Baker Books, 2007.

Kombo, Donald, and Delno Tromp. *Proposal and Thesis Writing: An Introduction*. Nairobi: Paulines Publications Africa, 2006.

Kothari, C.R. *Research Methodology: Methods and Techniques*. 2nd ed. Daryaganj, New Delhi: New Age International (P) Ltd., Publishers, 2004.

Kraus, Hans-Joachim. *Reich Gottes: Reich Der Freiheit, Grundriss Systematische Theologie*. Neukirchen: Neukirchener Verlag, 1975.

Kruse, Colin. *John: An Introduction and Commentary*. Vol. 4. Downers Grove, IL: InterVarsity Press, 2003.

Küng, Hans. *The Church*. Translated by Ray and Rosaleen. Ockenden, New York: Sheed & Ward, 1967.

Kunhiyop, Samuel. *African Christian Ethics*. Hippo Books, 2008.

_____. *African Christian Theology*. HippoBooks, 2012.

_____. "Towards a Christian Communal Ethics: The African Contribution." *Cultural Encounters* 6, no. 2 (2010).

Lange, Johann. et al. *A Commentary on the Holy Scriptures: 1 Corinthians*. Bellingham, WA: Logos Bible Software, 2008.

———. *A Commentary on the Holy Scriptures: Ephesians*. Bellingham, WA: Logos Bible Software, 2008.

Leithart, Peter. *The End of Protestantism: Pursuing Unity in a Fragmented Church*. Grand Rapids, MI: Brazos Press, 2016.

LenkaBula, Puleng. "Beyond Anthropocentricity-Botho/Ubuntu and the Quest for Economic and Ecological Justice in Africa." *Religion and Theology* 15 (2008): 383.

Lenski, R.C.H. *The Interpretation of St. John's Gospel*. Minneapolis, MN: Augsburg Publishing House, 1961.

———. *The Interpretation of St. Paul's Epistles to the Galatians, to the Ephesians and to the Philippians*. Columbus, O.: Lutheran Book Concern, 1937.

———. *The Interpretation of St. Paul's First and Second Epistle to the Corinthians*. Minneapolis, MN: Augsburg Publishing House, 1963.

Levinson, H.S. *Discourse Features of the New Testament Greek*. 2nd ed. Dallas: International Academic Bookstore, 2000.

Liefeld, Walter. *Ephesians*, vol. 10 Eph 2:13–19. Downers Grove, IL: InterVarsity Press, 1997.

Lincoln, Andrew. *Black's New Testament Commentary: The Gospel According to Saint John*. London: Continuum, 2005.

———. *Word Biblical Commentary*, vol. 42: Ephesians. Edited by Ralph Martin. Dallas, Texas: Thomas Nelson, 1990.

Lloyd-Jones, David. *God's Way of Reconciliation: Studies in Eph. 2*. Evangelical Press, 1972.

Lonergan, Bernard. *Method in Theology*. Toronto: University of Toronto Press, 1971.

Louw, Johannes, and Eugene Nida. *Greek-English Lexicon of the New Testament Based on Semantic Domains*, 2nd ed., vol. 1: Introduction & Domains. Edited by Rondal Smith and Karen Munson. New York: United Bible Societies, 1989.

Lowery, Stephanie. *Identity and Ecclesiology: Their Relationship Among Select African Theologians*. Eugene, Oregon: Pickwick Publications, 2017.

Maluleke, Mikateko. "Culture, Tradition, Custom, Law and Gender Equality." *PER / PELJ* 15, no.1 (2012): 2.

Mandela, Nelson. *Long Walk to Freedom*. New York: Little, Brown & Company, 1995.

Markus, Hazel, and Shinobu Kitayama. "Culture and the Self: Implications for Cognition, Emotion, and Motivation." Psychological Review 98, no. 2 (April 1991): 226, 227.

Marshall, Bruce. "Who Really Cares About Christian Unity?" Accessed October 9, 2017. https://www.firstthings.com/ ... / who-really-cares-about-christian-unity.

Martey, Emmanuel. *African Theology: Inculturation and Liberation*. Eugene, OR: Wipf and Stock Publishers, 2001.

Martin, Dale. *The Corinthian Body*. New Haven and London: Yale University Press, 1995.

Mbandi, Paul. *A Theology of the Unity of the Church in a Multi-Ethnic Context: Toward a Theological Understanding of the Unity of the Church in Relation to Ethnic Diversity*. Saarbbrucken: Dr. Muller, 2010.

Mbefo, Luke. *Towards a Mature African Christianity*. SNAAP Press Ltd, 1989.

Mbiti, John. *African Religions and Philosophy*. London: Heinemann Educational Books Ltd, 1969.

———. "African Theology." In *Initiation into Theology: The Rich Variety of Theology and Hermeneutics*. Pretoria: Van Schaik, 1998.

McDonald, Lee. *The Biblical Canon: Its Origin, Transmission, and Authority*. Grand Rapids: Baker Academic, n.d.

McKelvey, R.J. *The New Temple: The Church in the New Testament*. Oxford: Oxford University Press, 1969.

Mead, Sidney. "Denominationalism: The Shape of Protestantism in America." In *Denominationalism*. Eugene, OR: Wipf and Stock, 2010.

Meeks, Wayne. *The First Urban Christians*. New Haven, Conn: Yale University Press, 1983.

Meiring, Lieze. "Exploring Ubuntu Language in Bridging Gaps: A Narrative Reflection on Discussions between Members of Two Reformed Churches in a Rural Town of South Africa." PhD Diss., University of Pretoria, 2016.

Meyendorff, John. Catholicity and the Church. Crestwood, New York: St. Vladimir's Seminary Press, 1983.

Milne, Bruce. *The Message of John: Here Is Your King! With Study Guide*. Leicester, England: Downers Grove, IL: InterVarsity Press, 1993.

Mitchell, Margaret. *Paul and the Rhetoric of Reconciliation*. Tübingen: Mohr, 1991.

Moffat, James. *The First Epistle of Paul to the Corinthians*. The Moffat New Testament Commentary. Hodder & Stoughton, 1947.

Moehler, Johann. *Symbolism: or Exposition of Doctrinal Differences Between Catholics and Protestants, as Evidenced by their Symbolic Writings*, 2nd ed, Vol. 2 . London, 1847.

Moll, Sebastian. *The Arch-Heretic: Marcion*. Tubingen: Mohr Siebeck, 2010.

Moltmann, Jürgen. *Experiences in Theology: Ways and Forms of Christian Theology*. London, Great Britain: SCM Press, 2000.

Moore, Art. "Does 'The Gift of Salvation' Sell Out the Reformation?" *Christianity Today* 42, no. 5(April 27, 1993): 21.

Moripe, S. "The Notion of Independence and Rendering of Service to the African Independent/Indigenous Churches." 49, no. 4 (1993): 800–900.

Morris, Leon. *1 Corinthians: An Introduction and Commentary*. Vol. 7. Downers Grove, IL: InterVarsity Press, 1985.

Mott, Stephen. *Biblical Ethics and Social Change*. New York: Oxford University Press, 1982.

Msafiri, Aidan. "The Church as a Family Model: Its Strengths and Weaknesses."

Accessed August 24, 2020. https://pdfs.semanticscholar.org/6b59/ 813e7 f8f7789c4fb39a3a2e5cec6a427486a.pdf?ga=2.119494602. 2116468974. 1598167077-1515817833.1598167077.

Mugambi, Jesse, and Laurenti Magesa, eds. "Introduction." In *The Church in African Christianity: Innovative Essays in Ecclesiology*. Nairobi: Initiatives Publ., 1990.

Munyenyembe, Rhodian, and Johannes Hofmeyr. "Lofty But Not Powerful: A Critical Analysis of the Position of the General Assembly in the Union of the Church of Central Africa Presbyterian (Malawi)." *Studia Historiae Ecclesiasticae* 42, no. 3 (2016): 1–21.

Murdock, George. *Social Structure.* New York: Macmillan, 1949.

Murphy-O'Connor, Jerome. *Paul: His Story.* Oxford: Oxford University Press, 2004.

———. *St. Paul's Corinth: Texts and Archaeology.* 3rd ed. Good News Studies. Michael Glazier, 2002.

Murray, Paul. *Receptive Ecumenism and the Call to Catholic Learning: Exploring a Way for Contemporary Ecumenism.* Oxford: Oxford University Press, 2010.

Myers, Allen "The Kingdom of God, Kingdom of Heaven." In *The Eerdmans Bible Dictionary*, 347, 625. Grand Rapids, MI: Eerdmans, 1987.

Nasimiyu-Wasike, Anne. "Acceptance of the Total Human Situation as a Precondition for Authentic Inculturation." In *Inculturation: Abide by the Otherness of Africa and the Africans.* Edited by Turkson and Wijsen, Frans. Netherlands: Kok Publishers, 1994.

Nche, George, et al. "Revisiting the Concept of Inculturation in a Modern Africa: A Reflection on Salient Issues." *HTS Teologiese Studies/Theological Studies* 72, no.1 (2016): 1–20.

Ndung'u, Nahashon. "Persistence of Features of Traditional Healing in the Churches in Africa: The Case of the Akurinu Churches in Kenya Thought and Practice." *A Journal of the Philosophical Association of Kenya* 1, no. 2 (December 2009): 87–104.

Newbigin, Lesslie. *The Gospel in a Pluralist Society*. Grand Rapids, Michigan: Eerdmans, 1989.

Ngona, Dieudonne. "Inculturation as a Face of African Theology." In *Faces of African Theology*, 134–181. CUEA Interdisciplinary Series. Nairobi, Kenya: CUEA, 2003.

Nkansah-Obrempong, James. *Foundations for African Theological Ethics*. Langham Monographs, 2013.

———. *Visual Theology: Some Akan Cultural Symbols, Metaphors, Proverbs, Myths, and Symbols and Their Implications for Doing Christian Theology*. Saarbrucken: VDM Verlag Dr. Muller, 2010.

Nyamiti, Charles. *African Theology: Its Nature, Problems and Methods*. Kampala: Gaba Publications, 1971.

———. *Christ as Our Ancestor: Christology from an African Perspective*. Gweru, Zimbabwe: Mambo Press, 1984.

———. "The Church as Christ's Ancestral Mediation: An Essay on African Ecclesiology." In *The Church in African Christianity: Innovative Essays in Ecclesiology*, 129–177. Nairobi: Initiatives Publishers, 1990.

———. *The Way to Christian Theology in Africa*. Eldoret, Kenya: Gaba Publication, n.d.

O'Brien, Peter. *The Letter to the Ephesians*. Grand Rapids, MI: W.B. Eerdmans Publishing Co., 1999.

Odinga, Oginga. *Not Yet Uhuru: An Autobiography of Oginga Odinga*. African Writers Series 38. London, United Kingdom: Heinemann, 1967.

O'Donovan, Wilbur Jr. *Biblical Christianity in African Perspective*. Carlisle: Paternoster, 2000.

―――. *Biblical Christianity in Modern Africa*. Carlisle, Cumbria: Paternoster Press, 2000.

Oduyoye, Mercy. *Hearing and Knowing: Theological Reflections on Christianity in Africa*. Maryknoll, N.Y.: Orbis Books, 1986.

―――.Oduyoye, Mercy. "The Value of African Religious Beliefs and Practices for Christian Theology." In *African Theology Enroute*, 110–111. Edited by Kofi Appiah-Kubi, and Sergio Torres. New York: Orbis Books, 1979.

Ogola, Margaret A. *The River and the Source*. Nairobi, Kenya: Focus Publishers Ltd, 1994.

Ogot, Bethwell. *History of the Southern Luo: Migration and Settlement, 1500-1900*. Vol. 1. Peoples of East Africa. Nairobi: East African Publishing House, 1967.

Okafor, Godson, and Chukwuemeka Okoye. "Social Media Use and Real-Life Social Relationships: A Study of Nnamdi Azikiwe University." *Creative Artist: A Journal of Theatre and Media Studies* 8, no. 2 (2014): 1–14.

Okure, Teresa. "Africa: Globalization and the Loss of Cultural Identity." In *Globalization and Its Victims*, 67–74. London: SCM, 2001.

Olabisi, Aina, Joshua Aransiola, and Clementina Osezua. "Sexual Health and Sexual Rights within Marriage." *African Research Review: An International Multi-Disciplinary Journal* 3, no. 1(2009): 27–46.

Onwubiko, Oliver. *Building Unity Together in the Mission of the Church: A Theology of Ecumenism*. Nsukka: Fulladu Publishing Company, 1999.

Orobator, Agbonkhianmeghe. *From Crisis to Kairos: The Mission of the Church in the Time of HIV/AIDS, Refugees, and Poverty*. Nairobi, Kenya: Paulines Publications Africa, 2005.

———. "Perspectives and Trends in Contemporary African Ecclesiology." *Studia Missionalia* 45 (1996): 267.

Orodho, John. *Essentials of Educational and Social Sciences Research Method*. Nairobi: Masola Publishers, 2003.

Osborne, Grant. "Baptism." In *Baker Encyclopedia of the Bible*. Vol. 1, 258. Grand Rapids: Baker Book House, 1988), 258.

———. *The Hermeneutical Spiral: A Comprehensive Introduction to Biblical Interpretation*. Downers Grove, IL: InterVarsity Press, 1991.

Osuchukwu, Peter. *The Spirit of Umunna and the Development of Small Christian Communities in Igboland*. Frankfurt: Peter Lang, 1995.

Ottah, Gabriel. "African Culture and Communication Systems in the Coronation of Ata Igala, North Central Nigeria." *International Journal of Arts and Humanities* 4, no.15 (September 2015): 208–228.

Ozkan, Betul. "Using NVivo to Analyze Qualitative Classroom Data on Constructivist Learning Environments." *The Qualitative Report* 9, no. 4 (2004): 594.

Parkin, David. *The Cultural Definition of Political Response: Lineal Destiny Among the Luo*. London: Academic Press, 1978.

Pictet, Bénédict. *Christian Theology*. Translated by F. Reyroux. Philadelphia: Presbyterian Board of Publication, n.d.

Pirson, Dietrich. "Communio Als Kirchenrechtliches Leitprinzip," *Zeitschrift fur evangelisches Kirchenrecht* 29 (1984): 35-45.

Pope, William. *A Compendium of Christian Theology: Being Analytical Outlines of a Course of Theological Study, Biblical, Dogmatic, Historical*. Vol. 1. 1-3 vols. London: Beveridge and Co, 1879.

———. *A Compendium of Christian Theology: Being Analytical Outlines of a Course of Theological Study, Biblical, Dogmatic, Historical*. Vol. 3. 1-3 vols. London: Beveridge and Co, 1879.

Pratt, Richard Jr. *I & II Corinthians*. Vol. 7. Nashville, TN: Broadman & Holman Publishers, 2000.

Prestige, George. *God in Patristic Thought*. London: S.P.C.K, 1956.

Prior, David. *The Message of 1 Corinthians: Life in the Local Church*. Leicester, England: Downers Grove, IL: InterVarsity Press, 1985.

Quinn, James. "Pluralism and the Unity of the Church," n.d. www.theway.org.uk/Back/15Quinn.pdf.

Radner, Ephraim. *A Brutal Unity: The Spiritual Politics of the Christian Church*. Waco, Texas: Baylor University Press, 2012.

Ramm, Bernard. *Protestant Biblical Interpretation*. Boston: Wilde, 1950.

Ramose, Mogobe. *African Philosophy through Ubuntu*. Harare: Mond Books Publishers, 2002.

Reid, Daniel et al. In *Dictionary of Christianity in America*. Downers Grove, IL: InterVarsity Press, 1990.

Richards, Lyn. "Data Alive! The Thinking Behind NVivo." *Qualitative Health Research* 9, no. 3 (1999): 412.

Robertson, Archibald, and Alfred Plummer. *A Critical and Exegetical Commentary on the First Epistle of St. Paul to the Corinthians*. New York: T&T Clark, 1911.

Robertson, Archibald. *Word Pictures in the New Testament (1 Co 12:13–27)*. Nashville, TN: Broadman Press, 1933.

———. *Word Pictures in the New Testament (Eph 2:13–22)*. Nashville, TN: Broadman Press, 1933.

Robinson, Joseph. *St. Paul's Epistle to the Ephesians: Translation and Exposition*, 2nd ed. Macmillan and Co., 1907.

Rusten, Sharon, and Michael Rusten. *The Complete Book of When & Where in the Bible and Throughout History*. Wheaton, IL: Tyndale House Publishers, Inc., 2005.

Ryrie, Charles. *Basic Theology: A Popular Systematic Guide to Understanding Biblical Truth*. Chicago, IL: Moody Press, 1999.

Sabine, James. *A Concise History of the Christian Church: From the Birth of the Saviour to the Commencement of the Nineteenth Century*. 3rd ed. London: Burton and Briggs; Law and Whittaker, 1816.

Sandnes, Karl. *Paul—One of the Prophets? A Contribution to the Apostle's Self-Understanding*. Tübingen: J. C. B. Mohr [Paul Siebeck], 1991.

Sarpong, Peter. "Can Christianity Dialogue with African Traditional Religion?" Accessed April 22, 2015. http://www.afrikaworld.net/ afrel/sarpong.html.

Savage, Peter, and C. Padilla, eds. "The Church and Evangelism." in *New Faces of Evangelism: An International Symposium on the Lausanne Covenant.* Downers Grove: InterVarsity Press, 1976.

Schaff, Philip. *Christ and Christianity.* New York: Charles Scribner's Sons, 1885.

Schnackenburg, Rudolf. *Baptism in the Thought of Paul.* Oxford: Blackwell, 1964.

———. *Epistle to the Ephesians: A Commentary.* Translated by Helen Heron. Edinburgh: T&T Clark, 1991.

Schineller, Peter. "Inculturation and Syncretism: What Is the Real Issue?" *International Bulletin of Missionary Research* (1992): 50–53.

Setiloane, Gabriel. *African Theology: An Introduction.* Cape Town: Lux Verbi, 2000.

Shute, A. "Ubuntu As the African Ethical Vision." In *African Ethics – An Anthropology of Comparative and Applied Ethics.* Scottsville: University of KwaZulu Natal Press, 2009.

Silleck, Jeffrey. "A More Radical Proposal." *Lutheran Forum* 32, no.1 (Spring 1998): 28–35.

Snyder, Howard. *The Community of the King.* Downers Grove: InterVarsity Press, 1977.

Sohm, Rudolph. *Wesen and Ursprung des Katholizismus*, 2nd ed. Leipzig: Teubner, 1912.

Southall, Aidan. *Lineage Formation Among the Luo.* London, New York, Toronto: Oxford University Press, 1952.

Stinton, Diane. *Jesus of Africa: Voices of Contemporary African Christology*. Nairobi: Paulines Publications Africa, 2004.

Stott, John. *The Message of Acts*. The Bible Speaks Today. Nottingham, England: Inter-Varsity Press, 1991.

———. *God's New Society: The Message of Ephesians*. Downers Grove, IL: InterVarsity Press, 1979.

Strong, Augustus. *Systematic Theology*. Philadelphia: American Baptist Publication Society, 1907.

Sutton, John, and Mark Chaves. "Explaining Schism in American Protestant Denominations, 1890–1990." *Journal for the Scientific Study of Religion* 43, no. 2 (2004): 171–190.

Tertilt, Michele. "Polygyny, Fertility, and Savings," *Journal of Political Economy* 113, no. 6 (2005): 1341.

Theissen, Gerd. *The Social Setting of Pauline Christianity: Essays on Corinth*. Edited and translated by J.H. Schutz. Philadelphia: Fortress Press, 1982.

———. "The Strong and the Weak in Corinth: A Sociological Analysis of a Theological Quarrel." In *The Social Setting of Pauline Christianity, 121-144*. Philadelphia: Fortress, 1982.

Thiselton, Anthony. *The First Epistle to the Corinthians: A Commentary on the Greek Text*. Grand Rapids, MI: W.B. Eerdmans, 2000.

Thornton, Lionel. *The Common Life in the Body of Christ*. Dacre Press, 1942.

Tien, Ngo. "The Church as Family of God: Its Development and Implications for the Church in Vietnam." PhD Thesis, Australian Catholic University, 2006.

Towner, Philip. "Households and Household Codes," *Dictionary of Paul and His Letters*, 417–419. Downers Grove, Illinois; Leicester, England: InterVarsity Press, 1993.

Uwah, Innocent. "Between Traditional Christian Theology and Moral Parables of African Popular Films: Communicating Gospel Values Contextually." *Unizik Journal of Arts and Humanities* (n.d.): 60.

Uzukwu, Elochukwu. *A Listening Church: Autonomy and Communion in African Churches*. Eugene, OR: Wipf and Stock, 2006.

Valliant, James, and Warren Fahy. *Creating Christ: How Roman Emperors Invented Christianity*. Crossroad Press, 2016.

Van der Borght, Eduardus. "Unity That Sanctifies Diversity: Cottesloe Revisited."*Acta Theologica* 31, no. 2 (2011): 315–328.

Vanhoozer, Kevin. "What Is Everyday Theology? How and Why Christians Should Read Culture." In *Everyday Theology: How to Read Cultural Texts and Interpret Trends*, 15–60. Grand Rapids, Michigan: Baker Academic, 2007.

Vincent, Marvin. *Word Studies in the New Testament*. Vol. 3. New York: Charles Scribner's Sons, 1887.

Viriri, Advice, and Pascah Mungwini. "African Cosmology and the Duality of Western Hegemony: The Search for an African Identity." *The Journal of Pan African Studies* 3, no. 6 (2010): 24–42.

Visser't Hooft, Willem, ed. *The Evanston Report: The Second Assembly of the World Council of Churches 1954*. London: World Council of Churches, 1955.

Volf, Miroslav. *After Our Likeness: The Church as the Image of the Trinity*. Grand Rapids: Eerdmans, 1998.

Vyhmeister, Nancy, and Terry Robertson. *Your Guide to Writing Quality Research Papers for Students of Religion and Theology*, 3rd ed. Grand Rapids, Michigan: Zondervan, 2014.

Waliggo, John. "The African Clan as the True Model of the African Church." In *The Church in African Christianity: Innovative Essays in Ecclesiology*, 110–127. Nairobi: Initiatives Publ., 1990.

Waruta, David. "Towards an African Church: A Critical Assessment of Alternative Forms and Structures." In *The Church in African Christianity: Innovative Essays*, 28–41. Nairobi: Initiatives Publ., 1990.

Wehmeier, Sally, ed. *Oxford Advanced Learner's Dictionary*. New York: Oxford University Press, 2005.

Welker, Michael. *Kirche Im Pluralismus*, vol. 136. Kaiser Taschenbucher Guttersloh: Kaiser, 1995.

Whitacre, Rodney. *John*. Vol. 4. Downers Grove, IL: InterVarsity Press, 1999.

Wiersbe, Warren. *The Bible Exposition Commentary*. Vol. 1. Wheaton, IL: Victor Books, 1996.

Wilkin, Robert. "The Gospel According to John." In *The Grace New Testament Commentary*. Denton, TX: Grace Evangelical Society, 2010.

Willis, Karen, and et al. "The Essential Role of Social Theory in Qualitative Public Health Research." *Australian and New Zeeland Journal of Public Health* 315 (2007): 438–443.

Wilmer, W. *Handbook of the Christian Religion*. 2nd ed. New York: Benziger Brothers, 1921.

Wilson, Geoffrey. *1 Corinthians.* Banner of Truth, 1978.

Winter, Bruce. *After Paul Left Corinth: The Influence of Secular Ethics and Social Change.* Grand Rapids, MI: Eerdmans, 2001.

Wong, Li. "Data Analysis in Qualitative Research: A Brief Guide to Using Nvivo." *Malaysian Family Physician* 3, no. 1 (2008).

Workman, Robert *Persecution in the Early Church.* London: Epworth Press, 1960.

Wuest, Kenneth. *Wuest's Word Studies from the Greek New Testament: For the English Reader*, vol. 4. Grand Rapids: Eerdmans, 1997.

Yung, Hwa. *Mangoes or Bananas: The Quest for an Authentic Asian Theology.* Oxford: Oxford Centre for Mission Studies, 2014.

Zizioulas, John. *Being as Communion: Studies in Personhood and the Church.* Crestwood, N.Y.: St. Vladimir's Seminary Press, 1985.

———. "Die Pneumatologische Dimension der Kirche." *Internationale Katholische Zeitschrift "Communio."* 2 (1973): 133–147.

———. "Episkope and Episkopos in the Early Church: A Brief Survey of the Evidence." In *Episcope and Episcopate in Ecumenical Perspective*, Vol. 102. Faith and Order Papers. Geneva: World Council of Churches, 1980.

———. "La Mystere de l'Eglise Dans La Tradition Orthodoxe." *Irenikon* 60 (1987): 321–335.

———. "The Bishop in the Theological Doctrine of the Orthodox Church." *Kanon* 7 (1985): 23–35.

"An Evangelical Appraisal." *Christian History Magazine*, 1997.

"Global Christianity—A Report on the Size and Distribution of the World's Christian Population," December 19, 2011. http://www.pewforum.org/2011/12/19/ global christianityexec/.

The Book of Confessions. Vol. 5. Louisville, Ky: Office of the General Assembly, Presbyterian Church, 1991.

"The Gift of Salvation." *Christianity Today* 41, no.14 (December 8, 1997): 35–38.

Milton Keynes UK
Ingram Content Group UK Ltd.
UKHW010626260424
441804UK00001B/56